India's Relations With The International Monetary Fund (IMF)
25 Years In Perspective 1991-2016

India's Relations With The International Monetary Fund (IMF)
25 Years In Perspective 1991-2016

V. SRINIVAS

Vij Books India Pvt Ltd
New Delhi (India)

Indian Council of World Affairs
Sapru House, New Delhi

Published by
Vij Books India Pvt Ltd
(Publishers, Distributors & Importers)
2/19, Ansari Road
Delhi – 110 002
Phones: 91-11-43596460, 91-11-47340674
Fax: 91-11-47340674
e-mail: vijbooks@rediffmail.com
web : www.vijbooks.com

Copyright © 2019, Indian Council of World Affairs (ICWA)

ISBN: 978-93-88161-62-6 (Hardback)

ISBN: 978-93-88161-63-3 (ebook)

All rights reserved.

No part of this book may be reproduced, stored in a retrieval system, transmitted or utilized in any form or by any means, electronic, mechanical, photocopying, recording or otherwise, without the prior permission of the copyright owner. Application for such permission should be addressed to the publisher.

The views expressed in this book are of the author in his personal capacity and do not represent the views of the ICWA.

This book is dedicated to my wife Smt. Satyasree Pamulaparthy and our two beloved children Snigdha and Pranav

CONTENTS

Foreword		ix
Preface		xiii
Acknowledgements		xvii
Chapter - I	The International Monetary Fund	1
Chapter - II	Major Financial Crisis: From Great Depression to The Great Recession	25
Chapter - III	India's IMF Programmes—1966 and 1981: An Analytical Review	49
Chapter - IV	India Circa 1991 – Origins of the Crisis	61
Chapter - V	The Union Budgets 1991-96	81
Chapter - VI	The IMF View - India's Stand-By Arrangement	97
Chapter - VII	Evolutionary Changes in India-IMF Relations	119
Chapter - VIII	The IMF's Article IV Consultations 1997 – 2016	135
Chapter - IX	Finance Secretaries, Governors of RBI, Chief Economic Advisors and Executive Directors	151
Chapter - X	My Years With The IMF	187
Chapter - XI	G20 – A Decade in Multilateralism	203
Chapter - XII	The Rise of China in the International Monetary System	221
Chapter - XIII	Conclusion	243
Index		257

FOREWORD

The word International Monetary Fund (IMF) evokes strong reaction among many people in India. It is viewed as an institution that interferes with the conduct of public policy in India. It is sometimes viewed as an institution that propagates capitalist ideology and globalisation to the benefit of advanced economies and to the detriment of developing countries like India. No doubt, there are some elements of truth in these reactions, but the reality is that India is itself an important member of the IMF, sort of one of owners contributing to its capital.

The origin of the IMF can be traced to the Breton-wood Conference convened in 1944 for purpose of formulating post-war currency system. India was invited to attend the meeting, though it was not yet independent. India, thus, became a founder member of IMF in December 1945 even before Independence. However, since Soviet Union did not join the IMF and the Peoples' Republic of China was not represented in the IMF, the institution was identified with the capitalist system as distinct from the socialist block led by Soviet Union. The picture, however, changed in 1980s with the expanded membership to include them.

India is not only a founder member, but for some time it was the 5th largest shareholder. In addition, it had been the leader of the voice of developing countries – a voice that has been disproportionately large relative to its voting power. In recent years, India has also emerged as an important player in the global economy and, therefore, in the functioning of the IMF.

IMF is in the nature of a club where member countries come together to observe some rules of the game relating to international monetary system. The members of the club are entitled to draw resources when needed. In some ways, IMF is a sort of lender of last resort. India has also been a beneficiary of resources from IMF in times of difficulties.

While IMF is a cooperative institution, the voting power of the members is not equal. The voting power represents broadly the importance of the country concerned in terms of share in global economic activity in trade, etc. The United States of America has effective veto power. Its governance represents unequal economic and political strengths of member countries in the world.

IMF is a creature of governments. Governments are political animals. A creature of such governments cannot but be political, to varying degrees.

The major issues relating to IMF are: a) the governance of IMF and associated ideological biases; b) its asymmetric treatment of countries in its surveillance; c) differentiated conditionality prescribed as between borrowing countries; d) its failure in recognising the contribution of borrowers; e) its incapacity to resolve sovereign debt restructuring issues; and finally f) developing a system to replace U.S. Dollar as a de facto global currency since 1970s.

There have been several controversies in regard to the IMF. Recent controversies relate to its failure in anticipating global financial crisis of 2008, its operations in Latin America, East Asia and Euro Zone. The impression has been that IMF has been somewhat soft in its conditionality in Latin America. IMF was severely criticised for the avoidable pain it imposed through conditionality in Asia. Its involvement in the Euro Zone crisis and making available resources to advanced economies with political overtones was, perhaps, the most controversial of its recent programmes. IMF is criticised for its ideological association with U.S.A. However, more recently it has demonstrated dilution of its adherence to pre-conceived ideas. This is evident from its approach to capital account management.

At one stage on run-up-to-the global financial crisis in 2008, IMF did not have enough income to pay for its up-keep. As a result of great moderation, there was no demand for resources from IMF. There was a suggestion that the world no longer needs IMF and that it could be wound up since there were no takers for its money or services. However, the dominant view was that it should continue to be supported in case the need arises. So, to get over the difficulties, gold in IMF's stock of reserves was monetised. India is one of the countries that bought the gold.

In 1991, India pledged gold to manage the crisis, and IMF gave support. By 2008, India was ready to buy IMF's gold. These should be convincing illustrations of productive partnership between IMF and India.

As it happened, IMF became a focal point for global coordination in the global economy facing prospects of serious depression in 2008, and India has been a strong supporter of multilateralism.

In all these deliberations, India's leadership including professional inputs was conspicuous by its presence. The conclusion seems inevitable. Contrary to the popular beliefs, the partnership between India and IMF has been one of great mutual benefit.

Mr. V. Srinivas has done an excellent service by bringing on record in detail with insights, many of the interactions between India and IMF. The Book fills a serious gap in the existing literature on the subject by providing an updated analytical and objective account of India and IMF relationship. It should be of great interest to academics, policy makers and indeed general public too.

September 24, 2018

Y.V. Reddy

Chairman, 14th Finance Commission of India

Governor Reserve Bank of India (2008-2013)

PREFACE

The 2002 Annual Meetings witnessed unprecedented large-scale protests against the policies of the IMF and World Bank. The Anti-Globalization Protestors blocked Pennsylvania Avenue. The Washington Post dated September 27, 2002 said that anti-globalization protests were against the IMF programs in Brazil, Argentina, and IMF's maniacal support for privatization policies. Millions of protestors cried out that they were pushed into unemployment, poverty and debt by the IMF programs.

2002 was my first visit to the International Monetary Fund, as Private Secretary to Finance Minister, I was a member of the Indian delegation led by the Finance Minister to the Fund-Bank Annual Meetings. India had played several roles in the Fund, as a Founding Member and Owner; as a Borrower and then as a Creditor Nation. India's continuous engagement with the IMF has been mutually beneficial. Some of India's most distinguished civil servants, economists and central bankers have served as Executive Directors of India to the IMF.

The Fund looks resplendent in Annual Meetings with delegations from 184 member countries, comprising of Finance Ministers, Central Bank Governors, Financial Sector Specialists, Development Economists and representatives of Non-Governmental Organizations. The Fund-Bank meetings represent the best elements of multilateralism and functional democracy. They are also the biggest gathering of top financial leadership of the world. There are several sub-components of the Fund-bank Annual Meetings–the IMFC (International Monetary and Finance Committee) meetings, the World Bank Governors meeting, the Plenary Meetings, the G7 meetings, G24 meetings, G20 Central Bank Governors meetings, bilateral meetings on the sidelines of the Annual Meetings, meetings with the Managing Director IMF and President World Bank and some of the top American think tanks.

The world of Finance Ministers is driven by macroeconomic stability, control of inflation, promoting economic growth and boosting investments. In 2002, India's economic growth was on an upswing and there was buoyancy in the economic outlook. The Finance Minister presented a rosy picture of India's economic progress at the meetings of the IMFC, G20 and G24. At the IMFC, Indian Finance Ministers, largely stayed the course with the IMF's themes of fiscal integrity, monetary restraint and structural reform with support for trade liberalization, and exchange rate management.

India never held the chairmanship of the IMFC despite being an original member of the IMF. The IMFC is the apex committee to oversee the work of the Executive Board, headed by a Finance Minister who is elected to office in his home Nation and continues to hold chairmanship of the IMFC till such time he demits office of the Finance Portfolio. Gordon Brown, as Chancellor of Exchequer of United Kingdom, had one of the longest stints in recent years as IMFC chairman. When he demitted office of Chancellor of Exchequer and along with it the position of Chairman IMFC, the IMF chose the Egyptian Finance Minister and then the Finance Minister of Singapore and subsequently the Governor of the Central Bank of Mexico as Chairman. It is rather surprising why India, currently the fastest growing major economy in the world never held chairmanship of IMFC even as other emerging market economies have held the highly influential position.

For 5 years, I attended the Fund-Bank Spring and Annual Meetings in my capacities as Private Secretary to Finance Minister and subsequently as Advisor to the Executive Director (India) to the IMF. I attended an average of 17 Executive Board meetings every month for 38 months in my tenure in Washington DC.

Globalization challenges were a constant theme of discussions. Many countries were concerned that globalization policies were not working. Globalization of finance was to result in capital flowing from advanced economies to the developing economies. Instead capital moved from poor countries to advanced countries. Reduction of tariffs and global free trade were assumed to be the growth model for developing economies. Instead even Advanced Economies were not very enthused by free trade and looked at protectionist policies. Globalization was to enhance employment opportunities in countries with low wages. Instead in many cases massive job losses were witnessed and transnational Companies shifted capital with little accountability.

There was a constant discussion in the Executive Director's office if India had got anything more from the IMF than its due. We received technical assistance in the form of an RBI-IMF Institute at Pune, our quota was not entirely in accordance with the size of the economy, and India's program financing was in accordance with the permissible quota norms. India never received exceptional financing like Korea or Argentina or Brazil. India never defaulted on IMF loans unlike many other borrowing countries. The IMF's balance sheet in 2003 showed an outstanding loan of US $ 28 billion to Brazil, US $ 24 billion to Turkey, US $ 15 billion to Argentina and US $ 10 billion to Indonesia. Not all IMF loans are repaid and not all are repaid quickly.

The Fund is a highly legalistic organization driven by rigid compliance of the Articles of Agreement and the Guidelines on Conditionality. The Articles of Agreement of the IMF are synergetic with the ideological viewpoints of economic liberalism and democracy. There are a number of Indians who served the IMF as Staff. They are brilliant economists well versed in the ideals of Keynesian Macroeconomics. The collective intellectual firepower of macroeconomists that the IMF carries is unmatched by any organization in the world. As the lender of the last resort and as the confidential advisor to the member countries on macroeconomic policies, the Fund's views are taken seriously by Governments and Central Banks in addressing the external imbalances.

India has had the unique distinction of a number of staff exchanges. Several Chief Economic Advisors of India have been IMF Staffers. Ashok Lahiri, Raghuram Rajan, Arvind Subramanyam have all served at the IMF. One of the major reasons for the seamless implementation of the 1991 program was the synergy between the India's top bureaucracy and the IMF Staff. There was an intellectual convergence of ideas on structural reforms and Fund conditionality.

There were a lot of Indians who worked as staffers on the IMF. They were a part of an international bureaucracy and had reached high positions as high meritocracy in an organization dominated by Americans and Europeans. Shailendra Anjaria, Anoop Singh, Sidharth Tiwary, Kalpana

Kochhar, Ratna Sahay and several others served with high distinction on the IMF. In the Independent Evaluation Office Montek Singh Ahluwalia served as Director. A few of them returned to India to serve in the Ministry of Finance.

ACKNOWLEDGEMENTS

It is not an easy task for a serving civil servant to write a book. A subject of the complexity of India and IMF required a lot of research work and interactions with a number of senior officials who were involved with IMF. I was deeply driven to timely completion of my research work, and worked tirelessly to reach the end goal. My research work commenced on March 22, 2017 and concluded on July 8, 2018. Every day I wrote, every weekend, I worked for 12-14 hours on the book research. The IMF represented the greatest institution that I had served in, a global institution without parallel whose ideals of economic liberalism and democracy always inspired me. My wife and children put up with my obsession to write this book as I immersed myself into research and documentation for long hours. I am deeply grateful to them.

I was encouraged to take up this task by Ambassador Nalin Surie, Ambassador Bhaswati Mukherji and Smt. Kalyani Shankar. I discussed the subject of my Book Research Proposal with Ambassador T.C.A. Raghavan, who had always encouraged me to pursue academic excellence since I first served with him in the Ministry of External Affairs. Following discussions with Ambassador T.C.A. Raghavan, I decided to submit a book research proposal titled "India and the International Monetary Fund" to the Indian Council of World Affairs (ICWA). Ambassador Nalin Surie was extremely kind to sanction the project from ICWA and advised me frequently on the modalities of the study.

A book on India-IMF relations needed considerable inputs from India's Central Bankers, Ministry of Finance officials and Chief Economic Advisors. Dr. Y.V. Reddy was extremely forthcoming in his guidance and outlined his vision for India-IMF relations, emphasizing that there was a convergence of views between the IMF staff and India's Civil Servants during the 1991 economic reforms. Dr. Y.V. Reddy advised me to meet Dr.

M. Narasimham to understand the 1981 IMF program. I visited Chennai to meet Dr. C. Rangarajan, he was kind to share with me his views on India's 1991 IMF program, that the economic reforms were entirely home-grown. I met Dr. M. Narasimham at the Administrative Staff College Hyderabad, and spent an hour discussing India's 1981 IMF program. My interactions with Dr. M. Narasimham were quite significant and I incorporated an additional chapter on India's 1966 and 1981 IMF programs. Subsequently, I met Dr. Duvvuri Subbarao who advised me that the study of "India and IMF" has to take into consideration the "Rise of China in the International Monetary System" and "G20 – A Decade of Multilateralism". I found the suggestions very forward looking and incorporated 2 separate chapters on both these topics. I also met Dr. Bimal Jalan and Dr. Rakesh Mohan, who were extremely forthcoming in their views on India's economic reforms.

I met a number of former Chief Economic Advisors of India – Dr. Nitin Desai, Dr. Deepak Nayyar, Dr. Shankar Acharya, Dr. Ashok Lahiri and Dr. Arvind Virmani and I am extremely grateful for their support.

I met several colleagues in the Executive Director's Office of IMF, Shri Bhaskar Venkatramany, Shri Kanagasabapathy Kuppuswamy, Shri Partha Ray and Shri Krishnan Saranyan for their inputs and guidance. I spoke to Executive Director (India) IMF Dr. Subir Gokarn a number of times to understand the changing role of the Fund post 2008.

I had the opportunity to meet Dr. Montek Singh Ahluwalia and Dr. Rahul Khullar who served as Finance Secretary and Private Secretary to Finance Minister during the 1991 India-IMF program.

The study of India-IMF relations is an area of considerable interest to several academic institutions. I was invited by a number of elite academic institutions for orations and talks. Some of the significant orations that I delivered included "Rise of China in the International Monetary System and Implications for India and Other Countries" at the Chennai Centre for China Studies, Chennai, "India and IMF" at the Kobe University, Osaka, Japan and at the Thammasat University, Bangkok, "Finance Commissions, NITI Aayog and GST Council" at the India International Centre, New Delhi, "Rise of China in the International Monetary System" at Indian Council of World Affairs, Sapru House, New Delhi, "G20: A Decade of Multilateralism" at the Nehru Memorial Museum & Library, Teen MurtiBhavan, New Delhi; "India at 70: Relations with IMF" at the India

International Centre, "Fiscal Federalism in India" at the Institute of Social Sciences, New Delhi, "World Economic History: Major Financial Crisis 1932-2017" at the National Archives of India, "Archiving the History of the Reserve Bank of India" - the International Archives Day Oration at the Reserve Bank of India Pune, and "India's Economic History" at the 92nd Foundation Course, Lal BSNAA Mussoorie. The Executive Director(India) IMF invited me for an address at the IMF Headquarters, Washington DC in October 2018.

I received immense support from the Library Staff of ICWA where I spent 120 days from 9 am to 6 pm, Shri A.O. Khan and Smt. Shashi Rawat in particular were extremely helpful in identifying the old newspaper collections dating back to 1966. I spent a number of days in the Library rooms at the National Institute of Public Finance and Policy and the Nehru Memorial Museum and Library going through several documents of historical value. I must mention the support given by Shri Mohammad Asif Khan in my work at the National Institute of Public Finance and Policy. I also visited the Parliament House Library for the Lok Sabha and Rajya Debates on 1991 economic reforms. Shri D.Ramesh the Library Assistant helped with identifying the various debates in Parliament in 1991-1996 period.

I was posted as Chairman Board of Revenue for Rajasthan Ajmer and Chairman of the Rajasthan Tax Board from July 2017 and my office staff of Shri Satyamanyu Singh and Shri Naveen Anandkar supported me with the various inputs during this period to complete the work.

(V. Srinivas)

October 1, 2018

CHAPTER - I

THE INTERNATIONAL MONETARY FUND

This chapter deals with the evolution of the International Monetary Fund for promotion and maintenance of monetary and financial stability in individual countries and at the international level. India is an original member of the International Monetary Fund. This chapter also provides an introduction to the mandate and functions of the International Monetary Fund as lender of the last resort in handling the economic crisis.

The International Monetary Fund is amongst the most conservative financial Institutions in the world. Central Bankers and Macroeconomists are serious individuals. The 24 member IMF Executive Board meets three days a week, Mondays, Wednesdays and Fridays and considers 4 agenda items every day. The management of the Fund is the collective responsibility of the Managing Director and 4 Deputy Managing Directors. The Executive Board is the main decision-making body of the Fund, sitting in continuous session, with each of the 24 Executive Directors representing constituencies by their nationalities. Each member country is assigned a quota that determines the voting right and borrowing limits. The Executive Board exercises the onerous responsibilities of bilateral and multilateral surveillance, implementation of Stand-by Arrangements and Poverty Reduction and Growth Facilities and oversees Technical Assistance Programs. It is difficult to envisage a more driven organization with a global agenda than the International Monetary Fund.

India is an original member of the IMF. Its bustling democracy and reform-oriented leadership always received support from the Fund management. As a member of the G 20 and G 24 member countries, with a chair at the IMF since 1944, India's contribution to the IMF has been phenomenal. India lends a powerful voice of support for African member countries on PRGF programs in the IMF Board. It acts as a bridge between the G 7 member countries and Emerging Market economies, a supporter for reforms in the CIS member States and above all a voice for economic progress and development in all of South Asia.

India's quota was the fifth largest in 1945. There were serious concerns in Parliament over the utility of membership of the IMF especially when the whole system of quotas worked to give predominance to the United States of America while undermining the economic significance of India. That said, it was felt that India should lend its support to an Institution which was intended to put an end to the disastrous practices of competitive depreciation of currencies by establishing exchange rates. India's membership to the Fund was duly ratified by the Legislative Assembly on 29th October 1947. Following the 7th Quota review, India lost its nominated seat on the IMF and had to settle for an elected seat. India's position on the elected category was further eroded when the Government of the People's Republic of China sought to re-enter the Fund in April 1980. Today, China has the 3rd largest quota on the IMF and India has the 8th position.

IMF's Managing Directors in India

Christine Lagarde the Managing Director IMF was in New Delhi to address the students of Lady Shriram College on March 16, 2015 on the subject "Seizing India's Moment". This is what she said.

> "Here is your country. This is a special moment for India. Just as many countries around the world are grappling with low growth, India has been marching in the opposite direction. This year already, India's growth rate is expected to exceed that of China, and by 2030, India will overtake China as the most populous country in the world. The conditions are ripe for India to reap the demographic dividend and become a key engine for global growth. We look forward to seeing India becoming even more active on the global stage—in fora such as the G-20 and the IMF. The IMF is a global multilateral institution where countries like India deserve a bigger say. We are working precisely on that—on implementing reforms that would lift India to the top 10 shareholders at the IMF...Today, the elements are all

aligned to make India a global powerhouse. **This is India's moment. Seize it. Chak De India!"**

Dominique Strauss Kahn one of the most charismatic Managing Directors of IMF echoed similar sentiments too. In a 2010 speech at the FICCI in New Delhi Strauss Khan said the following:

> "Since my last visit to India—about three years ago—the world has suffered the worst financial crisis since the 1930s. India has weathered the crisis remarkably well, thanks in large part to sound macroeconomic and financial policies. Now, India's growth is amongst the highest in the world—making it a driving force of the global recovery. India has traveled a remarkable distance over the last generation. Rapid growth has lifted hundreds of millions out of poverty. And innovation has put India in the vanguard of technologically advanced nations. India has truly become an economic superpower. The time has come for India—and Asia more generally—to play its rightful role in the global framework of economic governance."

For decades India had lent its voice to the IMF promoting the values of democracy and liberalism. It had joined the Fund despite grave reservations from its delegation members at the Bretton Woods conference in 1944. The IMF was an institution that India had sustained and helped it grow to the global Institution that it is today.

In 2009 India committed to invest US$10 billion in IMF notes. The IMF welcomed the announcement of India's intention to support the Fund's lending capacity through the purchase of up to US$10 billion worth of IMF notes. The Fund said that the investment will help underpin the international financial system by ensuring the Fund has adequate resources to meet the financing needs of its membership, demonstrating the commitment of the Indian authorities to multilateral cooperation.

The Evolution of IMF

The IMF was established in 1944 following the Bretton Woods Conference. The world economy has witnessed dramatic changes since that time. For instance, the IMF's membership has grown four-fold, from around 40 to 184. The IMF has continually evolved to meet the needs of its members and the international economic system. In the first half of the 20th century, nationalism and protectionism disrupted this integration, setting off the

Great Depression and contributing to World War II. The IMF—and the World Bank—were established to restore an open system of trade and finance, help countries rebuild from the war and, in the process, hopefully, build a new era of world peace and prosperity. In 2008 following the Great Recession, the IMF has led the international policy cooperation dialogue for stabilizing the global economy. The world's financial landscape has dramatically altered over the past 70 years, with the rise of private international capital flows.

The IMF's mandate is promotion and maintenance of monetary and financial stability, in individual countries and at the international level. The IMF discharges this mandate in a variety of ways. It provides the framework and mechanisms for international economic cooperation through the annual IMFC and G-24 meetings. Second, the IMF helps countries design macroeconomic policies that achieve and maintain high levels of employment and income. The promotion of open economies and trade is a key element of these policies. Third, the IMF helps in the orderly correction of a country's balance of payments problems by providing temporary financing.

The International Monetary Fund represents an institution of immense asymmetric economic power. The IMF's active lending role requires sustained involvement in countries facing an economic crisis, in the formulation of macroeconomic policies. The major events that shaped the IMF namely the Paris peace conference, the Great Depression, and the Second World War, made the creation of a multilateral financial institution possible and largely determined the form it would take. Subsequent events caused the IMF to alter its practices in various ways to stay relevant in a changing world. The absence of the Soviet Union Block of countries made the IMF, largely a capitalist club that helped stabilize market-oriented economies. The bulk of IMF analysis has always been mainstream and centrist, viewed from the perspective of the dominant strain of Anglo-Saxon economics. The leading universities of North America, the United Kingdom, and Australia have been the main training grounds for much of its professional staff.

The IMF evolved over the years and underwent a number of changes. Its strengths are the depth of its surveillance in accordance with the needs of the member countries. The Fund represents the most conservative of global institutions, its ambience always projecting an environment of seriousness of purpose. For an organization with a global mandate as the lender of last resort, it has a small establishment, with about 1100 economists. The Fund's economists work in various departments with India being handled by the Asia Pacific Department.

The Fund's development in the 1970s was marked by a series of challenges. The global oil crisis made restoration of pre-crisis economic growth rates, reduced inflation and management of exchange rates for member countries a priority issue. The Fund was also called upon to finance current account deficits for oil importing countries. By 1980s the fiscal deficits in a majority of countries across the world had enlarged. There was a sharp increase in lending rates from 1 percent in the 1970s to 6 percent in 1980s. As a result, a number of countries were not able to service their external debts. There was a surge in IMF funding to developing countries, the quality of adjustment programs and Fund's financial portfolio was under stress. The surveillance procedures were weak as the Executive Board was reluctant to establish procedures that would cast a shadow on the member's economic policies. The global debt crisis of 1982-83 was the product of massive shocks to the world economy and serious misjudgments in the conduct of economic policy. The 1982 Debt Crisis changed the approach of the Fund significantly.

The Washington Consensus was to reduce the state ownership and control. The Fund's assessment of the correct level of real exchange rate was based on a model linking the level of macroeconomic policies to the behavior of the nominal exchange rate. The Fund recognized that macroeconomic adjustment alone would not be sufficient to cure the structural imbalances. It focused on reducing the roles of state ownership and control without exposing developing countries to instability and domination by more established economies and multilateral corporations. The Fund programs focused on Fiscal Integrity, Monetary Restraint and Structural Reforms.

In the 1980s the demand for Fund resources rose rapidly with 73 of the 152 members having financial obligations and 22 countries implementing Stand-by Arrangements. Poland, Romania, Hungary, Mexico, Argentina and Brazil all witnessed severe debt crisis. The Fund's approach was reduction in subsidies, raise taxes, reduce public sector borrowings, increase domestic interest rates and successive mini-devaluations. Surveillance was intrusive and deep as donors did not have separate instruments for surveillance and relied extensively on Fund inputs. Delays in implementation of reforms made donors skeptical. Negotiations with creditors occurred on many fronts from creditor countries to banks. The Fund often found it difficult to distinguish strategies of one country from the other.

African Independence resulted in significant enlargement of IMF membership. Only three of the IMF's 40 original members were in Africa: Egypt, Ethiopia, and South Africa. 53 African countries joined the IMF as members by 1990. The fall of communism in 1991 resulted in further expansion of the IMF membership taking the total membership to 172. The IMF Executive Board expanded from 22 to 24 Members in 1991 where it stands till date.

The IMF functions on a specific set of economic ideas. The primary amongst them is Keynesian macroeconomics emphasizing the use of countercyclical monetary and fiscal policies. The second is the Jacques Polak model of monetary approach to balance of payments. This approach designed in the 1950's says that if a country has balance of payments deficit, it can be resolved by reducing the domestic credit of banking system by fiscal and monetary means. The other major ideas that dominate the Fund's policy are Flexible Exchange Rates, Supply side macro-economics and inflation targeting.

The IMF's purposes, and its operational activities were designed with a key objective of fostering healthy national economies, linked by finance and trade, as the foundation for a robust global economic system. Global per capita income has more than tripled since 1944, and amongst the biggest gainers have been the developing nations —whose ranks include Brazil, Chile, China, India, Korea, and Mexico— which were able to double their share in world trade, raise per capita incomes, and lift millions out of poverty.

The Fund's oversight of the global financial stability is three-pronged (a) Surveillance (b) Monitoring of Financial sector and capital markets and (c) Financing and Lending.

Surveillance involves monitoring of economic and financial conditions, both at the global level and in individual countries. For the IMF, surveillance is a central instrument for maintaining monetary and financial stability. By obliging each IMF member to engage in a regular consultation on its economic policies, the surveillance process also explicitly recognizes the role that all countries play in maintaining global stability.

The IMF has often stated the central task of the Fund surveillance lies in a stronger and better-focused surveillance process. IMF surveillance provides the foundation for cooperation among member nations in the promotion of stability and growth in the global economy. Systemically important countries are given special attention. Further, the IMF has been carrying out comprehensive financial sector surveillance covering the financial sector and capital markets. The IMF conducts Financial Sector Assessment Program (FSAP) exercises for all participating member countries of systemic importance.

The IMF's lending role is focused on assisting members with balance of payments adjustments. Through the temporary provision of funds, the IMF lending gives members breathing room to implement policy measures to overcome underlying economic problems. For the poorest countries, financing may be provided on concessional terms, and with longer maturities. The availability of IMF funds to assist in economic adjustment gives confidence to members and the international system as a whole.

The Fund has played a traditional role in financing and lending to help prevent capital account crises and their contagion effects. To succeed in this role, the IMF exercises selectivity in supporting only those adjustment programs that will put the relevant members firmly on the path to external viability. The existence of robust domestic institutional frameworks, and strong national ownership of programs, are the key. Building on these principles, the IMF seeks a consensus between the member country and lenders on the appropriate circumstances and scale for IMF lending, the possible need for additional financial instruments, and the adequacy of the present framework for the orderly resolution of sovereign debt problems.

The Fund also provides technical assistance. Technical advice and assistance is provided to member countries in areas of the IMF's expertise, primarily in macroeconomic and financial policymaking. By helping to build institutional and human capacity for the making of sound economic policies, IMF technical assistance contributes to the building of strong economies and stable growth.

Creation of IMF – India, an Original Member

The United Nations Monetary and Financial Conference at Bretton Woods in July 1944 witnessed a consensus between 44 countries for the creation of the International Monetary Fund and the World Bank. India was represented at the Bretton Woods Conference by a six-member delegation including the Finance Minister Sir Jeremy Raisman, the Governor of the Reserve Bank of India Sir C.D. Deshmukh, and Mr. A.D. Shroff. The Indian delegation made a plea for adequate representation in the management of the Fund, and a workable agreement with the Government of the United Kingdom for liquidation of her sterling balances.

Mr. A.D. Shroff in his statement at the Bretton Woods Conference said that:

> "What I ask for is a multilateral settlement of a portion of our balances. The purpose set out in our agreement are two: To secure a multilateral convertibility for a reasonable portion of our balances and secondly to devise a formula so as not to place undue strain on the resources of the Fund. We have not disguised from the Conference the very strong feeling in our country on this question. It may be that unfortunately situated as we are politically, perhaps the big guns in the Conference may not attach great importance to a country like India. But I am bound to point out this, if you are prepared to ignore a country the size of India, with four hundred million population and with natural resources though not fully developed, yet not incomparable to the natural resources of some of biggest powers on this earth, we cannot be expected to make our full contribution to the strengthening of the resources of the Fund. Suppose you don't accept our position, you are placing us in a situation, which I may compare to the position of a man with a million-dollar balance in the bank but not sufficient cash to pay his taxi fare. That is the position you put us in."

The United States delegation expressed its sympathetic understanding of the importance of India's problem but took the view that the problem of wartime indebtedness will be settled directly by the countries concerned directly in a spirit of mutual understanding. The United Kingdom delegation said that they were grateful to those Allies and particularly to our Indian friends who put their resources at our disposal without stint and themselves suffered as a result. Lord John Maynard Keynes said that "we appreciate the moderate, friendly and realistic statement of the problem, which Mr. Shroff put before you today. Nevertheless, the settlement of these debts must be a matter between those concerned."

Despite having lost the battle for orderly liquidation of sterling balances, India still participated in the Fund and the World Bank. The membership of the International Monetary Fund proved beneficial to India in the longer run. India benefitted from the Fund's technical advice in Article IV discussions, participated in the international monetary discussions, gained valuable information and also established training institutions in India in collaboration between the Reserve Bank of India and the International Monetary Fund. Another important advantage India gained by becoming a member of the Fund is the membership of the World Bank. No Nation can become a member of the World Bank without being a member of the Fund. India received substantial loans for financing several developmental projects from the World Bank.

The charter for the International Monetary Fund (IMF) was drawn up by John Maynard Keynes, the head of the British delegation at Bretton Woods, and by Harry Dexter White, the principal member of the U.S. delegation. Over the next 6 decades, the IMF became the leading international financial institution in the world acting as a lender of the last resort in all major economic crisis.

IMF's Articles of Agreement

The purposes of the International Monetary Fund are laid down in Article I of the Articles of Agreement. So often was Article I referred to, in discussions on the Executive Board that Managing Directors often carried the Article I of the Articles of Agreement in their pockets for ready reference.

The Fund is mandated to promote international monetary cooperation through consultation and collaboration; to promote exchange stability, to maintain orderly exchange arrangements among members, and to avoid competitive exchange depreciation; to assist in the elimination of foreign exchange restrictions which hamper the growth of world trade. Further, the

Fund has to give confidence to members by making the general resources of the Fund temporarily available to them under adequate safeguards, thus providing them with the opportunity to correct maladjustments in their balance of payments. In accordance with the above, the Fund has to shorten the duration and lessen the degree of disequilibrium in the international balances of payments of members.

The Fund is mandated to oversee the effective operation of the international monetary system. In order to fulfill its functions, the Fund shall exercise firm surveillance over the exchange rate policies of members, and shall adopt specific principles for the guidance of all members with respect to those policies. Each member shall provide the Fund with the information necessary for such surveillance, and, when requested by the Fund, shall consult with it on the member's exchange rate policies. The principles adopted by the Fund shall be consistent with cooperative arrangements by which members maintain the value of their currencies in relation to the value of the currency or currencies of other members. These principles shall respect the domestic social and political policies of members, and in applying these principles the Fund shall pay due regard to the circumstances of members.

Quota Reform

In December 2015, the US Congress adopted legislation to authorize the IMF 2010 quota and governance reforms and all the conditions for their implementation were met in January 2016. These wide-ranging historic reforms represented a crucial step for the Fund's role in supporting global financial stability. Implementation of Quota reforms has enabled a more representative and modern IMF that is better equipped to meet the ends of its member countries in the 21st century. Under the quota reforms, more than 6 percent of the IMF quota shares were shifted to dynamic emerging market economies and developing countries; from over-represented to under-represented members. The four emerging market economies – Brazil, India, China and Russia are today amongst the IMF's 10 largest member countries joining the United States, Japan, and the four largest European countries – France, Germany, Italy and the United Kingdom. The Advanced European economies committed to reducing their combined Executive Board representation by 2 chairs. Accordingly, the Belgium-Netherlands chairs have been merged and the Nordic Countries chair has been merged reducing the representation by 2 chairs. For the first time, all seats on the IMF Executive Board are held by Executive Directors elected by IMF member countries. Previously, five of the seats of the Executive Board were reserved for Directors appointed by members with five largest quotas. Further, multi-country constituencies with seven or more members have been permitted to appoint a second Alternate Executive Director so that their constituencies are better represented on the Executive Board.

The quota shares of the 10 largest members of the IMF as of 2016 are the following:

S NO	COUNTRY	QUOTA
1	USA	16.66%
2	JAPAN	6.21%
3	CHINA	6.14%
4	GERMANY	5.37%
5	FRANCE	4.07%
6	UNITED KINGDOM	4.07%
7	ITALY	3.05%
8	INDIA	2.66%
9	RUSSIA	2.61%
10	BRAZIL	2.24%

Exchange Arrangements and Surveillance

The IMF's oversight of the international monetary system and the economic and financial policies of members is called surveillance. Fund surveillance covers 184 member countries. Article IV requires the Fund to conduct both bilateral and multilateral surveillance. Multilateral and bilateral surveillance are mutually supportive and reinforcing and accordingly have been operationally integrated despite being legally distinct.

Under the Articles of Agreement, the IMF Member Countries shall notify the Fund of any changes in their exchange rate arrangements. In cases where a member pegs a currency, the member would notify the Fund of all changes in the peg. In the case of a flexible exchange arrangements, the members would communicate to the Fund any discrete exchange rate changes that are not consistent with the set of indicators. All members maintaining flexible exchange arrangements have to notify the Fund whenever the authorities have taken a significant decision affecting such arrangements and in all cases of decisions where public policy statements have been issued. The Managing Director is empowered to consult a member if no such notification is received and if considered appropriate can seek a notification from the member.

The 2008 Great Recession and global financial crisis exposed the inconsistencies in the Fund surveillance necessitating significant changes. In July 2012, the IMF took an Integrated Surveillance Decision for Modernizing the Legal Framework for Surveillance. The decision said that there have been significant developments in the global economy that have highlighted the extent of trade and financial interconnections and integration and the potential benefits and risks spillovers across national borders. The Fund took the view of integrating bilateral and multilateral surveillance, including through the adoption of an integrated surveillance decision.

The Fund clarified that there were no new obligations created for members other than the existing obligations. Article IV consultations would be used for both bilateral and multilateral surveillance with an enhanced scope of coverage and a careful prioritization of topics to be covered. Such an integration was expected to fill the important gaps in surveillance. The Fund reiterated the importance of dialogue and persuasion, clarity and candor, even handedness and due regard for member countries' individual circumstances as part of Article IV consultations. The Fund stated that it would focus on those policies of members that can significantly influence present or prospective balance of payments and domestic stability. The Fund will assess whether exchange rate policies are promoting balance of payments stability and whether domestic policies are promoting domestic stability and advise members on the policy adjustments necessary for the purposes.

The 2014 Triennial Surveillance Review was conducted by the Executive Board in September 2014. The Fund identified five operational priorities for the 2014-2019 Surveillance. The priority areas were identified as risks and spillovers, macro-financial surveillance, macro-critical structural policy advise, cohesive expert policy advise and client focused approach to surveillance.

Risks and spillovers represented a major issue for the Fund, even after the global crisis had subsided. The Fund sought a systemic analysis of outward spillovers and spillbacks in systemic countries, and greater quantification of the impact of risks and spillovers and spillbacks in systemic countries; and in recipient countries, including through the presentation of alternate risk scenarios in Article IV Consultations. The Fund sought a deepening of analysis for sources and transmission of risks.

Micro-Financial Surveillance was included as an integral part of Fund Surveillance along with Structural Policies. The Fund sought an analysis of macro-prudential policies and also micro-financial policies given the relationship between the financial sector and the real economy. Fund Surveillance was also to cover macro-critical structural issues and their macro-economic importance.

As part of the cohesive expert policy advise, the Fund focused on strengthened efforts to improve the understanding of the inter-sectoral linkages and policy interactions, with focus on fiscal policy, growth and sustainability implications. A client-focused approach, effective communication and evenhandedness in surveillance were long-standing Fund approaches to Surveillance.

The Fund has adopted modalities for Surveillance over Euro Area Policies in the context of Article IV Consultations with member countries to cover monetary and exchange rate policies, regional perspectives and discussions with Euro Area institutions. Similarly, the Fund has adopted modalities for surveillance over Central African Economic and Monetary Union Policies, Eastern Caribbean Currency Union Policies, West African Economic and Monetary Union Policies.

The Fund's Surveillance had long recognized the importance of capital flows and policies to manage them. Massive surges and disruptive capital outflows posed serious policy challenges to the global economy post-2008. The Fund had an Institutional view of promoting capital flow liberalization for many decades. Amongst the major shifts in IMF positions in recent years was been the 2012 Institutional view on Trade Liberalization and Management of Capital Flows.

The Fund took the Institutional view that it needs to remain flexible on issues of liberalization and management of capital flows taking into account specific country circumstances to be reviewed periodically. Capital flows have important benefits by enhancing financial sector competitiveness, facilitating productive investment and easing the adjustment of imbalances. There were considerable risks associated with the size and volatility of capital flows and premature liberalization had adversely affected many countries. The Fund took the view that capital flow liberalization needs to be well planned, timed and sequenced so as to minimize the possible adverse domestic and multilateral consequences. Further, the Fund took the view that in certain circumstances the capital flow management measures can be useful and appropriate. The circumstances include situations in which the room for macroeconomic policy adjustment is limited, or appropriate policies take undue time to be effective.

Technical and Financial Services

The Fund undertakes financial stability assessments (FSAP) where the financial sector of a member is systemically important under Article IV. The scope of the financial stability assessment contains an evaluation of the source, probability and potential impact of the main risks to macro-financial stability in the near term for the relevant financial sector. Such an evaluation involves an analysis of the structure and soundness of the financial system, trends in both financial and non-financial sectors, risk transmission channels and features of the overall policy framework that may amplify financial stability risks. It also undertakes an assessment of the effectiveness of the authorities' financial sector supervision, the quality of financial stability analysis and reports, the role and coordination between various institutions involved in financial stability policy, and the effectiveness of monetary policy.

In 2016, India's financial sector was ranked 9th in size, 29th in Interconnectedness and has a 14th overall rank. United States was ranked 1st in size, 10th in interconnectedness and 3rd overall, while the United Kingdom was ranked 3rd in size, 1st in interconnectedness and 1st in overall rank.

The IMF's FSAP's provide an in-depth assessment of stability risks and systemic resilience. After 2010, FSAP's have been made mandatory for countries with systemically important financial sectors as a response to the global financial crisis.

Country Ownership of Fund Programs

The IMF extends credit to countries with an external imbalance, conditional on the country's commitment to implement economic policies that will restore equilibrium. Fund conditionality serves two purposes – first it ensures the IMF's financial resources are used for intended purposes to the benefit of the country and secondly it ensures that the IMF will operate as a revolving fund for the benefit of all member countries. The country authorities usually prefer conditional assistance as it comes relatively free of distorting influence of short-term political constraints that limit rational policy making. The willingness of creditor countries to influence the program may be enhanced by the perceived discipline conveyed by policy conditionality.

The Fund has defined National Ownership as:

> "Ownership is a willing assumption of responsibility for an agreed program of policies by officials in a borrowing country who have responsibility to formulate and carry out the policies, based on an understanding that the program is achievable and is in the country's interest."

Clearly establishing ownership is a two-way process, involving flexibility and responsiveness on the part of authorities of the borrowing country and the Fund and external creditors. Given that several Fund programs have gone beyond the resolution of external financing problems, ownership and flexibility needs have increased. The Fund has a specific process of interaction between the international agency and the country based on partnership and flexibility. The initial discussions and negotiations commence with a letter of intent from the country authorities to the Managing Director of the IMF followed by a set of prior actions by the country authorities for fund approval. The letter of intent is followed by dialogue with the Fund for designing a program that is most suitable for speedy restoration external balances.

Use of Fund Resources

The IMF's various loan instruments are tailored to different types of balance of payments need (actual, prospective, or potential; short-term or medium-term) as well as the specific circumstances of its diverse membership. Low-income countries may borrow on concessional terms through facilities available under the Poverty Reduction and Growth Trust. Concessional loans carry zero interest rates until the end of 2018.

The IMF's instruments for non-concessional loans are Stand-By Arrangements (SBA); the Flexible Credit Line (FCL); the Precautionary and Liquidity Line (PLL); for medium-term needs, the Extended Fund Facility (EFF); and for emergency assistance to members facing urgent balance of payments needs, the Rapid Financing Instrument (RFI). All non-concessional facilities are subject to the IMF's market-related interest rate, known as the "rate of charge," and large loans (above certain limits) carry a surcharge. The rate of charge is based on the SDR interest rate, which is revised weekly to take account of changes in short-term interest rates in major international money markets. The maximum amount that a country can borrow from the IMF, known as its access limit, varies depending on the type of loan, but is typically a multiple of the country's IMF quota. This limit may be exceeded in exceptional circumstances. The Stand-By Arrangement, the Flexible Credit Line and the Extended Fund Facility have no pre-set cap on access.

Stand-by Arrangements

The Stand-by Arrangements are not expressly provided for by the Fund's Articles of Agreement. They have been developed within the framework of the Articles and adapted with considerable flexibility to meet a variety of needs. The Stand-by Arrangements are a major feature of the Fund's operations and a flexible instrument of financial assistance. The essential purpose of a Stand-by Arrangement is to assure a member of the Fund that the member can use the financial resources upto the quota held by the member in the Fund. The Stand-by Arrangement is entered into after consultations between the Fund and a member. The only document for a Stand-by Arrangement is a member's letter or memorandum setting forth the policies and intentions utilization of Fund's resources. Use of Fund's resources, are not classified as loans. The words "Loan" and "Repayment" are carefully avoided in the Articles of Agreement. If a member needs to augment its foreign exchange resources in order to cope with its foreign payments problems, it purchases the currency or currencies of other members from the Fund and pays an equivalent amount of its own currency to the Fund. In order that the Fund's resources may continue to revolve for the benefit of all members, the member is required to see that the transaction does not remain outstanding for a long period of time.

Conditionality

The goal of conditionality on IMF credit arrangements is to promote a combination of internal and external economic balance in borrowing countries. In its lending practices, the Fund seeks to help members to attain, over the medium term, a viable payments position and exchange rate stability, a sustainable growth rate, and a liberal system of multilateral payments.

The Fund reviews the Guidelines on Conditionality on a periodical basis. Fund Conditionality is established on the basis of measures that are reasonably within a member's direct or indirect control and that are of crucial importance for achieving the goals of the member's program. Conditionality covered only those areas which are part of the Fund's core areas of responsibility. These included macroeconomic stabilization, exchange rate policies, fiscal policies and measures related to functioning of institutions associated with these policies.

The IMF handled a number of major crisis in 1980s and 1990s. The most important are the 1982 debt crisis in Mexico, Brazil and several countries of Latin America. This was followed by1992 Tequila Crisis in Mexico. The East Asian Crisis of 1998, the Korean Crisis 1998 and the Brazil and Argentina Crisis in 2002. Turkey had a large IMF program in 2003-06 period. A detailed discussion on the world's major financial crisis is taken up in the following chapter.

Fund's role in Low Income Countries

The environment affecting low-income countries (LICs) and the Fund's role in these countries have evolved considerably since the establishment of the Poverty Reduction and Growth Facility (PRGF), Poverty Reduction Strategy Paper (PRSP) process, and Enhanced Heavily Indebted Poor Countries (HIPC) Initiatives in the late 1990s. Macroeconomic policies and performance in LICs improved markedly and many LIC's benefitted from the highest growth and lowest inflation rates in decades. The Fund provided an important contribution to these gains as it refined its LIC involvement, placing emphasis on growth and poverty reduction. Debt sustainability became a central tenet of good macroeconomic management. The instruments to assist LICs were also modified and new ones created, including the Policy Support Instrument (PSI) and the Debt Sustainability Framework (DSF).

There have been refinements and increased flexibility in the Fund's approach in several key areas which played a part in sustaining growth and poverty reduction. Fund policy advice and program design have entailed greater flexibility in inflation and fiscal targets. This prudent accommodation of larger fiscal and external deficits in the context of scaled-up aid and debt relief, have allowed increased spending in priority areas. The Fund has also supported LICs in ensuring debt sustainability and avoiding a new unsustainable debt build-up. Shifting conditionality to measures critical for macroeconomic stability has helped improve country ownership.

The Fund's engagement in LICs is outlined in its mission statement which aims to help LICs achieve macroeconomic and financial stability needed to raise sustainable growth and have a durable effect on poverty reduction. The main channels for Fund's engagement are macroeconomic policy advice, capacity-building assistance, and concessional balance of payments support. As in other member countries, the Fund focuses on its core areas of expertise, macroeconomic stabilization and fiscal, monetary, financial, and exchange rate policies. The Fund's work draws on country-owned development strategies, and its advice and engagement tailored to the specific characteristics of countries.

Criticism of the IMF

By 2002, the Fund was under severe criticism from economists Joseph Stiglitz, Alan Meltzer, Martin Feldstien, John Taylor and George Schultz and also by civil society that the IMF has outlived its mission and the time has come for it go into oblivion. The clarion call of the critics was "fifty years are long enough". The issues pertain to the absence of adequate quota and voice for developing countries, resulting in the imposition of stringent conditionality for borrowings from the Fund exacerbating the problems in emerging market economies.

Critics felt that major issues and policies were not evolved in the Fund but in the G7 meetings with close to one half of the voting power of the Fund. They argued that the international monetary system would function better without the IMF as the leverage is with the G7. The counterfactual remains true that in the absence of the IMF, there will not be any other organization to finance countries in economic crisis.

The Independent Evaluation Office (IEO) of the IMF has conducted an important study regarding the prolonged use of Fund resources in the case of Pakistan, Philippines and Senegal. The IEO defined prolonged use as any country that has been in Fund programs for atleast 7 years out of 10. The IEO said that the causes of prolonged use are partly the result of evolving Fund policies but are also due to lack of clarity in the Fund's approach to the nature of the financial constraint and the design of Fund programs. Besides, in the 1990s the fund had set up a number of concessional financing instruments which had limited availability of funding, necessitating long term involvement. The IEO also pointed out that in Stand-by arrangements, there was considerable over optimism with regard to projections of terms of trade, tax revenues, exports and there was a prolonged use of Fund resources in cases where the achievements were much lesser than projected. The IEO says thus:

> "The case studies show that during long period of IMF program involvement, significant progress towards solving these countries' economic difficulties was eventually achieved in Philippines and Senegal and even more so in Morocco, although with a mixed record across areas of economic policy and at a much slower pace than originally envisaged. The record in Pakistan and Jamaica was more disappointing. In all cases substantial challenges remained at the end of the prolonged use period reviewed, especially as regards institutional reforms in tax administration and the broader public sector."

The IEO also addressed the question of Fund conditionality adversely affecting borrowing developing countries and impoverishing them. Fund conditionality comprises of prior actions and performance criteria which a country must meet to have access to Fund resources. On this the IEO said that the specific structure of conditionality is much less important than an underlying political commitment to core policy adjustment. Excessively detailed conditionality does not appear to have been effective in enhanced implementation. The IEO also found evidence that the conditionality focused on rules and procedures rather than onetime actions which was ultimately more effective. The IEO further said that ownership and implementation were the weak spots in Fund programs for prolonged users. The reason for this was the underestimation of the technical and political limits to implementation and the consequent over-optimism about the speed of success. The Fund also plays a gate keeper role providing signals to the private creditors that a clear assessment of that the member's policies are strong enough to be supported.

References

1. Lagarde, Christine, IMF Managing Director, Speech "Seizing India's Moment" Lady Shri Ram College, New Delhi, March 16, 2015www.imf.org

2. Strauss-Kahn, Dominique, IMF Managing Director Speech, "India and the Global Recovery: Key Policy Challenges", delivered at Federation of Indian Chambers of Commerce and Industry (FICCI) dated December 2, 2010www.imf.org

3. Press Release No 09/300 IMF Managing Director Dominique Strauss-Kahn Welcomes India's Commitment to Buy up to US$10 Billion of IMF Notes, September 5, 2009www.imf.org

4. De-Rato, Rodrigo, IMF Managing Director Key Note address, "The IMF in a Changing World", at the IMF/ Bundesbank symposium, Frankfurt, June 8, 2005www.imf.org

5. Press Release No. 16/91: IMF Executive Board Discusses Principles for Evenhanded Fund Surveillance and a New Mechanism for Reporting Concerns dated March 4, 2016www.imf.org

6. Report of the Coordinating Committee dated July 21, 1944 Bretton Woods Conference accessed from RBI Archives, Pune ACC No 44784 DEAP pages 27, 29-30, 31-32, 55-56

7. Kapuria R.S. "The Indian Rupee – A Study in retrospect and prospect", 1967 Vora and Co Publishers Pvt Ltd. pp 115-130

8. Boughton, James M., American in the Shadows : Harry Dexter White and the Design of the International Monetary Fund IMF WP/ 06/6 January 2006www.imf.org

9. Boughton, James M., "The IMF and the force of History : Ten Events and Ten Ideas that Have Shaped the Institution" IMF WP/ 04/75; May 2004www.imf.org

10. Boughton, James M., "Who's in Charge? Ownership and Conditionality in IMF Supported Programs" IMF WP 03/191; 2003www.imf.org

11. Reinhart, Carmen M., and Christoph Trebesch. "The International Monetary Fund: 70 Years of Reinvention." The Journal of Economic Perspectives, vol. 30, no. 1, 2016, pp. 3–27www.imf.org

12. Gold, Joseph., "The Law and Practice of the International Monetary Fund with Respect to Stand-By Arrangements" International and Comparative Law Weekly, January 1968www.imf.org

13. Public Information Notice No 08/125: IMF Executive Board Concludes Discussion on The Role of the Fund in Low-Income Countries, September 26, 2008www.imf.org

14. Selected Decisions and Selected Documents of the International Monetary Fund, Thirty Eighth Issue Washington DC, February 29, 2016 pp 25-26www.imf.org

15. Khatkhate, Deena. "Turning the Light Inward: Evaluation of IMF." Economic and Political Weekly 37, no. 46 (2002): 4627-632.

16. Eichengreen, B., & Woods, N. (2016). The IMF's Unmet Challenges. The Journal of Economic Perspectives,30(1), 29-51

17. Miller, Calum. "Pathways Through Financial Crisis: Turkey." Global Governance, vol. 12, no. 4, 2006, pp. 449–464.

18. Petras, J., & Brill, H. (1986). The IMF, Austerity and the State in Latin America. Third World Quarterly,8(2), 425-448.

19. Auvinen, J. (1996). IMF Intervention and Political Protest in the Third World: A Conventional Wisdom Refined. Third World Quarterly,17(3), 377-400.

20. Dreher, Axel, Silvia Marchesi, and James Raymond Vreeland. "The Political Economy of IMF Forecasts." Public Choice 137, no. 1/2 (2008): 145-71.

21. Lombardi, D., & Woods, N. (2008). The Politics of Influence: An Analysis of IMF Surveillance. Review of International Political Economy,15(5), 711-739

22. Dreher, Axel, and Roland Vaubel. "The Causes and Consequences of IMF Conditionality." Emerging Markets Finance & Trade 40, no. 3 (2004): 26-54.

23. Copelovitch, M. (2010). Master or Servant? Common Agency and the Political Economy of IMF Lending. International Studies Quarterly,54(1), 49-77.

24. Conway, Patrick, and Stanley Fischer. "The International Monetary Fund in a Time of Crisis: A Review of Stanley Fischer's 'IMF Essays from a Time of Crisis: The International Financial System, Stabilization, and Development." Journal of Economic Literature, vol. 44, no. 1, 2006, pp. 115–144.

25. Kapur, Devesh. "The IMF: A Cure or a Curse?" Foreign Policy, no. 111 (1998): 114-29.

26. Khan, Mohsin S., and Sunil Sharma. "IMF Conditionality and Country Ownership of Adjustment Programs." The World Bank Research Observer 18, no. 2 (2003): 227-48.

27. Thacker, Strom C. "The High Politics of IMF Lending." World Politics 52, no. 1 (1999): 38-75.

28. Yoon, Il-Hyun. "The Changing Role of the IMF: Evidence From Korea's Crisis." Asian Perspective 29, no. 2 (2005): 179-201.

29. Decision on Bilateral and Multilateral Surveillance Decision No. 15203 – (12.72) dated July 18, 2012 Selected Decisions and Selected Documents of the International Monetary Fund, Thirty Eighth Issue Washington DC, February 29, 2016 pp 25-26www.imf.org

30. The Acting Chair's Summing up – The Liberalization and Management of Capital Flows – An Institutional View, Executive Board Meeting 12/105 November 16, 2012 Selected Decisions and Selected Documents of the International Monetary Fund, Thirty Eighth Issue Washington DC, February 29, 2016 pp 55-56www.imf.org

31. The Chairman's Summing Up – 2014 Triennial Surveillance Review, Executive Board Meeting 14/90, September 26, 2014 Selected

Decisions and Selected Documents of the International Monetary Fund, Thirty Eighth Issue Washington DC, February 29, 2016 pp 41-45www.imf.org

CHAPTER - II

MAJOR FINANCIAL CRISIS: FROM GREAT DEPRESSION TO THE GREAT RECESSION

To understand the role of the IMF, it is important to present the major financial crisis that were handled by the Fund since its inception. The 9 crises presented in this chapter are the Great Depression 1932; the Suez Crisis 1956; the International Debt Crisis 1982; the East Asian Economic Crisis 1997-2001; the Russian Economic Crisis 1992-97, the Latin American Debt Crisis in Mexico, Brazil and Argentina 1994-2002, the Global Economic Recession 2007-09 and the European Crisis 2010. The G7 Finance Ministers with the IMF and World Bank formulated lending policies to enable crisis-ridden countries to regain macroeconomic stability.

Large macroeconomic imbalances represented by current account deficit and fiscal deficit contributed to vulnerability in Emerging Market Economies (EMEs). In most crisis countries, EME's financed the twin deficits with short-term foreign currency debts. A financial crisis driven by excessive loan growth was normally preceded by currency crisis, high inflation and debt defaults resulting in high capital outflows. Financial crisis also resulted from poor banking regulation, macroeconomic distortions to promote excessive investment and external shocks like commodity price volatility deteriorated a country's terms of trade. The Great Depression, the Suez Crisis, the International Debt Crisis, the East Asian Crisis, the Latin American Debt Crisis and the Great Recession were episodes in which a large number of countries simultaneously experienced crisis. In each instance, the global crisis was preceded by elevated growth rates and collapses in the year of financial turmoil.

THE GREAT DEPRESSION

On October 25, 1929 the New York Stock Exchange saw 13 million shares being sold in panic selling. During the 1920s the American economy grew at 42 percent and stock market values had increased by 218 percent from 1922 to 1929 at a rate of 20 percent a year for 7 years. No country had ever experienced such a run-up of stock prices which attracted millions of Americans into financial speculation. Nobody had seen the stock market crash coming and Americans believed in permanent prosperity till it happened.

There was no rational explanation for the collapse of the American markets in October 1929. Nearly US $ 30 billion were lost in a day, wiping out thousands of investors. In the aftermath of the US stock market crash, a series of bank panics emanated from Europe in 1931 spreading financial contagion to United States, United Kingdom, France and eventually the whole world spiraled downward into the Great Depression. The Great Depression lasted from 1929 to 1939 and was the worst economic downturn in history. By 1933, 15 million Americans were unemployed, 20,000 companies went bankrupt and a majority of American banks failed.

Early in 1928, the US Federal Reserve began a monetary contraction to reduce stock market speculation. This coupled with declining value of bank assets resulted in a rush of bank withdrawals. As Americans held onto liquidity, the ability of the Banking system to generate money through deposits was curtailed. The US Banking system could have been saved by a massive recapitalization of Banks but the Federal Reserve did not intervene. In that period, the United States maintained significant current account surplus and Germany a substantial current account deficit. Borrowings by German public and private sector occurred in foreign currencies through dollar denominated bonds and credits from United States, routed through banks in the Netherlands, Switzerland and Austria. Monetary contraction in the United States culminated in a depression in Germany. The Reichsbank's foreign reserves of gold and foreign exchange declined sharply.

In May 1931, Austria's largest Bank, the Kreditanstalt collapsed. As investors feared that their moneys would be frozen or lost, there was a huge capital exodus. Germany failed to obtain the foreign credits needed to halt the crisis. To halt the capital outflow, Germany had to close banks, devalue the mark, negotiate standstill agreements with foreign creditors and impose exchange controls. In the period 1930-32, money supply in the United States fell by 26 percent, Germany by 27 percent, in United Kingdom and France by 18 percent.

The German currency and banking crisis impacted the British pound. Vulnerabilities emerged in the British economy, given the United Kingdom's large short term indebtedness and slim gold reserves. European Banks whose assets were frozen by the German standstill agreements were making significant withdrawals from the United Kingdom resulting in a weakening of the pound. On September 16, 1931 United Kingdom suspended gold convertibility and allowed the pound to float. The Bank of England revalued its gold stock and expanded its domestic credit enabling a faster recovery than in United States and Germany. France felt the impact of the Great Depression once the pound became a floating currency and the dollar devalued. The French Franc was forced off the gold standard in 1936.

By 1933, 35 Nations had abandoned gold and gold-exchange standards. The trade of countries with stable currencies – France, Germany and United States declined substantially higher than the trade of countries with depreciated currencies – the United Kingdom and Canada. The decreases in value of exports in 1932 from the previous year was 35 percent in France, 40 percent in Germany and 33 percent in the United States as compared to 7 percent in United Kingdom and 19 percent in Canada. It was broadly felt that currency depreciation would stimulate a country's exports if other conditions are favorable. The United States promulgated the Tariff Act authorizing the President to raise or lower tariff rate by a maximum of 50 percent to ensure that the foreign currency depreciation did not result in millions of Americans losing their employment.

The United States did not lead the recovery in 1933. Economic recovery as indicated by industrial activity was visible in Great Britain, France and Germany, with the United States witnessing a rapid industrial upturn during April and May 1933. The "New Deal" of President Franklin

Roosevelt brought in a sweeping reformation of the US economy, laying the foundations of the American welfare state – federal aid to the unemployed, stiffer regulation of industry, legal protections for workers, and the Social Security program. The "New Deal" was the first step in the United States muscular emergence from the Great Depression, and the beginning of the country's rise to become the undisputed "leader of the free world."

THE SUEZ CRISIS

On July 26, 1956, Egypt nationalized the Suez Canal Company and assumed control of the canal from the international consortium that had run it for nearly a century. France, Israel and United Kingdom initiated joint military action, with Israel invading the Sinai on October 29, 1956. The military action lasted two months and the Suez-canal was closed for 6 months impacting the current account balances of all 4 countries. All four countries, had to seek IMF financial assistance in the face of an impending macroeconomic crisis. It also had a lot of political consequences - Egypt's independence, Israel's Nationhood, and a devastating blow to British empire.

In September - October 1956, Egypt, Israel and France approached the IMF with financing requests. In 1956, Britain had a significant current account surplus. The pound sterling came under heavy speculative pressure and United Kingdom witnessed short-term capital outflows. The Bank of England was forced to deplete its US dollar reserves to defend the fixed value of the pound sterling against the dollar. By December 1956, the risk of currency devaluation was real. The United Kingdom did not qualify for financial assistance from the IMF. The IMF's Articles of Agreement prohibit its lending finance to "large and unsustained" outflow of capital, which Britain faced. The Bank of England had enough resources to credit and fend off the outflow without IMF assistance. That said, the IMF financed all 4 countries on a stand-by basis. This involvement gave IMF the role of an International Crisis Manager. The Suez Crisis was the first major financial crisis of the post-war era.

Egypt was borrowing from the IMF for the second time. It was a financing request for US $ 15 million and politics did not intrude in the IMF financing of Egypt. The United States spoke in favor, France consented by noting the absence of any legal basis for objecting, Britain and The

Netherlands abstained. The IMF decision stated that the IMF expresses no objection to the financing request.

Israel had joined the IMF in 1954 and the economy was not stable enough to sustain a fixed exchange rate for its currency. After resisting for several months, the IMF agreed to set a par rate of 1.8 Israeli pounds to the dollar. It was felt that Israel drawing from the IMF could help supplement its foreign exchange reserves and setting a par value for the Israeli currency was a step in this direction. Israel had a quota of US $ 7.5 million from the IMF in 1957 and the developments in the Mediterranean with consequent rise in military spending contributed to a worsening of the balance of payments situation. With the lone abstention from Egypt, the IMF financing for Israel was approved on May 15, 1957 at 50 percent of its quota.

By September 1956, France witnessed a situation of low and depleting foreign exchange reserves. The French Franc was subjected to a flight of capital. France sought a financing arrangement for 50 percent of its quota of US $ 263.5 million. France was also fighting a war in Algeria and had a sharply reduced agricultural output that year due to frosts. These adverse influences disrupted France's balance of payments position significantly. France's current account position deteriorated by US$ 1.1 billion in 1956 from US $ 409 million surplus to US $ 700 million deficit. In October 1956, the IMF approved France's financing request.

Britain had a significant current account surplus and the second largest quota in the IMF after United States. The Bank of England had a parity of US $ 2.80 to the US Dollar and given the speculation, there was pressure to abandon the sterling parity. Britain viewed the US $ 2.80 as appropriate for trade purposes, regarded exchange rate stability as essential for preserving the sterling area as a preferential trade zone and as a reserve currency. Britain wanted to keep a minimum balance of US $ 2 billion reserves, and to fall through that floor would be interpreted as a signal that devaluation or even float was to be seriously considered. As market sentiments had shifted against the Pound Sterling, British authorities knew that they could not hold the pound at US $ 2.80 per dollar without support of the United States. The IMF financing was to address the psychological impact of a political crisis on financial markets.

The financial pressures drove Britain to accept a ceasefire and full withdrawal in the Mediterranean. The Suez Crisis was suddenly over. Following the ceasefire, American resistance to a British financing arrangement was out of the way and British request for a financing arrangement upto 75 percent of its quota was considered. Britain required US $ 1.3 billion to stem speculation against the pound. It was felt that given the United Kingdom's role as a banker for a large trading area and the status of sterling as an international currency, the IMF agreed to lend in a situation of a large and sustained capital flows.

The Suez Crisis was the first time the IMF played a significant role in helping countries cope with the international crisis. The IMF adopted a rapid response to the crisis which impressed the financial markets and convinced speculators. Britain had faced a speculative attack on a stable currency despite sound economic policies. Britain was unable to restore the level of foreign exchange reserves till 1958.

THE INTERNATIONAL DEBT CRISIS 1982 - 1989

The international debt crisis began on August 20, 1982 when the Mexican Finance Minister informed the bankers in New York that Mexico could not repay the loan that was due. The Mexican authorities had informed the IMF that without an immediate rescue, Mexico had no option but to default. This was the commencement of a decade long international debt crisis.

In March 1981, Poland informed its bank creditors that it could not repay its debt obligations. A number of Europe's largest commercial banks were heavily exposed with loans to Poland, and European governments had little choice but to rescue these banks. Poland pushed several other countries into the precipice – Romania, Hungary and Yugoslavia also requested for rescheduling the terms of repayment. The monetary contraction in the United States in the 1970-80 period resulted in a sustained appreciation of the US dollar. It made repayments in dollar terms difficult for most countries of Eastern Europe and Latin America. The commercial debt crisis erupted in 1982 and lasted till 1989.

In the 1970s, developing countries borrowed freely in the rapidly growing international credit markets at low interest rates. Banks had grown cash rich with large deposits from oil-exporting countries and there was increased lending to oil-importing countries. The loans were used on investment projects or to boost current consumption. Several developing countries had reached borrowings 12 percent of their national income, resulting in major debt-servicing difficulties. The monetary contraction in the United States in 1979-80 and the second oil shock resulted in sustained appreciation of the dollar. The May 1980 World Economic Outlook (WEO) said that the outlook for oil-importing developing countries was "frightening" and that current account deficits for those countries were not financeable under the existing development assistance. There was a concern in the WEO bordering on urgency, gravity and insistence about the potential problems in most heavily indebted countries.

The overwhelming view was that debt accumulation was beneficial. No one saw the crisis coming, or who might be affected. Commercial banks believed that sovereign lending to developing countries was a highly profitable activity. Mexico and Poland were the first manifestations of the impending crisis. Soon after Mexico, several countries in Latin America – Argentina, Brazil, Chile, Ecuador, Peru and Uruguay encountered debt-servicing problems. This accelerated the eruption of crisis in other continents also. Clearly, too many Governments were pursuing unsustainable economic policies in the contracting economic policy environment of the 1980s. Sub-Saharan African countries with official debts too faced economic crisis. The tremors were felt in Asia with India, Pakistan and China drawing on Fund's support for ambitious development and reform plans. Korea was able to service its debt without restructuring by an effective adjustment and reform program.

The International Debt Crisis lasted from 1981 to 1989. It covered nearly 20 countries around the world. The 3 major East European countries affected were Poland, Romania and Hungary and the 3 major Latin American countries affected were Argentina, Brazil and Chile. Each one faced serious debt problems but each one had unique problems in origin and implications. Long-term growth in most heavily indebted countries required a broader strategy. The Baker Plan was formulated to strengthen growth prospects of indebted countries and was followed by the Brady Plan.

Inability to service debt was only a symptom of deeper economic mismanagement in most developing countries. Feasible economic reform programs were put in place by a series of IMF programs under the Stand-By Agreements, Extended Fund Facility and Brady Plan. The strategy drawn up by the IMF and the creditor countries envisaged financing a small portion of the debt through official programs. Traditional IMF relations with Commercial Banks were characterized by arms-length mutual dependency, with Banks financing strong economic policy programs recommended by the Fund. Post-Debt Crisis there was a major change in relations between the IMF and the Commercial Banks. Officials of the IMF participated in meetings between the Commercial Banks and Country authorities. Large Stand-By Arrangements and Extended Financing Facilities were put in place to persuade Commercial Banks against rapid withdrawal.

The International Debt Crisis of 1982-89 was a threat to both creditors and debtors. The crisis could only be solved by cooperation between debtors and creditors. The coordination efforts were led by the International Monetary Fund. The systemic crisis gradually subsided by 1983, although debt-servicing difficulties remained. The period 1985-87 was a period of sustained growth and developing countries could reduce the burden of servicing debt. By 1989, there was a marked improvement in the external economic environment facing many of the indebted countries which brought an end to the international debt crisis.

THE EAST ASIAN CRISIS

A major economic crisis struck many East Asian economies in 1997. The East Asian economies, which were witnessing rapid growth and improvement in living standards, got embroiled in a severe financial crisis. Interrupting a decade of unparalleled economic growth, prosperity and promise, the crisis revealed the precariousness of the systems of economic governance in the region. No one had foreseen that these countries which were widely envisaged as economic models for many other countries could suddenly become embroiled in one of the worst financial crisis of the postwar period. The crisis was a result of large external deficits, inflated property and stock market values, poor prudential regulation, lack of supervision and exchange rate pegs to the US dollar resulting in wide swings to the exchange rates making international competitiveness unsustainable.

The Southeast Asian currency collapse began in Thailand. Thailand's current account deficit and the interest on foreign obligations had exceeded 4 percent of Thailand's GDP. Creditors believed that Thailand's large current account deficit reflected high business investment, as it was backed by high savings rates and government budget surplus. Thailand maintained a fixed exchange rate relative to the dollar. Foreign funds kept coming to Thailand given the high interest rates on Thai baht deposits and the fixed exchange rate at 25 baht per dollar. But the Baht's fixed value to the dollar could not be sustained. In 1996 and 1997 the Japanese Yen declined by 35 percent to the dollar. Wide swings in the dollar/ yen exchange rate contributed to the build-up in the crisis through shifts in the international competitiveness which proved unsustainable. As foreign investors began selling bahts, Government intervened to support its value. However, the currency could not be sustained and eventually, the Thai currency collapsed.

Contagion beset Indonesia and Korea as financial investors became worried about large current account deficits. On July 2, 1997, the Thai baht was floated and depreciated by 15-20 percent. On July 24, 2017 East Asia witnessed a "Currency Meltdown" with severe pressure on the Indonesian rupiah, the Thai baht and the Malaysian ringgit. The 1997 Indonesian economic crisis brought an end to 30 years of uninterrupted economic growth, and was amongst the worst faced by any country in the world in the 20th century. The economic crisis was exacerbated by a political transition which played out with widespread riots and resulted in the election of a new President. The Indonesian rupiah depreciated from about 2500 rupiah per US dollar in May 1997 to around 14000 rupiah per US dollar by January 1998 with imminent hyperinflation and financial meltdown. The closure of 16 banks created panic. The Indonesian authorities responded with steps to provide blanket guarantee for all depositors and creditors, creation of an Indonesian Bank Restructuring Agency and assurances to carry forward corporate restructuring.

In 1997, Korea was the 11th largest economy in the world, with inflation rate less than 5 percent, unemployment rate less than 3 percent and GDP growth was 8 percent per annum. The Korean economic crisis emerged because its business and financial institutions had incurred short term foreign debts of nearly US$ 110 billion which were 3 times of its foreign exchange reserves. Massive financial bailouts were necessitated, as countries suspended debt payments to private creditors. The Korean won came under severe pressure and Korea opted for an IMF bail-out. Korea required a US$ 57 billion IMF program, Indonesia required a US$ 40 billion IMF program.

The social costs of the IMF programs in Indonesia, Thailand and Korea were severe. Sharp price rises were witnessed in all 3 countries as a result of large exchange rate depreciations and massive job losses were seen. Food prices went up by 35 percent. Unemployment levels reached 12 percent in Indonesia, 9 percent in Korea and 8 percent in Thailand. Of the 3 crisis countries, only Korea had formal unemployment insurance, the other countries did not offer social protection arrangements.

The IMF programs in East Asian countries addressed the challenges of prolonged maintenance of pegged exchange rates, lack of enforcement of prudential rules, inadequate supervision of the financial systems, and problems of governance. Capital account liberalization became one of the core purposes of the IMF. There was a significant change in the thinking about the sustainability of fixed exchange rates. It was felt that monetary policy must be firm enough to resist excessive currency depreciation. The IMF programs promoted restructuring and recapitalization of financial institutions. Governance models for public and private sector were improved with transparency and accountability being strengthened. The IMF programs focused on fiscal policies which reduced the countries' reliance on external savings and taking into account the cost of restructuring and recapitalizing banking systems.

THE RUSSIAN ECONOMIC CRISIS

In the mid 1990s, Russia was coming out of post-Soviet period to a market economy. There was massive social dislocation, fall in living standards, inflation in excess of 300 percent. Many Russians did not have savings for basic necessities of life. Barter was prevalent in several parts of the economy and the concept of debt repayment or legal enforcement was yet to be established. The source of inflation lay in a lack of fiscal discipline – Government ran huge budget deficits financed by the Central Bank of Russia. There was large scale tax evasion and huge capital flight. Fiscal discipline in the run-up to the 1996 election was not forthcoming and the Government did not show any resolve to tackle the budget deficits. The

Government lacked the enforcement power to collect taxes from the major industrial and energy sector tax-payers.

Feeble attempts to cut the budget deficits were made in 1995. The Government sought to control the money growth by keeping the exchange rate of the ruble vis-a-vis the US dollar within a pre-announced band. Thus money growth was controlled to maintaining the exchange rate. Russia had effectively surrendered large parts of monetary independence in deciding to use the exchange rate as a nominal anchor for monetary policy. The tightening of monetary policy supported by the exchange rate anchor produced an impressive reduction of inflation in the short term and an improvement in the confidence of the ruble. Inflation was lowered to less than 50 percent by 1996 and to under 15 percent by the onset of the Asian crisis. Russia accessed international capital markets and foreigners acquired government issued paper. The strong external current account, rising international reserves and an appreciation in exchange rate, covered up the challenges of high debt servicing costs, short term structure of maturities and impact that a sudden depreciation of exchange rate could have on the Nation.

The weakening of the oil prices coupled with the onset of the East Asian crisis in 1997, resulted in a sharp and sudden deterioration in Russia's terms of trade. There was a 25 percent fall in the total exports and there were lower inflows from international capital markets with rising cost of access to international capital. Between 1997-98, faced with a deteriorating balance of payments situation, Russia faced international debt repayments of US $ 20 billion. The Central Bank of Russia intervened in the market, selling foreign exchange reserves to defend the exchange rate. Market sentiment had deteriorated rapidly and despite borrowings from International Financial Institutions, there was a rapid decline in the reserves position. It was clear that Russia could have avoided the massive disruption it faced if the Government had maintained fiscal discipline. There was a lack of coherence between institutions as the Duma rejected the key elements of the fiscal program recommended by the IMF. There was no credible macroeconomic policy response in the first 6 months of the Russian crisis. By February 1999, the Ruble had lost 70 percent of its value against the dollar and inflation had reached 90 percent. There was no banking crisis as banks largely served as the payments system and impact of the crisis on balance sheets of enterprises was modest.

Russia declared across the board suspension of debt-service payments including ruble denominated debt and suspension of private sector external payments. The authorities adopted a free floating exchange rate by abandoning the exchange rate anchor and preserved the remaining foreign exchange reserves. The policy focused on keeping the payments system operational. The political impasse between the President and the Duma made budgetary revisions impossible in 1998. Government adopted strict cash management and cut non-essential expenditures. By 1999, a credible economic stabilization program was put in place, with a prudent budget which was passed by the Duma.

The specter of seemingly unmanageable external debt and the threat of an uncontrollable hyper-inflation instilled a sense of fiscal discipline into the 1999 Russian Budget. There was an improvement in the oil prices by the third quarter of 1999 enabling Russia to build reserves quickly. Russia recovered quicker than other crisis hit countries in the same period largely due to increase in oil and gas prices. The positive effects of the high oil prices on the Russian economy coupled with fiscally prudent budgets continued up to 2003. These policy corrections enabled Russia to cover the burden of debt service repayments. Fiscal restraint in the face of burgeoning oil revenues enabled the government to rebuild international reserves while slowing the appreciation of the ruble. As the confidence in the ruble and the banking system increased, gradual reduction in inflation was also achieved. Russia adopted wide ranging structural reforms in taxation and legal enforcement. The Soviet era labor and land codes were dismantled. The number of licensed activities were brought down, pension reforms, bankruptcy laws, agricultural land laws were passed. Russia recovered quicker than what any of the observers had predicted.

LATIN AMERICAN DEBT CRISIS - MEXICO, BRAZIL AND ARGENTINA

In the 20th century, Latin America witnessed a major crisis in 1982 – Mexico's default, 1994/ 95 – the Tequila crisis, in 2001/02 Argentina's default, 1999/03 – Brazil's crisis and 2008/09 Global Financial Crisis.

In February 1995, Mexico approached the IMF for a US $ 17.8 billion stand-by arrangement for an 18-month program. This was the largest ever financing package approved by the IMF for any member country. The exceptional action was necessary to provide an adequate international response to Mexico's financial crisis and giving confidence to the international financial system. Mexico had achieved a remarkable economic transformation in 1980s on the basis of far reaching structural reforms. The Government's program had resulted in a sharp reduction in fiscal imbalances, a reduction in the role of the State in the economy, a lowering of inflation to close to international levels. During 1994, investors' concerns about the sustainability of the current account deficit began to increase, against the background of dramatic adverse political events in Mexico. To stem capital outflows, the authorities raised interest rates and depreciated the peso. Nevertheless, there was a significant loss of external reserves and there was tremendous pressure on foreign exchange and financial markets precipitated a financial crisis. The Mexican financial crisis contributed to serious pressures in financial and exchange markets in a number of other Latin American countries.

In 1998, Brazil came under significant pressure in the aftermath of the East Asian crisis, as contagion resulted in a dramatic worsening of the international financial environment. Brazilian authorities took emergency fiscal and monetary policy measures – revenue raising and expenditure cuts equivalent to 2 ½ percent of GDP and doubling the domestic lending rates to 43 ½ percent. By August 1998, the capital account came under serious pressure in the aftermath of the Russian crisis, necessitating additional expenditure cuts and fiscal tightening measures. Despite these measures, foreign exchange reserves declined from US $ 70 billion to US $ 45 billion in 3 months from July to October 1998, and Brazil was in need of a major economic restructuring program. Brazil approached the IMF for an US $ 18 billion stand-by arrangement for 36 months. The program was largely preventive in nature with the objective to assist Brazil face a period of deep uncertainty in the international financial markets.

In 2001-02 Argentina experienced one of the worst economic crisis in its history. GDP fell by 20 percent over 3 years, inflation reignited, Argentina defaulted on its sovereign debt, the banking system was paralyzed and the Argentine Peso which was pegged to the US Dollar reached lows of Arg $ 3.90 to US dollar in June 2002. Less than a year earlier Argentina was cited as a model of successful economic reform, inflation was in single digits, GDP growth was impressive, and the economy had successfully weathered the storm of the Tequila crisis. Argentina was considered a model reformer of the 21st century economic governance. The 2002 Argentina crisis was not driven by large money financed deficits and hyper-inflation but by fragility in the public sector debt dynamics. The currency board arrangement precluded direct money financing of budget deficits. In the run-up to the crisis, there was price deflation and banking system appeared sound and well capitalized.

The currency board arrangement played a central role between Argentina's transformation from a star performer to a crisis country. Initially, the currency board played a role in achieving disinflation, once Argentina slid into recession, the currency board arrangement limited Argentina's ability to prevent a tightening of monetary policy and the public debt dynamics ruled out loosening of fiscal policy. The entire onus of macroeconomic stabilization was on fiscal policy. Argentina seemed trapped in a monetary policy regime that constrained policy choices. Rising fiscal deficits, government's high off budget activities and extensive transfers of over 30 percent to provinces from Federal budgets and interest repayments severely constrained Argentina's policy options. The share of exports in Argentina's economy was limited and the country could not export its way out of the crisis. Debt service payments were absorbing 3/4th of the exports earnings. Amidst dramatically mounting debt, given the currency's free fall, Argentina defaulted on government debt and the currency board collapsed.

Argentina crisis required an IMF Stand-By Arrangement of US $ 14 billion and an international support package of US $ 40 billion. The macroeconomic stabilization program sought to bring public sector surplus to 1 ½ percent of GDP from ½ percent of GDP and reduce fiscal deficit from (–) 6.4 percent to 3 percent of GDP. Despite these interventions, GDP growth continued to decline, falling by 11 percent in 2002 and unemployment rose above 20 percent with significant inflation. Argentina passed a zero deficit law, and made radical policy changes as it ran out of funding options.

THE GREAT RECESSION

In 2008 severe recession unfolded in the United States and Europe which was the deepest slump in the world economy since 1930 and first annual contraction since the postwar period. The financial crisis which erupted in 2007 with the US sub-prime crisis deepened and entered a tumultuous phase by 2008. The impact was felt across the global financial system including in emerging markets. The 2008 deterioration of global economic performance followed years of sustained expansion built on the increasing integration of emerging and developing economies into the global economy. Lax regulatory and macroeconomic policies contributed to a buildup in imbalances across financial, housing and commodity markets. The international financial system was devastated.

The United States GDP fell by nearly 4 percent in the 4th quarter of 2008 with the broadest of US market indices, the S&P 500 down by 45 percent from its 2007 high. World GDP growth slowed down from 5 percent in 2007 to 3 ¾ percent in 2008 and 2 percent in 2009. The IMF estimated the loan losses for global financial institutions at US $ 1.5 trillion. The Lehman Brothers collapsed in September 2008. The credit freeze brought the global financial system to the brink of a collapse. Weakening global demand depressed commodity prices. Oil prices declined by over 50 percent as also food and other commodity prices. Emerging equity markets lost about a third of their value in local currency terms and more than 40 percent of their value in US dollar terms. Comprehensive policy actions were implemented to address the root causes of the financial crisis and to support demand. Faced with an imminent meltdown, the US Federal Reserve and the European Central Bank injected US $ 2.5 trillion into the credit markets. The United States passed an economic stimulus legislation to use public funds to purchase troubled assets from banks and several European countries implemented stimulus packages to manage the financial damage.

Policymakers around the world faced the daunting challenge of stabilizing financial conditions while simultaneously nursing their economies through a period of slower growth and containing inflation. Multilateral efforts were particularly important. During this period, China's geopolitical standing enhanced significantly. As the G8 member countries grappled with the crisis, it was important that given its mandate and wealth China had to be included in the discussions. The G20 framework representing 19 of the world's largest economies and the European Union became the coordinating body for handling the global crisis. The policy actions included programs to purchase distressed assets, use of public funds to recapitalize banks and provide comprehensive guarantees, and a coordinated reduction in policy rates by major central banks. Advanced economies as also emerging market economies witnessed moderation of inflation pressures due to rapidly slowing economic activity. There was scope for monetary easing and discretionary fiscal stimulus to support growth without undermining fiscal sustainability. Multilateral efforts were initiated to plug gaps in regulatory and supervisory infrastructure, fostering energy conservation and greater oil and food supplies, and enhanced efforts for unwinding the global imbalances. The effective appreciation of the renminbi and shifting resources of China and Middle East Oil Exporters to internal demand were pursued.

By October 2009, economic growth turned positive as wide ranging policy intervention supported demand and lowered the uncertainty of systemic risks to the financial system. Although the pace of recovery was slow, there was a rebound in commodity prices, pickup in manufacturing and a return of consumer confidence with firmer confidence in housing markets. The triggers for the rebound were strong public policies across the advanced economies and emerging market economies which supported demand and eliminated fears of a global depression. Central Banks reacted with exceptionally large rate cuts and Governments launched major fiscal stimulus programs. As the world economy ended 2009, the key policy challenge was to maintain supportive macroeconomic policies till the recovery was on firm footing. The withdrawal of the fiscal stimulus posed a risk in the near term, and the challenge was to map the timing of tightening of accommodative monetary policy conditions. The other policy challenge was to heal the financial sector while reforming the prudential framework. There were structural and social challenges of rising unemployment and poverty. Each of these challenges required international policy collaboration and cooperation which was achieved through the G20.

By April 2010, the world GDP growth was projected to rise to 4 ¼ percent based on highly accommodative monetary policies and supportive fiscal policies. The recovery had proceeded better than expected, and the world economy had reached a stage where monetary accommodation could be unwound cautiously with nominal exchange rate appreciation. Reform and repair of the financial sector remained a top priority for a number of advanced economies. This was taken up in the subsequent years.

THE EUROPEAN CRISIS

The year 2010, the European crisis unfolded. The euro area economy was in chaos. The euro currency area had become too large and diverse – with the anti-inflation mandate of the European Central Bank too restrictive. There were no fiscal mechanisms to transfer resources across regions. A group of European Emerging Market Countries required financial support in 2008-09. The group included Georgia, Hungary, Iceland, Latvia, Ukraine, Armenia, Bosnia and Herzegovina, Romania and Serbia. The euro area crisis countries of Greece (2011, 2012), Ireland (2010), Portugal (2011) and Cyprus (2013) faced problems of problems of public and private balance sheet vulnerabilities with large current account imbalances within the Euro Area.

In Greece, the homeless stood in lines at soup kitchens, pensioners committed suicide, the sick could not get prescription medicines, shops were shut and scavengers picked through dustbins – conditions almost reminiscent of the post war Europe. Every person under 25 was unemployed. Greece economy was collapsing due to heavy public debt and loss of market access. High fiscal deficits and dependency on foreign borrowing fueled demand. Entry to Euro Area had enabled Greece to access low cost credit, boost domestic demand with an average growth rate of 4 percent. Greece also ran pro-cyclical fiscal policies with tax cuts, increasing spending on wages and ran fiscal deficits of 7 percent for the period 2000-2008. Health care and pension costs were very high at 4.5 percent and 12.5 percent of GDP respectively. Further, Greece had a poor business environment, high inflation well above the Eurozone average and low productivity. The governance systems were poor, hardly any inward FDI and public sector was highly inefficient.

The Greece authorities made feeble attempts initially to address vulnerabilities like reducing the fiscal deficit. The efforts were not convincing and concerns about fiscal sustainability deepened with a further weakening of the market sentiment. Foreign funding dried up and there was a loss of confidence in the banking system. There were sovereign downgrades by rating agencies, sharp increases in non-performing loans, and decline in viability of banks. Greece was misreporting its fiscal data for access to foreign borrowing. The fiscal deficit for 2008 was revised from 5 percent of GDP to 7.7 percent of GDP and the fiscal deficit for 2008 was revised from 3.7 percent of GDP to 13.6 percent of GDP. The 2009 public debt data was revised from 99.6 percent of GDP to 115.1 percent of GDP. Greece needed a strong and sustained adjustment program to lower fiscal deficits, to decline its debt ratio and improve its competitiveness. The IMF stand-by arrangement in 2010 for Greece was Euro 28 billion and bilateral program assistance was provided by Greece's 15 partner Eurozone countries, in ratio of their shares in the European Central Bank capital. Greece required an additional program with the IMF in 2012 amounting Euro 30 billion. The Greece program aimed at restoring confidence and fiscal sustainability to regain market access, restore competitiveness and safeguard financial sector stability.

The unprecedented crisis in the Euro Area also affected Ireland and Portugal. In Ireland, the global crisis had major repercussions on the Irish Banking sector. This was coupled with the bursting of the real market bubble resulting in a 41 percent collapse of investment and a severe economic downturn, resulting in rising bank losses and growing difficulties for banks to secure wholesale financing. The lack of market funding access and large outflows of wholesale deposits by corporates, made banks increasingly reliant on Central Bank funding to replace maturing liabilities. Ireland's exposure was Euro 90 billion through European Central Bank and at Euro 150 billion through the Central Bank of Ireland. The initial crisis response from the Irish authorities was insufficient to stabilize the economy and Ireland required an IMF program of Euro 22.5 billion.

Against the backdrop of crisis in Greece and Ireland and fear of euro area contagion, Portugal also faced a sudden drop in financing in 2011. Portugal had the lowest per capita income of founding member countries when it joined the euro area. Easy financing with euro accession sparked a spending boom and build-up of debt. Portugal failed to adhere to the fiscal rules of EU's stability and growth pact. By 2010, when financing began to dry up, Portugal had twin deficits – current account and fiscal, of 10 percent of GDP, and public and private debt, which were amongst the highest in the euro area. Portugal required an IMF financing program of Euro 26 billion.

The crisis in the Euro Area was unprecedented, coming against the backdrop of global financial crisis, the risks of contagion were very high. The key challenges included abrupt loss of market access, need for orderly adjustments in countries with deep imbalances, no recourse to exchange rate policies, and absence of euro area firewalls. The stabilization programs were successful in giving time to build firewalls, preventing the crisis from spreading and restoring growth and market access. That the Euro Area remains together represents a collective success story for the IMF, the International Partners and the Program Countries.

Conclusion

Pre-World War I, the highly credible gold standard provided long-term exchange rate stability and eliminated exchange rate risk. The October 1929, the Great Depression meant a sudden stop of foreign capital flows to United States and Europe. As the pound was devalued, massive capital flight occurred resulting in competitive devaluations, exchange restrictions, capital controls and trade barriers. The 1944 Bretton Woods Conference resulted in the creation of the International Monetary Fund and formulation of a set of rules to address the challenges.

By 1972, the Bretton Woods Agreement had collapsed and the IMF's Articles of Agreement were amended to legitimize floating exchange rates. Capital account crises were witnessed in several emerging market countries in 1980s, 1990s to 2000s like the International Debt Crisis 1982-1989, Latin American Countries - Mexico, Brazil and Argentina 1994-2003, the East Asian Economies in 1997-1998, the Russian Federation in 1998, and the European Countries – Greece, Portugal and Ireland in 2010-2012. Each of these crisis caused immense hardships – from 15 million Americans were unemployed in the Great Depression, to every person under 25 being unemployed in Greece in the European Crisis – millions suffered. The Great Recession occurred in 2008. During the Great Recession, as in the Great Depression, the world economy witnessed volatile capital flows, scramble for reserves, an asymmetric burden of adjustment and concerns about currency wars.

In a world of increasing capital flows, regulatory challenges have thrown up policy trilemmas. The first trilemma is the incompatibility of capital flows with monetary policy autonomy and fixed exchange rate. The second trilemma is the incompatibility between financial stability and capital mobility. The third trilemma is the interplay between fiscal policy, monetary policy and capital mobility. The East Asian crisis had its origins in the financial liberalization in Thailand when the Bangkok International

Banking Facility was established which allowed a substantial number of foreign banks to operate an international banking business. These banks engaged in heavy foreign exchange borrowing which they then used to expand credit domestically. A banking crisis resulted. The Great Recession and the European crisis were also in the backdrop of liberalized financial systems, weakened financial institutions, which provided more room for the buildup of financial imbalances.

The issue of international policy coordination requires increased multilateralism. One of the steps for increased multilateralism is the cooperation through the BRICS framework – the BRICS countries established a Contingent Reserve Arrangement (CRA) which is a foundation for protection of their economic from a financial crisis. The CRA along with Chiang Mai initiative are efforts to establish monetary cooperation without the United States. That said, the financial leadership of the United States cannot be substituted. Financial crisis require foreign exchange reserves in the dollar denominated global monetary and financial infrastructure. Otherwise, Nations have to turn to the IMF, which was built as a cornerstone of the international financial system. However, in a world of increasing private capital flows, the IMF itself faced an existential crisis in 1990s and had to sell gold reserves for operational viability. The Great Recession and the European Crisis brought forth the multilateral cooperation efforts to address imminent global financial meltdowns. The G20 framework representing 19 of the world's largest economies and the European Union became the coordinating body for handling the global crisis. Collectively the global comity of Nations was successful in building firewalls, overcoming crisis and restoring growth and market access.

References

1. Foreign Affairs., "The Age of the Great Depression 1929-1941" by Dixon Wecter Reviewed by Robert Gale Woolbert January 1949 issue. www.imf.org

2. Foreign Affairs., "The Great Depression" by Edwin F. Gay July 1932 issue. www.imf.org

3. IMF., "From Suez to Tequila: The IMF as Crisis Manager" IMF Working Paper WP/ 97/90 by James Boughton, August 7, 1997. www.imf.org

4. IMF., Finance & Development September 2001 – Was Suez in 1956 the First Financial Crisis of the 21st Century? James Boughton September 1, 2001. www.imf.org

5. IMF., Summary of the Silent Revolution: The International Monetary Fund 1979-1989 by James Boughton October 1, 2001. www.imf.org

6. IMF., Finance & Development June 1998., What Lessons Does the Mexican Crisis hold for Recovery in Asia? By Guillermo Ortiz Martinez. www.imf.org

7. Silent Revolution: The IMF 1979 – 1989, October 2001, Chapter 7 – The Mexican Crisis: No Mountain Too High? www.imf.org

8. IMF., The IMF and the Challenges of Globalization – The Fund's Evolving Approach to its Constant Mission: The Case of Mexico – Address by Michel Camdessus., November 14, 1995 www.imf.org

9. IMF., Brazil Letter of Intent, November 13, 1998 www.imf.org

10. IMF., Independent Evaluation Office (IEO) of the IMF –IMF and Recent Capital Account Crisis: Indonesia, Korea and Brazil, September 12, 2003 www.imf.org

11. IMF., Lessons from the Crisis in Argentina., prepared by Policy Development and Review Department., Timothy Geithner, October 8, 2003 www.imf.org

12. IMF., "Should Countries like Argentina be able to Declare Themselves Bankrupt?, A Commentary" by Anne Krueger, First Deputy Managing Director, IMF January 18, 2002www.imf.org

13. IMF., "IMF Did Help Argentina" A letter to the Editor by Thomas C.Dawson Director External Relations Department IMF, February 25, 2002www.imf.org

14. IMF., Finance & Development, June 1999 – Lessons of the Russian Crisis for Transition Economies, YegorGaiderwww.imf.org

15. IMF., Overview of Structural Reforms in Russia after 1998 Financial Crisis., S.A.Vasiliev, February 16, 2000www.imf.org

16. IMF., Russia Rebounds., Edited by David Owen and David O.Robinson 2003www.imf.org

17. IMF., World Economic Outlook (WEO) – Financial Stress, Downturns and Recoveries, October 2008www.imf.org

18. Foreign Affairs., "The Great Crash 2008 : A Geopolitical Setback for the West" by Roger C. Altman., January/ February 2009 issue

19. IMF., World Economic Outlook (WEO) – Crisis and Recovery, April 2009www.imf.org

20. IMF., World Economic Outlook (WEO) – Sustaining the Recovery, October 2009www.imf.org

21. IMF., World Economic Outlook (WEO) – Rebalancing Growth, April 2010www.imf.org

22. Foreign Affairs., "Big Ben: Bernanke, the Fed and the Real Lessons of the Crisis" by Adam S.Posen January/ February 2015 issuewww.imf.org

23. IMF., From Great Depression to Great Recession: The Elusive Quest for International Policy Cooperation., by Atish R. Ghosh and Mahvash S. Qureshi 2017www.imf.org

24. IMF Survey: Europe: Learning Lessons from the Crisis., Marek Belka's analysis., February 24, 2010 www.imf.org

25. IMF., Greece: Ex-Post Evaluation of Exceptional Access under the 2010 Stand-By Arrangement., June 5, 2013 www.imf.org

26. IMF., Ireland: Ex-Post Evaluation of Exceptional Access under the 2010 Stand-By Arrangement., January 29, 2015 www.imf.org

27. IMF., Portugal: Post Crisis Challenges., June 15, 2016 roubini economonitor, www.imf.org

CHAPTER - III

INDIA'S IMF PROGRAMMES—1966 AND 1981: AN ANALYTICAL REVIEW

India was one of the most closed economies in the world during the period of 1947–1991. India's fiscal deficits were high, and foreign exchange reserves were precipitously low and the exports were non-competitive. On three occasions, India had to avail external assistance from the International Monetary Fund (IMF) to overcome the balance of payments (BOP) crisis. India negotiated IMF programmes in 1966, 1981 and 1991. This chapter presents an analytical review of India's IMF programs of 1966 and 1981.

In 2017, India is among the fastest growing major economies in the world. With US$400 billion foreign exchange reserves, a stable exchange rate regime and considerable global integration of the economy, India is one of the bright spots representing democracy and global growth. The dark days when the Indian economy faced severe balance of payments (BOP) crisis and had to seek external financing are distant memory. That the Indian economy has moved significantly forward on the reforms path is a tribute to the Indian policymakers in the Reserve Bank of India (RBI) and the Ministry of Finance.

Since 1947, India has availed three International Monetary Fund (IMF) programmes:

1. In the Fourth Plan, India felt that there was a need for external assistance for import liberalisation. Discussions were held between Ashok Mehta, Minister of Planning and Pierre-Paul Schweitzer,

Managing Director, IMF on 20 April 1966, in Washington, DC, following which India had agreed on 36.5 per cent rupee devaluation to bring domestic prices in line with external prices, to enhance competitiveness of exports to address the country's trade and BOP. Along with devaluation, several existing special export promotion schemes providing import entitlements against exports, and the scheme for tax credit certificates were abolished.

2. In 1981, India entered into an arrangement with the IMF to borrow in SDR 5 billion over a 3-year period under the Extended Fund Facility (EFF) Arrangement. The improvement in the BOP was faster than expected. This enabled the Government to terminate the IMF arrangement in May 1984 after drawing SDR 3.9 billion out of the SDR 5 billion originally envisaged.

3. The BOP crisis of 1991 was one of the biggest challenges in India's economic history. The rupee was devalued in two stages on 1 July and 3 July 1991 and the cumulative devaluation was about 18 per cent against major currencies. Along with the exchange rate adjustment, significant structural reforms were introduced in India's trade policy. The third major reforms were the changes introduced into the framework of industrial licensing, role of public sector, MRTP Act, and foreign direct investments and foreign technology agreements. These measures were accepted as part of the conditionalities accepted with the IMF loan in July 1991.

This chapter covers the 1966–1968 and the 1981–1983 programmes. The 1981–1983 programme was implemented at a time of low or no conditionality period in the Fund when the Fund was eager to meet the financing request of non-oil-producing member countries and conditionality was not as strong or effective as it later became.

The 1966 Program

The Indian Economic scene from 1965–1966 to 1967–1968 remained grim. The year 1965 witnessed war with Pakistan and a major drought. India's BOP position was under pressure throughout 1965, and the difficulties continued into 1966, necessitating a sizeable use of Fund resources despite severe tightening of restrictions. As the year 1965 opened, exchange reserves had already been reduced to a low level by increased payments for food inputs occasioned by the shortfall in domestic production and by delays in the repatriation of export proceeds. In March, a stand-by arrangement of US$200 million was approved by the Fund.

Inflation was 12 per cent in 1965–1966 and 15 per cent in 1966–1967. Despite high inflation rates, interest rates were low. It did not help, as both exports and imports fell by about 12 per cent in 1966–1967. Public expenditure declined by 5 per cent in 1966–1967 and 11 per cent in 1967–1968.

To slow down the monetary expansion, the government took a number of steps including raising the bank rate to 6 per cent adopting a substantially less expansionary budget for the fiscal year beginning 1 April 1965 and imposing a 10 per cent surcharge on all but the most essential imports. In August, a supplementary budget was adopted including additional domestic taxation and simplification and rationalisation of import tariff, which also had the effect of increasing further the duties on most imports. However, the tempo of monetary expansion continued unabated, in part because of unexpected developments affecting the union government's budgetary position and deficits in state governments' budgets.

Exports failed to increase in 1965. On the other hand, debt service payments continued to increase. In the latter part of 1965, exchange reserves increased steadily because of the disappearance of earlier delays in repatriating export proceeds, some inflow of banking capital, and tight import restrictions - which, however, soon began to affect domestic industrial production adversely. Moreover, by the end of the year, the basic payments position was seriously aggravated by a pause in the inflow of external assistance and by a domestic drought of unprecedented severity, which sharply increased requirements of imported food grains. In order to meet the BOP of the drought, a drawing of US$187.5 million was made from the IMF in March 1966. Reflecting this, and the Remittance Scheme, foreign exchange reserves increased substantially further in the 5 months of 1966. The Remittance Scheme which operated from November 1965 to May 1966 affected a more depreciated exchange rate to certain inward remittances by providing for the issuance of transferable certificates against which import licences up to 60 per cent of the value of remittances could be issued.

The Government had no choice except to seek a Fund arrangement and currency devaluation. Rupee was devalued by 36.5 per cent to bring domestic prices in line with external prices, to enhance the competitiveness of exports and to address the country's trade and BOP problems on 6 June 1966. The US dollar that was equivalent to Rs. 4.75 now rose to Rs. 7.50 and the pound sterling rose from Rs. 13.33 to Rs. 21. Special export promotion schemes were abolished as part of trade reforms on the same day. The devaluation of the rupee was seen as India succumbing to Western pressure. The government declared a plan holiday. The Fourth Five-Year plan was abandoned in favour of three annual plans in the wake of disruptions in the economy on account of 2 years of drought, two wars, and the devaluation of the rupee. The annual plans guided development with an immediate focus on stimulating exports and searching for efficient uses of industrial assets.

The United States allocated 900 thousand tonnes of grain under PL 480 to help India fight the famine in Bihar consequent on 3 years of drought. President Lyndon Johnson signed a Congressional resolution on 20 April 1966 and said that the Indian government would use the time gained by foreign assistance to mount a determined and effective drive to raise the country's agricultural output.

There was tremendous political pressure on the government. The Prime Minister tried to reassure the Nation that India's economic policy was not sold out under Western pressure or that Indian economy is unlikely to be dominated by foreign capital, saying that the commanding heights of the economy will always be in public domain. The Prime Minister reiterated that the government is fully committed to the objective of socialist and democratic society, but it was not wedded to any dogma. Further, it was reiterated that Indian socialism was one that was related to the country's needs and aspirations and the reality of the Indian situation.

The World Bank and the IMF hailed the decision. On 6 June 1966, the Finance Minister Sachindra Chaudhuri firmly rejected suggestions that the Government of India yielded to external pressure and agreed to devalue the rupee. The Finance Minister said that the government spent long hours considering if there was any alternative to devaluing the rupee, and ultimately, it was decided that no measure would yield the remedy they sought. The Governor of the Reserve Bank of India (RBI), P.C.

Bhattacharya, said that devaluation was not a panacea for all evils but only a beginning to enable the country to promote further development, and all efforts would be made to contain inflationary pressures and promote internal discipline. The IMF stated that it had concurred to the devaluation of the Indian rupee to a new par of Rs. 7.50 to the US dollar. The IMF hoped that devaluation of the rupee would bring about a substantial increase in Indian exports, which up to now had grown at a very small rate. Much would depend, the IMF stated, on foreign economic aid being mobilised for that purpose.

The RBI history notes that despite the package of policy measures announced in June 1966, aid commitments never approached the levels which the Indian government had earlier been given to understand it could expect from the World Bank and other members of the consortium. India and the World Bank were agreed on the need for non-project assistance of US$900 million annually for 3 years after the devaluation, in addition to project assistance of US$300 million and the latter committed itself to raising the amount. The first US$900 million was slow in coming and was received in November 1966. This was followed by protracted delays in the release of the committed funding for the second year resulting from delays in IDA replenishment. India received US$295 million in 1967–1968 and US$642 million in 1968–1969. With devaluation, there was a sharp price rise in 1966–1967 and growth in industrial production dropped sharply. Devaluation was accompanied by import liberalisation measures but imports failed to revive. The failure of the devaluation resulted in slowing down of reforms and moderation of growth targets.

But it was clear that the rupee devaluation, the single big step that the Aid India Consortium pushed for granting foreign aid to India did not meet its objectives. According to the Reserve Bank's explanation at the time, the 'adjustment in relative prices, costs and pattern of investment' necessitated by the devaluation proved 'even more difficult because of serious drought' which affected Indian economy for the second year in succession. The promised foreign aid did not materialise. Devaluation was expansionary and inflationary, particularly food prices already reeling under the impact of two successive droughts shot up steeply. There was a drastic fall in non-food aid disbursements as most of the moneys promised by the Aid India Consortium did not materialise. Exports did not become competitive and imports declined as rupee became weaker.

It was rather difficult to cut food subsidies at a time of severe drought. The expenditure contraction largely happened in public expenditure as subsidy cuts were not feasible. There was also a decline in private investments.

Newspapers were quite supportive of the government. The Hindu stated that continued pressure on the BOP position has been aggravated by the aftermath of the Chinese and Pakistani aggression and the severe drought of the past year. With exports remaining sluggish and a slowing down of foreign aid, Indian industries dependent on imported raw materials or components were working well below their capacity. It is against this background that the devaluation decision must be viewed. It is just possible that it could have been avoided if the Aid India Consortium had taken a more sympathetic and understanding view of the Indian situation—which had taken an extremely difficult turn as a result of the India–Pakistan conflict and suspension of foreign aid. Projects with high proportion of foreign exchange should be given a back seat for the present. The media also said that a modest plan on the basis of available internal and external resources and keeping in readiness a number of schemes which could be taken up when additional resources were available could be the better option.

Although export volume declined slightly during the 2 years following the devaluation, it was primarily due to drought. Correcting for this factor, exports improved though mildly. The import substitution was by no means negligible. Yet imports fell by 19 per cent. Despite a steep increase in prices caused by the drought, there was little evidence that the inflation was caused by devaluation. The devaluation had a contractionary effect on the economy. It reduced domestic economic activity, reduced private investments and had huge long-term negative implications for the economy. In the backdrop of this experience, several scholars recommended a moratorium on future devaluations or depreciations for India. It took India another 5 years to return the borrowings from IMF.

Presenting the Union Budget 1971–1972 (Interim), Finance Minister Y. B. Chavan (1971) said that India would be repaying all outstanding drawings on the IMF made during the critical years of 1966 and 1967. In addition, the obligations in relation to an increase in India's IMF quota from 750 million to 940 million dollars were also repaid. There was an overall improvement in India's foreign exchange position during the 1970s, yet there was no room for complacency with regard to BOP. The government looked at future policy options and felt the need for keeping firm rein over costs and prices, and for the deployment of fiscal instruments to regulate consumption. The priorities in investment had to be guided by the exigencies of the BOP.

The 1981 Program

After the second round of oil price increase in 1979, the shape of India's BOP which had fared reasonably well between 1972 and 1978 became a matter of concern. The BOP situation changed dramatically in 1979–1980 as agricultural growth suffered and industrial bottlenecks emerged owing to shortages of power, coal, cement and a deterioration of labour relations, difficulties with ports and railway transportation. Infrastructure inadequacies bedevilled the economy, and these were accentuated by a poor monsoon which affected hydel generation. Inflation soared from 3 per cent in 1978–1979 to 22 per cent in 1979–1980. The external terms of trade worsened significantly owing to higher prices for imported petroleum and fertilisers. Trade deficit zoomed. The government undertook deficit financing on an unprecedented scale with expansion of credit to trade, commerce and industry. Bank lending to both food and non-food sectors contributed to the rise in credit to the commercial sector.

India's second IMF loan was initially not supported by either the Finance Minister R. Venkatraman or Finance Secretary R. N. Malhotra. It was piloted by the Executive Director of India to the IMF. Dr M. Narasimham was the Executive Director of India to the World Bank who convinced the Prime Minister that India should get an IMF loan as the BOP outlook was not rosy due to oil price rise. It was only subsequent to the discussions between the Prime Minister and the Executive Director of India to the World Bank that the Finance Minister and Finance Secretary visited Washington, DC, for discussions with the IMF.

Was the IMF loan necessary? India's loan negotiations in the IMF for SDR 5 billion was opposed by the United States. The United States, which is IMF's largest shareholder, was not convinced about the BOP need. The United States felt that the IMF was getting into an investment financing contrary to the principle that Fund resources would have a revolving character for BOP crisis. The government maintained that India's policy on exchange rates would be guided by its BOP. It was clear that India did not walk into the Fund on a stretcher like it did in 1966. It was like walking into a clinic for a check-up. There were a lot of negotiations with the IMF management on the Fund arrangement from which India would draw—the Managing Director suggested a stand-by arrangement which was of shorter duration while the Indian authorities sought an EFF. There was fierce opposition in India for an IMF programme. A white paper titled 'The IMF Loan: Facts and Issues', by Ashok Mitra, the West Bengal Finance Minister in 1981, with a joint statement from twenty-three economists denounced the government's approach for IMF assistance. There was fierce opposition in Parliament and the Finance Minister assured the Lok Sabha that the government in its negotiations with the IMF would not do anything derogatory to Nation's self-respect or to the Nation's interest. The US Executive Director in the IMF conveyed to the Advisor to the Executive Director (India) that the United States could not support the EFF programme as the adjustment programme lacked specificity. The Americans were concerned that the moneys were to be used to buy Mirage aircraft.

After considerable negotiations, India's EFF loan for SDR 5 billion was approved by the IMF Executive Board. The focal point of the adjustment effort was reduction of the current account deficit by 2 per cent of GDP. The other quantitative performance criteria incorporated into the programme was the ceiling on external commercial borrowing. The Executive Board discussed India's EFF programme for a full day. The marathon debate concluded with the US abstaining. Through the programme period (November 1981 to February 1983), the RBI followed a policy of gradual devaluation of the rupee against a basket of currencies. India met all the performance criteria agreed upon and made each drawing on time.

To meet the short-term cyclical imbalance, India drew SDR 266 million under the compensatory financing facility (CFF) from the IMF, but even so, the country's international reserves slid down to three and a half months of imports. Clearly, it was a low-conditionality programme which did not entail substantial one-time devaluation. The government had successfully negotiated an IMF programme with the gradual devaluation of the rupee. The 1966 experience had convinced the government that large-scale devaluation should not be undertaken. After 3 years, India had drawn SDR 3.9 billion of the SDR 5 billion, leaving SDR 1.1 billion to be drawn following negotiation of the Fourth Year's programme.

An interesting affirmation in November 1981 was that the terms and conditions laid down by the IMF on the grant of the loan were no different from the strategy and thrust of India's own Sixth Five-Year Plan. What indeed was required by the IMF was that the Plan itself should be implemented and necessary discipline observed by the Indian authorities. The IMF conditionalities should, therefore, not be regarded as an imposition. They represented a convergence of outcomes and interests between those controlling the IMF and clients in India.

The Finance Minister's Budget Speech for 1982–1983 mentioned that there had been a substantial reduction in our BOP since 1979–1980 primarily because of sharp increases in import prices, particularly of oil and oil products. Anticipating these developments, the government made timely arrangements to negotiate a line of credit of SDR 5 billion from the IMF under its EFF. This was necessary to avoid the disruption in the Indian economy for want of essential imports and to gain time for re-adjustment to the new situation. The line of credit has been accepted in order to support an adjustment programme drawn from our strategy of planned development. It will help us implement our policies which have been sanctioned and approved by our people and Parliament.

The main elements of the government's strategy for restoring the viability of BOP in the coming years were, first and foremost, an increase in the domestic production of petroleum and petroleum products, fertilisers, steel, edible oils and non-ferrous metals. These accounted for nearly 60 per cent of total imports. The government had taken necessary action to step up production and investment in these and other critical areas. Exports have increased by 15.4 per cent during the first 8 months of the financial year, which is encouraging. However, in several areas, particularly in traditional exports, such as textiles fabrics, jute and tea, India continued to face unfavourable world market conditions. While sustaining exports of these and other traditional commodities, India needed much greater effort to expand these exports for which world markets were growing.

The RBI's history states that India's EFF experiment was a classic case of a country's readiness to accept self-imposed conditionality in adjusting its economy to a changed structural scenario and aimed at tackling the root cause of the problem. It could be claimed as a precursor for member-country's ownership of conditionality and adjustment programmes.

Several economists were surprised that gradualism ruled the 1981 programme. India went through the 1981 IMF programme without major reforms. In the 1981–1984 period, the government did start changes, for example, Export Oriented Units and SEZs were established. But the pace of reforms was slow. Following the 1984 elections, the reforms continued. But there were no major overhauling reforms. The various fears expressed by the Left that there would be dismantling of regulations such as industrial licensing, the MRTP Act and fiscal cuts were unfounded. There was tremendous political pressure on government not to liberalise imports, not to devalue and not to cut social sector spending. This is exactly what happened. The accent of liberalisation, private capital and market mechanisms which are the essential features of an IMF programme was not pursued.

Finance Minister Pranab Mukherji (1984), introducing the 1984–1985 budget, said: 'Our strategy for bringing balance of payments under control after sharp deterioration that occurred in 1979–1980, has paid rich dividends'. In view of the improvement in our payments position, the government has voluntarily decided not to avail of the balance of 1.1 billion SDR under the EFF of the IMF. While intervening in the debate on the IMF loan in this House in December 1981, the Prime Minister had this to say, and I quote:

It does not force us to borrow, nor shall we borrow unless it is in the national interest. There is absolutely no question of our accepting any programme which is incompatible with our policy declared and accepted by Parliament. It is inconceivable that anybody should think that we should accept assistance from any external agency which dictates terms which are not in consonance with such policies.

This was true then, and it is true now. Belying the prophesies of a self-styled Cassandra, the economy has emerged stronger as a result of the adjustment effort mounted by us. None of the dire consequences of that we were warned has occurred. We have not cut subsidies. We have not cut wages. We have not compromised on planning. We have not been trapped in a debt crisis. We have not faltered in our commitment to antipoverty programmes for the welfare of our people. We entered this loan arrangement with our eyes open. We came out with our heads held high.

We hope that our decision to forgo the balance of the amount available to us under the IMF loan would in a small way help the IMF to provide greater assistance to other developing countries. I must also take this opportunity to express our appreciation for the goodwill and mutual understanding that has marked our relationship with the IMF during the entire EFF arrangement.

The IMF programmes of 1966 and 1981 helped tide over periods of high inflation and difficult BOP position faced at that point of time. That stated, they were modestly successful in bringing economic reforms to the Indian economy. In the 1979–1981 period, the IMF itself was in a period of low conditionality for non-oil-producing countries and did not press for major structural reforms or performance criteria. The discovery of oil reserves in Bombay High led to complacency of possible reduction in oil imports and improvements in the fiscal and BOP positions. Although there was no devaluation of the rupee after 1966, the exchange rate policy was aimed at gradual depreciation of the rupee to maintain price competitiveness of the exports sector. Expansionary fiscal policy continued in the 1980s, and the automatic monetisation of budgetary deficits by issuing ad hoc Treasury bills strained credit policy. India entered the 1990s with structural rigidities and imbalances in the economy, pronounced macro-economic imbalances despite a significant growth rate of 5 per cent. Several adverse domestic and external developments precipitated in the BOP crisis in 1991. From this crisis, emerged a comprehensive reform agenda backed by an IMF programme which was effectively implemented.

References

1. Chavan, Y. B. (1971, March 24). Minister of Finance, introducing the interim budget for the year 1971–72.

2. Mukherji, P. (1984, February 29). Minister of Finance, introducing the Budget for the Year 1984–85 (Lok Sabha debate).

3. Sen, P. (1986, July 26). The 1966 devaluation in India: A reappraisal. The Economic and Political Weekly, XXI (30), 1323–1328.

4. The Hindu, (1966, June 7). Rupee Devalued: US Dollar to Cost Rs. 7.50 (p. 6).

5. The Hindu, (1966, April 25). India Seeks `5000 cr. Aid from Consortium (p. 1).

6. The Hindu, (1966, April 21) Western Aid Will Not Alter Basic Policy (p. 1).

CHAPTER - IV

INDIA CIRCA 1991 – ORIGINS OF THE CRISIS

This Chapter explains the origins of the economic crisis with large trade and current account deficits financed through depletion of foreign exchange reserves and growing recourse to foreign borrowings. The fiscal imbalance was the root cause of the twin problems of inflation and the difficult balance of payments position. The initial months of the IMF program were not effective. Then the turnaround happened.

The 1985-86 Long Term Fiscal Policy (LTFP) was formulated in pursuance of a commitment given by the Government as part of Union Budget 1985-86. The long term fiscal policy was to impart a definite direction and coherence to the annual budgets. Secondly, it was envisaged to shift to rules based fiscal and financial policies and less reliance on discretionary case-by-case administration of physical controls. It also envisaged an effective coordination of different dimensions of economic policy – fiscal policy, monetary policy, industrial policy and trade policy. The LTFP was to be an effective vehicle for strengthening operational linkages between the fiscal and financial objectives of the 7th Plan. The alleviation of poverty was the centrality of the Long Term Fiscal Policy.

The Long Term Fiscal Policy envisaged that Center's resources for 7th Plan period as 10.1 percent of GDP, of which 1.4 percent would be financed by net capital flow from abroad, 5.1 percent would be financed by domestic borrowings and 3.6 percent by public savings. The Budgetary deficit as a percentage of GDP was to decrease from 1.3 percent to 1.1 percent under the LTFP. In the face of persistent droughts and agrarian distress, the LTFP projections could not be sustained. The budgetary deficits for the 5 years were significantly off target, there was an expenditure boom and the tax collections were off targets. Although the Economic Surveys kept maintaining that the fiscal management in immediate future must aim at correcting these imbalances to stop inflation, contain balance of payments pressures, the policy pronouncements did not translate into effective implementation.

TABLE 2: PROJECTIONS FOR FINANCING OF CENTRAL AND UT PLANS (as a percent of GDP at 1984-85 prices)

	1985-86	1986-87	1987-88	1988-89	1989-90	7th Plan Period
Centre's Resources for Plan	10.2	10.1	10.1	10.1	10.1	10.1
Financed by						
Net Capital inflow from abroad	1.2	1.3	1.4	1.5	1.6	1.4
Domestic Borrowings	6.4	5.6	5.0	4.4	4.2	5.1
Public Savings	2.5	3.2	3.7	4.3	4.3	3.6

Source: Table 3, Long Term Fiscal Policy Ministry of Finance (Department of Economic Affairs) December 1985 pp 11

The Economic Survey for the year 1988-89 said thus:

"Though it has not been appreciated, it must be recognized that high levels of fiscal deficits tend to spill over and contribute to high current account deficits in the balance of payments. An improvement in the current account of the balance of payments requires a commensurate reduction in the overall savings –investment gap of the economy. In a situation such as ours where the recent widening of the savings-investments gap is largely attributable to deterioration in the budgetary performance will contribute substantially towards a sustained improvement in the balance of payments."

The Economic Survey[1] for the year 1989-90 said thus:

"India's balance of payments situation has remained under considerable pressure during 1989-90 despite a buoyant trend in exports and a slow-down in the growth of imports. Deterioration in our balance of payments position during the 7th Plan period is due to several unfavorable factors such as deceleration in the growth of domestic oil production bunching of repayment obligations to the IMF and other sources, limited availability of concessional assistance and a rise in debt service payments on external debt. The continuing strain on our balance of payments is reflected in steep depletion of foreign exchange reserves which stood at Rs. 5531 crores at the end of January 1990."

Prof Madhu Dandavate introduced the Union Budget for the year 1990-91. The scenario could not have been more grim. The Finance Minister presented to the Lok Sabha the ground realities of that period. The Central Government's budgetary deficit was Rs. 13,790 crores as on 1st December 1989, a level nearly double the deficit projected for the whole year in 1989-90 budget. Wholesale prices had risen by 6.6 percent since the beginning of the financial year. The balance of payment was under strain and foreign exchange reserves (excluding gold and SDRs) were down to around Rs. 5000 crores. Stocks of food grains had fallen to 11 million tons. The GDP growth was projected at 4-4.5 percent, industrial output growth projected at 6 percent and agricultural output growth projected at 1 percent. The price rise and pressure of inflation strained fiscal balance. Budget deficit was expected to be substantially higher than the projected Rs. 7337 crores and the growth rate of aggregate monetary resources was 16.5 percent in 1989-90.

Trade performance wasn't very encouraging either. Although exports grew by 38 percent and imports by 21 percent in rupee terms in the first nine months of 1990-91, the pressure on foreign exchange reserves continued and improvements in trade account were not sufficient to counter-balance the increase in debt-service obligations. Trade and current accounts deficits were financed through depletion of foreign exchange reserves and growing

---

1 Economic Survey 1989-90 pp 7-8

recourse to foreign borrowings. To combat the pressures on the balance of payments and to ensure a viable situation over the 8th Plan period, exports were accorded the highest priority. It was recognized that the alternative of higher foreign borrowing to finance essential import requirements runs the risk of mortgaging India's hard won economic independence, which was unacceptable. The Finance Minister outlined fiscal measures for promotion of export production for earning high net foreign exchange.

TABLE 4

PROJECTIONS OF CENTRE'S REVENUE RECEIPTS AND NON PLAN REVENUE EXPENDITURE OVER 7TH PLAN PERIOD (as percent of GDP at 1984-85 prices)

	1985-86	1986-87	1987-88	1988-89	1989-90
Tax Revenue (projected in LTFP)	7.8	8.2	8.7	9.2	9.4
Tax Revenue (actual)	8.1	8.3	8.4	8.4	8.9
Total Current Expenditure (projected in LTFP)	11.1	11.3	11.5	11.6	11.9
Total Current Expenditure (actual)	13.2	14.4	14.3	14.2	14.2
Budgetary Deficit (projected in LTFP)	1.3	1.2	1.1	1.0	0.9
Budget Deficit (actual)	1.3	3.1	1.7	2.3	1.9

Source: Tables 4 Long Term Fiscal Policy December 1985 pp 13 and Table 6.2 Economic Survey 1989-90 pp77

The budget recognized that the import bill for bulk items was increasing rapidly. The oil consumption was rising at around 8 percent resulting in a huge outflow of foreign exchange on this account. India's foreign debt had doubled in the period 1985-90 adding to vulnerability. The Government exhorted people to make sacrifices to meet challenges in order to preserve India's economic independence and spirit of self-reliance. The Nation prepared for a period of austerity and hardship in order to avoid excess foreign borrowings.

Fiscal imbalance was the root cause of the twin problems of inflation and difficult balance of payments position. Government said that the management of deficit required containment of expenditure growth. The restraint of expenditure required careful consideration of the areas of public spending involving explicit and implicit subsidies. On the revenue side, the major challenge was tax compliance. Tax evasion was rampant, generating black money with serious adverse effects on the economy fueling inflation and conspicuous consumption. Black money was also generated by shortages, artificially pegged prices and detailed physical controls. The leakages from public expenditure programs also caused serious distortions in the economic and social structure of the society.

The Reserve Bank of India's history says that the monetization of fiscal deficit resulted in higher liquidity growth over and above the overhang of liquidity carried from earlier years and the consequent expansionary impact on money supply. To some extent, the Union Budget for 1989-90 sought to correct the growing imbalances between revenues and expenditures. However, the outcome turned out to be much worse because the imbalances did not stem from any let-up in government revenue mobilization but due to increases in the government expenditure which in turn was financed by larger borrowings and the budget deficit. The Centre's budget deficit in 1989-90 (according to Reserve Bank records) was much higher, by about 30 percent, than the budgeted amount. Like-wise the Reserve Bank credit to Central Government was in 1989-90 more than twice the actual for 1988-89. The spill-over of fiscal deficit into current account deficit was visible. The aggregate absorption in the economy was in excess of domestically produced goods and services. The imbalances between aggregate demand and supply ultimately spilt over into the BOP and the gap had to be met by either running down the reserves or increasing debt. The fiscal deficit was nurtured by a large expansion in net Reserve Bank credit to Central Government against the issue of adhoc Treasury Bills, which was automatic monetization of deficit.

The Economic Survey[2] for the year 1991-92 said thus:

> "The first signs of the current payments crisis became evident in the second half of 1990-91 when the Gulf war led to a sharp increase in oil prices. Foreign exchange reserves began to decline from September 1990. They declined to a level of Rs. 5480 crores (US $ 3.11 billion) at the end of August 1990 to Rs. 1666 crores (US $ 896 million) on 16th January 1991. During the period the Government took recourse to the IMF by drawing Rs. 1177 crores (US $ 60 million) from the reserve tranche during July-September 1990. Again in January 1991, the Government made a drawing of Rs. 1884 crores (US $ 1.025 billion) under the compensatory and contingency financing facility (CCFF) and a drawing of Rs. 1450 crores (US $ 789 million) under a first credit tranche arrangement (FCT). The purchases from the International Monetary Fund in January 1991 amounted to Rs. 3334 crores (US $ 1.814 billion). Nevertheless the decline in reserves continued unabated."

The rapid loss of reserves had prompted the Government to take a number of counter measures in the second half of 1990-91. In October 1990, Reserve Bank of India imposed a cash margin of 50 percent on imports other than those of capital goods. Capital goods imports were allowed only against foreign sources of credit. In December 1990, Government imposed a surcharge of 25 percent on the prices of petroleum products except domestic gas. The Reserve Bank of India imposed a 25 percent surcharge on interest on bank credit for imports. These stringent measures had the effect of forcing a considerable degree of import compression. The non-oil imports came down by 23.1 percent in the April-June 1991 quarter.

Government launched a sustained and multi-pronged drive against proliferation of black money, by improving tax compliance and simpler tax laws. Government proposed introduction of a time bound scheme permitting undeclared incomes and hidden wealth on a flat rate of tax. Government proposed to abolish the Gold Control Act. On the direct taxes front, Government increased the exemption limit for personal income tax from Rs. 18000/- to Rs. 22000/-. The decision to raise the exemption limit involving substantial loss of revenue and narrowing the tax base was defended by the Government on the grounds that it was part of the National Front Government's manifesto. Even on the indirect taxes side, the Government gave a number of concessions. Coming at a time of severe

---

2 Economic Survey 1991-92 pp 4-17

financial crisis, the Union Budget 1990-91 did not produce the anticipated results.

TABLE 5

MOVEMENTS IN FOREIGN EXCHANGE RESERVES[3] (RS. CRORES)

Year	Foreign Exchange reserves at the end of the year@	Movement in Foreign Exchange Reserves	Net Drawals on IMF
1979-80	5934	113	-55*
1980-81	5544	-390	814**
1981-82	4024	-1520	637
1982-83	4782	758	1893
1983-84	5972	1190	1342
1984-85	7243	1271	63
1985-86	7820	577	-327*
1986-87	8151	331	-840*
1987-88	7687	-464	-1388*
1988-89	7040	-647	-1749*
1989-90	6251	-789	-1688*
1990-91	11416**	5165**	-2043*
1991-92	19392***	7976***	2169

*Includes Trust Fund loan drawals and repayments/**Effective October 17, 1990 gold was revalued close to international market price at the end of every month. For earlier periods gold is valued at official rate of Rs. 84.39 per 10 grams/ ***Includes purchase of gold of Rs. 494 crores and US $ 191 million from Government of India on December 23, 1991 and January 7, 1991/ @includes foreign currency assets of RBI, gold holdings of RBI, SDR holdings of Government.

---

3   Table 8.2, Economic Survey 1991-92 pp 62

Dr. Nitin Desai Chief Economic Advisor from 1988-1990 says:

In the period 1988-89, the Ministry of Finance was run by Prime Minister's Office. The Budget Meetings were convened in the PMO. Prime Minister would often chair the meetings with Finance Minister in attendance. The Prime Minister's economist was Montek Singh Ahluwalia.

Should we have gone to the IMF in 1988 and did not go to the IMF? 1988 was a little early to go to the IMF. It was mentioned but there was no serious consideration on the subject. Growth rate had increased and although the balance of payments and fiscal situation was not doing well, the major problems did not surface till 1989 when the rupee trade with the Soviet Union for commodities had collapsed.

The Prime Minister in 1988 was not worried about going to the IMF. There was no ideological problem abut going to the IMF. The IMF wanted a sharp fiscal correction in India. The political judgment was "we cant do it now, perhaps after the elections."

After the elections in 1989, with the new Government, there was an ideological opposition to an IMF program. The talk of an IMF program was more active because we were facing a near solvency crunch. An IMF program was not pursued as Government feared capitalist conditions would be imposed. The political base of the new Government was largely from backward sections of society. The crisis broke in 1991. In hindsight, if we went to IMF in 1989, we would have avoided the tight crunch of 1991, some of the decisions like pledging gold could have been avoided. We also were worried about that external discipline would be enforced on us. The public image of the IMF was that of a ruthless condition setter, as one that will reduce social expenditures.

In those days, the Chief Economic Advisor (CEA) also shouldered operational duties in the Ministry of Finance and not an independent advisor to Government. As CEA, I had adopted a more restrained approach in the Economic Surveys. Our Economic Survey of 1988-89 brought out the impending crisis in a subtle manner. The Government's formal communications with the RBI were limited as we enjoyed an informal relationship with the Secretary DEA being appointed as Governor RBI. Although there were communications from RBI on the impending crisis, there was no formal response from Government.

India in 1980s was fairly active in external commercial borrowings. We had never reneged on debt payments. Our solvency was a major problem for the credit agencies. The problem was exacerbated by an unbalanced current account deficit, not so much as debt. We were lulled into complacency by the oil discoveries at Bombay High Oilfields. With domestic oil production rising in the mid 1980s, oil import bills had shown a decline. Hence the complacency in export promotion. We could have done more in liberalization at that time. We remained a public sector dependent country.

If I were to look back and say the causes of the 1991 crisis, they would be four fold:

1. Complacency caused by Bombay High Oil discoveries

2. Lack of export competitiveness

3. High dependence on public sector

4. Collapse of Rupee-Rouble trade following the dismantling of the Soviet Union which was largely barter system because the rupee component was significant.

Could it have been staved off? Yes. In hind sight, an IMF program in 1988-89 could have helped us stave off the desperate measures we undertook in 1991. The reforms would have also come. The mood was right but they wanted to wait till the 1989 elections. In the run-up to the Union Budget 1989, we were looking at announcements that would enthuse the markets, liberalize the trade policy. There was a broad consensus for trade policy reform, industrial policy reform, but the mood was for gradual reforms. We also took some steps for reform of financial sector. SEBI was established, National Stock Exchange was established and dematerialization was introduced. Another step was the opening up of the mutual fund industry to private players. The gains from the opening up of financial sector were quite significant in the reform years.

1991 was the year when the full range of reforms scenario was witnessed, would not have been possible without an IMF program. The reforms of 1980s cannot be underestimated though. The boom in private sector investments, witnessed in the 1990s were from the financial sector reforms of 1980s. That said, like many other developing countries, we left it too late to go to the IMF. The reforms we got, were quite radical. The Government doing reforms as part of the IMF program was quite significant and no major opposition was witnessed. One of the reasons was that the Indian conditionality in the IMF program was not onerous. Fiscal adjustment was modest and we could cope with conditions. It can safely be said that without the IMF program there would have been a major disruption in our economy. The IMF program allowed us to have a smooth transition. Camdessus as Managing Director IMF was keen that the Fund program in India is successful.

Today the IMF represents part of the old global financial institutions. The scenario has changed significantly with the emergence of China and the rise of the G20.

India circa 1991 – Origins of the Crisis

On December 27, 1990 Finance Minister Yashwant Sinha made a statement in the Rajya Sabha on the Current Fiscal Situation on the strategic issues in the management of the Indian economy. The scenario presented the persistence of large fiscal imbalances, serious balance of payments and considerable inflationary pressures on the price level. The Finance Minister said that the performance of the economy during the second half of the 1980s was impressive in terms of growth rates, but this was associated with the emergence of macro-economic imbalances. The widening gap between income and expenditure led to mounting budget deficit. The fiscal deficit burden was met through borrowings. The burden of serving the debt became onerous. Interest payments in 1990-91 alone constituted 20 percent of total expenditure of central government and 4 percent of GDP as compared with 10 percent of total expenditure and 2 percent of GDP in 1980-81. The balance of payments situation was also under considerable strain. Current account deficit was 2.2 percent of GDP as compared with 1.3 percent of GDP during 6th Plan period. Current account deficits were financed by borrowings. The Finance Minister informed the House that it was clear that the Indian economy was facing a serious fiscal crisis and very difficult balance of payments position. The Gulf Crisis and the shortfalls in domestic crude oil production led to a further deterioration in the fiscal situation.

The Finance Minister said that the soft options stand exhausted and it was imperative to start making the necessary macro-economic adjustments. Additional taxation measures were introduced namely the gulf surcharge of 25 percent and a further surcharge of 7 percent on corporation tax. On the indirect taxes side, auxiliary customs duties were introduced. Expenditure controls and rationalization of subsidies were proposed so that the expenditures are better directed at the poor. Even in December 1990, the Finance Minister maintained that the Government would be in a position to overcome the crisis and manage the economic difficulties.

> On the Pledging of Gold, Dr. C. Rangarajan says,
>
> India's balance of payments situation had deteriorated sharply by the end of 1990. Even as attempts were being made to obtain normal and extraordinary funding from multilateral

institutions, private banks and other market players were also being approached. With frequent changes in government, the responsibility of RBI increased. Governor Venkitaramanan was so active that he was described by an economic daily as 'lone (loan) ranger'.

In the course of talking with various market players, one question that came up frequently was: 'what was India doing on its own to tide over the crisis?' The implication was simple. India had a fairly large stock of gold as reserves. Why could not India use it? This was not outside the thought of RBI as well. Several steps were being taken to activate the Banks' gold holding. The first step was to revalue the gold holdings at market price. This was done by government through an ordinance in October 1990 which later was approved by the parliament to become part of the Act. In January 1991 a proposal was mooted by SBI to raise foreign exchange through lease of gold held by government. In April 1991, government agreed to the proposal to utilise 20 tonnes of confiscated gold to raise foreign exchange and gold was despatched in four consignments in May 1991. This was actually executed in the form of sale with a repurchase option. RBI was involved totally in this arrangement. This was not enough. RBI was thinking of how to use its own gold to tide over the crisis.

In using RBI's gold, there were three sets of issues to be faced and cleared. First, at the policy level, a decision was needed. Given the sentimental attachment to gold, it was felt from the beginning that outright sale of gold was not an option. Pledging gold and raising a foreign exchange loan was the only thing contemplated. Second whatever was to be done had to be consistent with the provisions of RBI Act. Under the Act, RBI could borrow only from other currency authorities. Third, there were issues connected with the physical task of selecting, packing and sending gold out. It bristled with many problems.

The advice of RBI for pledging gold to raise a foreign exchange loan was accepted by government. It was a bold decision by a government which at that time was only a caretaker government.

Governor Venkitaramanan and I visited several central banks to sound out how far they would be helpful. Bank for International Settlements (BIS) had to be ruled out because it was not strictly a 'currency authority'. It turned out that Bank of England and Bank of Japan were two Central Banks who would be willing. But both the institutions insisted that the pledged gold must be kept outside India, despite India being a depository country under IMF. The RBI Act does permit keeping of gold outside India, but with some restrictions. To conform to the provisions of the Act with respect to borrowing, RBI had to transfer the asset from the Issue Department to Banking Department and this was done before transshipping gold. Since RBI is permitted to borrow only for a month, the borrowing had to be rolled over from month to month.

The third set of issues relating to the shipment of gold turned out to be more arduous than expected. Since the quantity of gold to be pledged was around 50 tonnes, it was decided to use the gold that was in stock in Mumbai. The gold that was in stock was in various forms. Not all of them satisfied London Good Delivery (LGD) specifications in terms of fineness and weight. It was decided to send the pure gold bars as they were and Bank of England was entrusted with the responsibility of converting non LGD bars into LGD bars. Packing, insuring and finally sending the gold through airlines had to be done in a short span of time without attracting much attention. This was an operation in which various departments of RBI such as External Investments & Operations (DEIO), Issue, Banking Operations and Legal had to come together and act.

Mr. P.B. Kulkarni, Chief of DEIO and his band of devoted colleagues did a tremendous job. In all, 46.91 tonnes of gold were dispatched in four consignments by air beginning July 4. The largest consignment was the second one which had to be transported through a chartered carrier. It is interesting to note that the actual dispatch happened after the new government of Mr. Narasimha Rao and Dr. Manmohan Singh took over. The new Finance Minister raised no objection and he in fact defended the action in parliament. The loan raised against the pledging of gold was repaid by November 1991. However, that gold was not brought back but kept abroad.

The entire episode is not without its drama. For example, when any Commodity is sent out of the country, the nature of the commodity has to be declared. I spoke with the Commissioner of Customs and a special authorization from the Finance Ministry was obtained to send gold without such a declaration. As one of the consignments had an intermediate stop-over, a sudden doubt arose whether this was covered by insurance. On a Sunday, I had the office opened to check the policy and was relieved to find that it had a 'Vault to Vault' insurance cover. Finally, when gold was moved from the vault of Bombay office to the airport, the movement along the road was closely monitored. It so happened in the case of one large consignment, the bullion van had to stop because of a suspected tyre burst of one of the cars in the convoy. Fortunately, before much commotion could happen, the convoy resumed.

The total loan raised against the pledge of gold was US $ 405 million. In today's reckoning it may look small. But that amount was crucial at that time to prevent a default. There was no intention on the part of the RBI or government to hide from the public the transaction. The RBI wanted to make it public once the operation was over. Otherwise there was some operational risk. The shipment of gold brought home to everyone the enormity of the crisis and paved the way for the Reforms.

By June 1991, it had become clear that import compression was proving counter-productive as an instrument for management of the balance of payments. The adverse impact of import compression was felt on the index of industrial production during 1991-92. Further compression would have entailed a sharper fall in industrial production, disruption of transport and a fall in exports as imports of inputs were reduced. Import compression reached a stage where it threatened widespread loss of production and employment and verged on large scale economic chaos.

The balance of payments crisis had become overwhelmingly a crisis of confidence – of confidence in the Government's ability to manage the balance of payments. The loss of confidence had itself undermined the Government's capability to deal with the crisis by closing off all recourse to external credit. A default in payments for the first time in India's history had become a serious possibility in June 1991.

To avoid a default in payments the Government leased 20 tons of gold out of its stock to the State Bank of India to enable it to sell gold abroad with the option to repurchase it at the end of six months. The Government allowed the Reserve Bank of India to ship 47 tons of gold to the Bank of England in July. This helped to raise US $ 600 million. The exchange rate of the rupee was adjusted in July 1991 to bring to a credible level where it could be defended. The Government moved quickly to implement a program of fiscal correction. Simultaneously a program of structural reforms in trade policy, industrial policy and public sector policies were also initiated.

In 1991, the IMF granted India a loan amounting to US$ 1786 million – US $ 777 million under India's first credit tranche and US $ 1009 million under the Compensatory and Contingency Financing Facility a week ago.

The IMF's press note said that "the Government of India is committed to continuing the adjustment process in the fiscal year 1991-92 beginning in April". The IMF was also given an assurance by the Government that it intends to implement a wide range of policies to improve the efficiency and competitiveness of the Indian economy. The Economic and Political Weekly said that this is just the beginning of the IMF's active involvement with the Indian economy which is going to last for next many years. Satisfaction of the IMF is going to be an important consideration for the Government in framing its budget for the next financial year.

On Devaluation of the rupee Dr. C.Rangarajan recollects the following:

The 'downward adjustment of the rupee' (an euphemistic expression for devaluation) in July 1991 continues to attract attention and excitement. Unlike the previous decisions on devaluation, the July 1991 decision was not announced by the government. It was done as part of the daily adjustment of the exchange rate that the RBI was making. No one had expected this and there hangs an important tale.

The deterioration in India's Balance of Payments during 1990 and 1991 is well documented. The sharp rise in crude oil prices as a consequence of the Gulf Crisis in mid 1990 gave a severe jolt to India's balance of payments situation which was already under stress. India's current account deficit had touched 2.7 per cent of GDP even in 1988-89. From the middle of 1990, financing the current account deficit became an arduous task. Traditional sources of financing started drying up. It became difficult to roll over short term finance. Non-resident deposits, the inflow of which contributed significantly to bridge the current account deficit started flowing out. Serious negotiations with IMF started only in December 1990, even though in a detailed letter RBI had urged government approaching IMF as early as August 1990. Had we done so, the process of negotiations would have been much smoother. By the time we went to IMF, the position had deteriorated so much that we were gasping for relief. By end December 1990, foreign exchange reserves were equal only to three weeks of imports. Deepak Nayyar and I went to Washington to begin negotiations. Initially the negotiations related only to Compensatory and Contingency Financing Facility. Later on it was widened to cover other type of facilities. There were other efforts to raise funds. Thus some help came. However, the position continued to remain grim.

As the new government took over by the end of June 1991, serious consideration had to be given to redeem the situation. Almost the first decisive action of the new government was with respect to the exchange rate. Discussions between the Ministry of Finance and RBI were held at the highest level. As far as I can recall, there was really no opposition to the move. The situation had deteriorated to a point that it had become inevitable. Discussion centered around the extent of the adjustment and the mode. In fact by a steady day to day adjustment, the rupee in terms of dollar had depreciated by 10.8 per cent between March 1990 and March 1991. Given the situation, a sharper and onetime adjustment was needed. Of course, every decision to 'devalue' the currency has a political connotation. The task of convincing the Prime Minister and the President was a task that Dr. Manmohan Singh as FM took on himself.

The decision was to effect a downward adjustment which was to be done in two stages with a gap of two to three days. As already indicated, this was to be done by RBI in the course of the daily fixation of exchange rate. Technically, the rate was to be fixed in relation to the value of a basket of currencies within a given margin. We had long before gone outside the margin. A sharp downward adjustment would take it even more outside the limit. Since the adjustment was to be made in two stages, the code name for the exercise was 'Hop, Skip and Jump". Why two stages? This was partly to test the market with an initial dose and then to follow it up. In a sense, the first announcement would prepare the market. After the political clearance, the signal was given to Governor Venkitaramanan and me to go ahead. At that time, I was in charge of exchange rate adjustment.

On July 1, 1991, I made the first change. The foreign exchange market while welcoming the move was a bit shaken. It took time for the participants to digest it. But then speculation started as to where the process would end. There were editorial comments which talked about devaluation much beyond what we had in mind. It was then we decided to advance the date and not give too much of a gap. So on July 3, the next adjustment was made according to the plan. The depreciation worked out to 17.38 per cent against the intervention currency Pound Sterling. Was there any rethinking on the part of the government during the intervening time? I certainly was not aware. Somehow, 'devaluation' is always regarded as a 'quasi' political decision. The new government hardly a few weeks old could have been subject to various pressures. I did not hear anything from FM. On July 3, however, I got a call from Dr. Manmohan Singh at around 9.30 a.m. He put me a neutral question regarding the situation and I simply said 'I have jumped'. He said 'fine'. and that was the end of that episode. Dr. Manmohan Singh gave interviews as well as spoke in the Parliament about why the decision to devalue had to be taken. After the announcement on July 3, 1991, the market has to be assured that there would be no further sharp downward adjustment. This was necessary to prevent exporters from postponing bringing in receipts or non-resident Indians postponing sending deposits. Our action in the next one week in terms of the adjustment of the value of the rupee reassured the market. In fact, on August 2, 1991, I addressed a gathering in Bombay providing a detailed account of the reasons behind the adjustments in the value of the rupee and reiterated that there would be no further sharp change. The lecture entitled "Recent Exchange Rate Adjustments: Causes and Consequences" was later published in the RBI Bulletin in September 1991.

The decision to make the downward adjustment was a bold decision. It required a lot of courage. But devaluation has been done in the past also. What was, in fact, bolder was the ushering in of reforms in general and particularly in the external sector. The dismantling of quantitative controls on imports; reduction in import tariff, introduction of EXIM

Scrips, adoption of dual exchange rate and finally moving to a market determined exchange rate system - all happened in a short span of eighteen months and transformed the external sector regime. The Indian currency became convertible on current account in 1994. India's external sector has never been as strong as it has been since 1991-92.

References

1. Long Term Fiscal Policy December 1985, Ministry of Finance (Department of Economic Affairs)

2. Prof Madhu Dandavate, Finance Minister, "Budget Speech for the year 1990-91".

3. Yashwant Sinha. "Statement by Finance Minister on Current Fiscal Situation" Rajya Sabha, December 27, 1990

4. Arun Ghosh, "IMF Borrowings: Some Myths Exposed", Economic and Political Weekly July 20, 1991

5. Interview with Dr. Nitin Desai

6. Interview with Dr. C.Rangarajan

CHAPTER - V

THE UNION BUDGETS 1991-96

The Government of India pursued a policy of fiscal consolidation and structural reform over a period of 18 months. The Union Budgets reflect the policy measures of opening up the Indian economy. This chapter outlines the economic reforms pursued from 1991-96.

The Union Budget for 1991-92 was presented on 24th July 1991. The Budget Speech of Finance Minister Dr. Manmohan Singh remains a classic in economic history of India. It formed the cornerstone of long reaching macro-economic policy changes and reforms. Trade reforms with rupee devaluation and abolition of export subsidies, subsidy reforms in food, fertilizer and petroleum sectors, industrial sector reforms with foreign direct investment permissions and constitution of the Foreign Investment Promotion Board, efforts to reduce tax evasion and improve tax compliance were key components of the Union Budget 1990-91. The Budget ended with the words *"Let the whole world hear it loud and clear. India is now wide-awake. We shall prevail. We shall overcome"* indicating the mood of the Nation in 1990-91.

On the macroeconomic situation the new Government had inherited an economy in deep crisis. The balance of payments situation was precarious. There was a sharp decline in capital inflows through commercial borrowing and non-resident deposits. As a result, despite large borrowing from the International Monetary Fund in July 1990 and January 1991, there was a sharp reduction in the foreign exchange reserves. The foreign exchange crisis constituted a serious threat to the sustainability of growth processes and orderly implementation of developmental programs. In sum, the crisis in the economy was acute and deep. The Nation had not experienced anything similar in the history of independent India.

The crisis of the fiscal system is a cause for serious concern. Fiscal deficit was estimated at more than 8 percent of GDP in 1990-91 as compared to 6 percent at the beginning of the 1980s and 4 percent in the mid 1970s. The fiscal deficit had to be met by net borrowing. The internal public debt of Central Government had accumulated to 55 percent of GDP. The burden of servicing the debt had become onerous and interest payments alone were about 4 percent of GDP and constitute 20 percent of the total expenditure of the Central Government.

Finance Minister said that the balance of payments situation is most difficult. The current account deficit had reached 2.5 percent of GDP in 1990-91. The deficits which were financed by borrowings from abroad, led to continuous increase in external debt estimated at 23 percent of GDP at the end of 1990-91. Consequently, the debt service burden was estimated at 21 percent of current account receipts in 1990-91. The strains were stretched to a breaking point on account of the Gulf crisis. The balance of payments lurched from one liquidity crisis to another since December 1990. The foreign exchange reserves in the range of Rs. 2500 crores would suffice to finance imports for a mere fortnight.

The price situation posed a serious problem and inflation had reached a double-digit level. The wholesale price index had registered an increase of 12.1 percent and the consumer price index had registered an increase of 13.6 percent. Inflation in 1990-91 was concentrated in essential commodities.

Macroeconomic adjustment long overdue could not be postponed any further as that would mean the balance of payments situation would become unmanageable and inflation would exceed limits of tolerance. The center piece of India's strategy was a credible fiscal adjustment and macroeconomic stabilization with continued fiscal consolidation over the next 3 years. In macro-management of the economy, over the medium term, the steps envisaged were to progressively reduce the fiscal deficit and move towards a significant reduction in revenue deficit and to reduce the current account deficit in the balance of payments. Government committed itself to make essential reforms in economic policy and economic adjustment as an integral part of the adjustment process. The thrust of the reform process was to increase the international competitiveness of industrial production, to increase the productivity of the investment and to ensure that India's financial sector rapidly modernized.

The policies for industrial development are closely related to policies for trade. To expose Indian industry to competition from abroad in a phased manner Government introduced changes in import export policy aimed at reduction in import licensing, vigorous export promotion and optimal import compression. The exchange rate adjustments on the 1st and 3rd July 1991 constituted the two major initial steps in the direction of trade policy reform.

Government decided to liberalize the regime for foreign direct investment in industry. Foreign Direct Investment in specified high priority industries with a raised limit for foreign equity at 51 percent, second, foreign equity upto 51 percent in trading companies was allowed and third, a special board was constituted to negotiate with a number of large international firms and approve foreign direct investment in selected areas. Thus was born the Foreign Investment Promotion Board.

Government further decided to disinvest 20 percent of government equity in selected public sector undertakings to mutual funds and investment institutions in the public sector as also to workers. Public enterprises which were chronically sick were to be referred to the Board for Industrial and Financial Reconstruction (BIFR).

Measures for strengthening the banking sector and financial institutions were initiated. Greater flexibility into the structure of interest rates was introduced with the empowerment of the Reserve Bank of India. Similarly, all statutory powers under the Securities Contracts (Regulation) Act and the Companies Act were transferred to the Securities and Exchange Board of India from the Controller of Capital Issues. To establish a transparent mechanism for fixing prices, the Tariff Commission was established. Government also initiated steps for total deregulation of Fertilizer Subsidies, increased the prices of Sugar and Petroleum products. On the taxation side, the emphasis was on ensuring better tax compliance and mobilizing revenues through the imposition of additional taxes.

The Lok Sabha took up the General Discussion on the Budget on 31 July 1991. The Finance Minister was under fierce attack from several Members of Parliament that the economic sovereignty of India has been destroyed.

The Finance Minister responded thus:

> "I think a great concern has been expressed about the economic sovereignty of this Nation. It has been said that this Budget seeks to destroy the economic sovereignty of this Nation, that it has been prepared at the behest of the IMF. I think it was one hon. Member, who went so far to say that I have been an employee of the World Bank. I would like to say that let us disagree but let us not be disagreeable. I submit to this House that I have never been an employee of the World Bank, I have no international pension. I have a minor pension of Rs. 2000 from the Government of India. Therefore, this thing that was mentioned that I am a pensioner of the IMF, that I have been an employee of the IMF or World Bank is totally untrue and it is not worthy of this House that these charges should be leveled. Now I would like to ask, how do you protect the economic sovereignty of a Nation, which is going bankrupt? The only way to protect the economic sovereignty of this Nation is to deal with those causes which have brought us to a virtual state of bankruptcy. ...The World respects strength, nobody cares about the weak. In the situation that we are in today, a country with 850 million people with reserves which are equal to two weeks, if you tell me that you have mechanisms of preserving the economic sovereignty of this Nation through imposing more drastic import controls, further squeezing imports I am afraid you have not understood the gravity of the situation. ..Therefore I repudiate this charge that this budget has been prepared at the behest of anybody outside India. This budget has been prepared by us, it is a response to the situation that the people of India face and if we had not taken strong corrective measures to correct this fiscal distortion, I think we would be reneging in our responsibility as an effective Government and I think that would be something which future generations of this country would never have forgiven us."

The policies of Government were widely endorsed in IMF Working Papers. A 1991 IMF Working paper examined public debt in India and concluded that steps must be taken to reduce the deficit there was a need for narrowing the scope of government activities, freezing government employment, and cutting subsidies. It further said that government should privatize public enterprises and close down or sell-off loss making public sector enterprises. A 1993 IMF Working Paper titled "A Framework for Assessing Fiscal Sustainability and External Viability with an Application to India mid-1991" said that the government undertook a comprehensive program of macroeconomic stabilization and structural adjustment.

The Lok Sabha took up the Industrial Policy in a short duration discussion on 7th August 1991. There was fierce resistance by Parliamentarians. Participating in the discussion M.S.Gurupadaswamy and Yashwant Sinha Member said that the Industrial Policy Resolution of Government was hasty and the problems on the fiscal front can be surmounted.

Gurupadaswamy went onto attack the Finance Minister thus

> "he is turning the clock back and undermining the very bed-rock of economic development which we have built up. He has shown himself before the world as a supplicant, a helpless dove, before the World Bank and the International Monetary Fund. He has denied he is acting at the behest of the World Bank and International Monetary Fund. I wish I could believe it. That is why there is a touch of hypocrisy here. He should have been candid and frank in saying that there has been a study by the World Bank and International Monetary Fund about our economy, I agree with those findings, I too follow their advice."

Yashwant Sinha said:

> "the industrial policy is a nefarious conspiracy which has been unleashed upon us by vested interests. Therefore I would like to warn everyone, including Government that we have to be very very cautious....I would like to say that this policy is not worth the paper it is written on. It is a hopeless document. It is a document of capitulation. It is a document of surrender. I do not know whether the IMF is behind it. I do not know whether the World Bank is behind it, but I certainly know that this is a product of pax American, and for God's sake, let us give it up."

In an article in January 1991, titled "Management of Economy and IMF Conditionalities", the Economic and Political Weekly said that the conditions used by the IMF on the Government of India especially those set out in paragraphs 28 to 33 of the Memorandum of Understanding with the IMF laid before the Parliament by the Finance Minister go far beyond those normally imposed by the IMF for an upper tranche stand-by credit. Adherence to these conditions will drag the country deeper into the morass of dependence on external support. The article held that devaluation of the currency and deflation are the standard IMF prescriptions for countries in balance of payments difficulties. The issues that were most contentious were the promises to review and relax all curbs on import of capital goods, decanalisation of imports and referring all sick public enterprises to the BIFR. The other contentious clause was the reform of the financial system. The Economic and Political Weekly held that the program chalked out by the IMF should be unacceptable to the people of India.

I.G.Patel writing in the Economic and Political Weekly said so great was the sense of excitement and the cloud of controversy about the new economic policies that it was almost obligatory for an economist to come clean on where he or she stands in relation to the grand debate on New Economic Policy.

I.G. Patel's scathing criticism of the fiscal policy of the day is captured in the following words:

"If the present crisis is the greatest we have faced since independence.... it is because what successive governments in the 1980s chose to abdicate their responsibility to the nation for the sake of short term partisan political gains and indeed out of sheer cynicism. It was already clear by 1986 that we were in an internal debt trap which would soon engulf us in an external debt trap. Rather than take any remedial action we went merrily along, borrowing more and more at home and on shorter and shorter terms abroad. The climate for official and concessional capital had turned irretrievably adverse for many years. Borrowing short term is like inviting sudden death – with the slightest adverse turn in confidence, these loans will not be renewed and we will be faced immediately with a liquidity crisis. Yet nothing was done to take corrective action or to buy time for example by going to the IMF. This was obviously politically inconvenient in 1988 and 1989 when winning the elections was the only concern. The new government of V.P. Singh could not be unaware of the writing on the wall. But it preferred to add its own fuel to the fire, farm loan waivers and the red herring of reservations. It was left to the feckless Chandra Sekhar government to start serious negotiations with the Fund when it was almost too late."

I.G. Patel remained a staunch supporter of the IMF program, a rather large drawal from the IMF as a part of the assistance was to be used for rebuilding reserves and reducing short term indebtedness. He felt that there was no need to be afraid of IMF conditionality as much of the IMF reasoning is sound and we share it. I.G. Patel also noted that there would be some pressure from the Americans, Germans and Japanese on the Fund for extensive unwanted privatization or hasty liberalization of imports or premature or excessive opening for private foreign investors. That said, reducing India's external indebtedness is an agenda for the 21st century.

Finance Minister Dr. Manmohan Singh presented his 2nd Budget on 29th February 1992. He said that Government had inherited an economy on the verge of collapse where inflation was accelerating rapidly, the balance of payments was in serious trouble and foreign exchange reserves were barely enough for two weeks of imports. Further, the foreign commercial banks had stopped lending to India, Non-Resident Indians were withdrawing their deposits and shortages of foreign exchange had forced a massive import squeeze, which had halted the rapid industrial growth of earlier years and had produced negative growth rates from May 1991 onwards. From this grim legacy, the Government had taken steps to restore macro-economic balance in the economy, control inflation and reduce the balance of payments deficit to a manageable level. The medium term objective was to place the economy back on the path of high and sustainable growth.

The Finance Minister detailed the Government's initiatives in pursuit of these objectives. Emergency measures were taken to prevent a default in external payments, which would have been highly disruptive. The process of restoring macro-economic balance by seeking to reduce the fiscal deficit which had grown very large in the previous year was undertaken. The Government embarked on a medium term program of structural reform, including new initiatives in trade policy and industrial policy aimed at improving the efficiency, productivity and international competitiveness of the Indian industry. Production was bound to suffer in a year of crisis and this has happened in 1991-92. Agricultural production was below target in the kharif season, but prospects for the rabi crop look good. Industrial production suffered because of severe import compression and tight credit conditions. However, the infrastructure sectors, which are the foundation on which future industrial growth depends, have done well. The GDP growth in 1991-92 was 2.5%. The Finance Minister expected a distinct improvement in 1992-93, and a return to high growth in 1993-94 subject to India continuing on the reform path.

The Finance Minister clarified the role of the IMF and the World Bank in the Indian economic policy making in his budget speech. He said

> "It has been alleged by some people that the reform program has been dictated by the IMF and the World Bank. We are founder members of these two institutions and it is our right to borrow from them when we need assistance in support of our programs. As lenders, they are required to satisfy themselves about our capacity to repay loans and this is where conditionality comes into the picture. All borrowing countries hold discussions with these institutions on the viability of the programs for which assistance is sought. We have also held such discussions. The extent of conditionality depends on the amount and the type of assistance sought. However, I wish to state categorically that the conditions we have accepted reflect no more than the implementation of the reform program as outlined in my letters of intent sent to the IMF and the World Bank, and are wholly consistent with our national interests. The bulk of the reform program is based on the election manifesto of our Party. There is no question of the Government ever compromising our national interests, not to speak of our sovereignty."

Following 8 months of implementation of the Stand-By Arrangement, India's foreign exchange reserves were rebuilt to about Rs.11,000 crores. Non-Resident Indians were no longer withdrawing their deposits. India had successfully concluded arrangements with multi-lateral financing institutions such as the IMF, the World Bank and the Asian Development Bank to obtain quick disbursing funds to support the balance of payments in the current year.

In 1992 also inflation remained a difficult problem, although it had come down from 16.7 percent in 1991 to about 12% in 1992. With higher foreign exchange reserves Government was in a position to relax the restrictions on imports. India needed a growing volume of imports of fuel, and other industrial inputs and also of capital goods embodying modern technology. Government moved towards convertibility of the rupee on the current account. The new system was designed to provide a powerful boost to India's exports as well as to efficient import substitution. The Finance Minister had achieved significant simplifications in trade policy.

Deepak Nayyar, the former Chief Economic Advisor, said that there were causes for concern about the sustainability of India's stabilization which was largely based on borrowing, both on inflation and balance of payments situation. He took the view that the slowdown in the rate of inflation is much less than what point to point rates suggest and the decline is largely attributable to the good monsoon and the impact on the prices of agricultural commodities. That said, the balance of payments situation was no longer precarious and the level of foreign exchange reserves had climbed from a meagre US $ 2.2 billion in end March 1991 to a comfortable US $ 5.6 billion in end March 1992 and remained in that range thereafter. The build-up of reserves was attributed to the import compression measures, the multilateral/ bilateral assistance from IMF, World Bank, ADB, Japan and Germany and the amnesties announced in the 1991-92 budget largely in the form of borrowings from non-residents through bonds and remittances.

Finance Minister Dr. Manmohan Singh presented his third Budget on 27th February 1993. As he rose to present the Union Budget, the Finance Minister said that

> "It is now twenty months since our Government took office: twenty eventful months in which we have worked ceaselessly to overcome the very difficult economic situation we inherited. In June 1991, the economy was in the throes of an unprecedented balance of payments crisis. A savage squeeze had been imposed on imports; international confidence had collapsed; industrial production was falling, and inflation was on the rise. The sense of crisis is now behind us. We have restored a measure of normalcy to our external payments."

The annual rate of inflation had been reduced from the peak of 17% in August, 1991 to below 7%. The growth of the economy, which had declined to 1.2% in 1991-92, was expected to be around 4% in 1992-93. India's economic strategy resting on the twin pillars of fiscal discipline and structural reform, had shown a decisive upward turn. Government had made progress by reducing the fiscal deficit from 8.4% of GDP in 1990-91 to about 5% in 1993-94. Trade and industrial policies were restructured, foreign investment norms eased and India was enabled to integrate with the global economy.

The Finance Minister said that without these reforms, India faced the certain prospect of entering the 21st century as just about the poorest country in Asia. Inflation was down and production was beginning to recover. Despite the virtual removal of import licensing in 1992-93, total imports in 1992-93 in US dollars were lower than in 1990-91. Although the rupee had been floated for most current account transactions, the market exchange rate has remained relatively stable. The investment climate had improved considerably. Fiscal imbalances continued to be large. The efficiency and resource generating capacity of public sector enterprises was quite inadequate. Inflationary expectations remained and could revive if fiscal discipline was relaxed. The economy was still vulnerable to external shocks and loss of confidence.

For 1993-94, Government laid down the priorities for economic policy, as continuation of fiscal correction, focus on poverty alleviation, industrial recovery, tax reform, supporting agriculture and exports. In the backdrop of the securities scam of April 1992, Government adopted the recommendations of the Narasimham Committee on financial sector reforms. The measures included provisioning for bad debts, prescription of capital adequacy requirements in line with Basel Norms, and new norms for income recognition. Government set up special tribunals to expedite legal action by the banks to enforce reserves. The Reserve Bank of India was asked to enhance supervisory arrangements of Banks by setting up a separate Board for Financial Supervision. The Securities and Exchange Board of India, was been entrusted with the task of bringing about capital market reforms. Government also initiated reforms in the insurance industry aimed at introducing a more competitive environment subject to suitable regulation and supervision.

Finance Minister Dr. Manmohan Singh presented his fourth budget on 28th February 1994. He said that three years are not enough to complete economic restructuring in a country as complex as India. That said the economic situation has shown substantial improvement. Progress on the external front has been dramatic and foreign currency reserves, which were a little over $1 billion in June 1991 were close to $ 13 billion. India's gold, which earlier had been pledged abroad, was back in India's possession. India's exports had increased by a remarkable 21 per cent in dollar terms in the first 10 months of 1993-94 as compared to a decline of 3 per cent in 1991-92 and a rise of 2 per cent in 1992-93. Liberalization did not lead to a flood of imports. The dollar value of India's imports during April-January 1993-94 was less than one per cent higher than imports during the corresponding period of 1992-93. The current account deficit in our balance of payments during 1993-94 was half a percent of GDP compared to over 3 per cent in 1990-91 and 2 per cent in 1992-93. The exchange rate for the rupee has remained remarkably steady. Foreign direct and portfolio investment, which was hardly $150 million in 1991-92, was likely to be around $3 billion in 1993-94.

Finance Minister said that the news on the domestic economy was encouraging. Inflation had reduced from a peak of 17 per cent in August 1991 to about half that level at present. Agricultural performance was strong. Food stocks were at their highest levels in seven years and provided invaluable insurance against any possible crop failure. Industrial growth was also recovering, and overall economic growth was estimated at about 4 per cent for the second year in a row. Fears that the reform program might lead to a large scale increase in unemployment had turned out to be unfounded.

However, it was not possible to contain the fiscal deficit to the level Government had originally targeted. The slower pace of industrial recovery in 1993-94 led to a shortfall in revenues and various expenditures had exceeded Budget estimates. The slippage in the fiscal deficit in 1993-94 was less damaging than might have been the case ordinarily, mainly because of the existence of sizeable idle industrial capacity and low investment levels.

In an article titled "Structural Reform in India 1991-93 Experience and Agenda" published in the Economic and Political Weekly dated November 27, 1993, Kaushik Basu presented a bird's eye-view of the Structural Reform Program from July 1991 to February 1993. India's debt service ratio had grown to 30 percent and the short term credit component had grown disproportionately. Trade performance was poor. The premise that India had always lived precariously on the international front but there was no precipitous decline in the 1980s is maintainable. The reforms were undertaken on two fronts: one on trade policy and the other on exchange rate policy. The Finance Minister first spoke of lowering import tariffs in the Budget of 1992 and fixed an upper ceiling of 110 percent for all goods and except hand baggage and liquor. The ceiling was lowered to 85 percent in the budget presented on February 27, 1993. The plan to ease the exit of sick public sector firms had progressed very sluggishly. Government had decided to refer all sick public enterprises to the Board of Industrial and Financial Reconstruction. Interventions for equity in the form of various programs required a lot of institutional and organizational restructuring.

The Finance Minister outlined the priorities for the 1994-95 Budget into six major tasks (a) acceleration of the reform and modernization of our tax system that began two years ago; (b) correcting the slippages in the fiscal deficit; (c) building on the demonstrable success already achieved in the external sector (d) a major stimulus for a strong industrial recovery, especially for investment and capital goods production; (e) reorientation of India's development policies and programs to address more effectively the problems of poverty, unemployment and social deprivation and (f) consolidate and deepen the progress made in restoring the health of the banking system.

India continued to make progress on a unified, market-determined exchange rate system and moved towards convertibility on the current account. Current account convertibility was aimed to substantially liberalise the access to foreign exchange for all current business transactions and eliminate reliance upon illegal channels for such transactions. Further, the Government approved direct investments for critical infrastructure sectors, and negotiated bilateral investment treaties with several investor countries.

Finance Minister said that India's debt position had been more than offset by the sharp increase in our foreign currency reserves. There was no question of India falling into a debt trap.

He went on to say that

> "Honourable Members are aware that some of our external debt is owed to the IMF. We had approached the Fund in our hour of difficulty. Now that our payments situation has improved considerably and our reserves have been rebuilt to comfortable levels, we are in a position to repay the Fund somewhat ahead of schedule. Repayments of principal and interest amounting to $1.4 billion are due to the Fund in 1994-95. Instead of following the regular

schedule of payments, we intend to pre-pay the entire amount at the beginning of the year. This decision to pre-pay in no sense detracts from the excellent relations we have with the Fund which has helped us immensely in our time of need. We will not hesitate to seek financial support again, if conditions warrant."

The Finance Minister Dr. Manmohan Singh presented his 5th Budget on 15th March 1995. He outlined to the Members of Parliament how far India had come since the grim days of 1991:

"The growth of our economy had fallen to less than one per cent in 1991- 92. We brought the economy back to a growth of 4.3 per cent per year in the two years thereafter, and growth has accelerated further to 5.3 per cent in 1994-95. Few countries can claim as quick and smooth a recovery from as deep an economic crisis. Industrial growth had collapsed to about half of one per cent in 1991-92. Today, Indian industry is experiencing a vibrant, broad-based recovery with industrial growth of 8.7 per cent in April-November, 1994. The manufacturing sector is growing even faster at 9.2 per cent and the capital goods sector is growing at 24.7 per cent.

Food-grain production had fallen to 168 million tons in 1991-92. This year, it will be an all-time record of 185 million tons. Our farmers have clearly benefited from the policy of offering remunerative prices and have returned a strong production performance. Public stocks of food-grain, had declined to 14.7 million tons three years ago. They have been rebuilt to a record level of 31 million tons, as on January 1, 1995. Growth has created new jobs for our people. In 1991-92, total employment grew by only about 3 million. In each of the two years thereafter, employment increased twice as fast, with about 6 million new jobs added each year. The increase is expected to be even higher in 1994-95.

At the time of the crisis, our external debt was rising at the rate of 8 billion dollars a year. In 1993-94, the increase in external debt was reduced to less than one billion dollars. In the first half of 1994-95, our external debt stock actually declined by almost 300 million dollars. Our foreign currency reserves had fallen to barely one billion dollars in June 1991. On March 10, 1995 they stood at over 20 billion dollars."

The Economic Survey of 1995-96 said that the economic reforms had led to a marked and favorable turnaround in the performance of the external sector since the crisis of 1991. There was a strong and sustained recovery in export growth, a pronounced rise in the ratio of exports to imports from the level prevailing at the turn of the decade. There was also a substantial decline in the current account deficit as proportion of GDP from the unsustainable level of 3.2 percent in 1990-91 and a strong growth in foreign direct investment flows since 1991-92 and in foreign portfolio investment flows since 1993-94 and an increase in foreign currency reserves from US$ 2.2 billion in March 1991 to over US $ 20 billion in March 1995.

In 2016, on the 25th Anniversary of the 1991 Reforms, Dr. Montek Singh Ahluwalia in an article in the Economic and Political Weekly examined the issues whether the reforms were home grown or pushed by the International Monetary Fund onto a helpless government as the price for financial assistance. The widely believed allegation that the reforms were pushed by the IMF was a constant refrain when the reforms were unveiled. This completely ignores the fact that there was a home grown process of rethinking on economic policy that had been underway and pointed towards many changes. These changes certainly formed a part of the conditionality of IMF assistance, because the IMF is expected to lend only in situations where the government has a credible adjustment program. The IMF obviously approved the reforms in that sense but that is not the same thing as saying it dictated the contents.

India had come a long way, from being a program country of the IMF. Whatever challenges remained were its own, for it to take forward in the comity of Nations.

References

1. Dr. Manmohan Singh Finance Minister, "Budget Speech for the Year 1991-92" dated July 24, 1991

2. General Discussion on Union Budget 1991-92, Lok Sabha Debates July 1991

3. Chellaih, Raja J. "The Growth of Indian Public Debt – Dimensions of the Problem and Corrective Measures", IMF Working Paper No. 91/72, July 1, 1991

4. Parker, Karen Elizebeth | Kastner, Steffen. "A Framework for Assessing Fiscal Sustainability and External Viability, with an Application to India", IMF Working Paper No. 93/78, October 1, 1993

5. Dr. Manmohan Singh Finance Minister, "Budget Speech for the Year 1992-93" dated February 29, 1992

6. Dr Manmohan Singh Finance Minister, "Budget Speech for the Year 1993-94" dated February 27 1993

7. Deepak Nayyar., "Indian Economy at the Crossroads – Illusions and Realities"., Text of a Public Lecture in the Frontier Lecture Series at the Indian Institute of Science Bangalore delivered on February 25, 1993., published in the Economic and Political Weekly April 10, 1993

8. Dr Manmohan Singh Finance Minister, "Budget Speech for the Year 1994-95" dated February 28, 1994

9. Dr Manmohan Singh Finance Minister, "Budget Speech for the Year 1995-96" dated March 15, 1995

10. General Discussion on Union Budgets 1992-93, 1993-94, 1994-95, 1995-96, Lok Sabha Debates

11. Rajya Sabha Discussion on Statement of Finance Minister on "Current Fiscal Situation" Rajya Sabha Debates dated January 4, 1991

12. Rajya Sabha Discussion on Statutory Resolution seeking Disapproval of the Foreign Exchange Regulation Amendment Ordinance 1993, Rajya Sabha Debates March 24, 1993

13. Rajya Sabha Short Duration Discussion on "Price Situation in the Country" Rajya Sabha Debates dated January 10, 1991

14. Rajya Sabha Short Duration Discussion on "The Working of the Ministry of Industry" Rajya Sabha Debates May 13, 1993

15. Rajya Sabha Short Duration Discussion on "Discussion on Dunkel Draft" Rajya Sabha Debates December 7, 1993

16. Rajya Sabha Calling Attention Motion to a Matter of Urgent Public Importance on "Steep Fall in the Value of the Rupee and Its Impact on Country's Economy" Rajya Sabha Debates December 4, 1995

17. Economic Survey 1995-96 An Update

18. Rajya Sabha Short Duration Discussion on "The Value of the Rupee" Rajya Sabha Debates dated June17, 1996

19. Basu, K. (1993). Structural Reform in India, 1991-93: Experience and Agenda. *Economic and Political Weekly, 28*(48), 2599-2605.

20. Sen, S. (1994). Dimensions of India's External Economic Crisis. *Economic and Political Weekly, 29*(14), 805-812.

21. Acharya, Shankar. "India's Medium-Term Growth Prospects." *Economic and Political Weekly*, vol. 37, no. 28, 2002, pp. 2897–2906.

22. Jalan, Bimal. "India's Economy in the 21st Century: A New Beginning or a False Dawn?" *India International Centre Quarterly*, vol. 38, no. 3/4, 2011, pp. 230–247

23. Patel I.G., New Economic Policies: A Historical Perspective, Economic and Political Weekly January 4-11, 1992 pp 41-46

CHAPTER - VI

THE IMF VIEW - INDIA'S STAND-BY ARRANGEMENT

The IMF's standby arrangement with India entailed stringent conditionality and exchange rate devaluation. Exchange rate devaluation and interest rate increases were adopted in July 1991 and provided important early successes. The two central elements of the Fund program of substantial reduction in central government deficit from 9 percent of GDP in 1990-91 to 5 percent of GDP in 1992-93 and significant progress in the dismantling of interventionist industrial, trade and financial policies were pursued. The budget deficit reduction was achieved through increases in petrol prices, decontrol of fertilizer prices and a satisfactory revenue performance. By end 1992, the IMF shifted India to a standard 12 month consultation cycle for Article IV surveillance.

The IMF teams led by Hubert Neiss held discussions in New Delhi and Bombay with Yashwant Sinha and Dr. Manmohan Singh the former and current Ministers of Finance from August 1-16, 1991. The IMF team also met Finance Secretary Shukla, Chief Economic Advisor Deepak Nayyar, RBI Governor Venkitaramanan and Deputy Governor Dr. Rangarajan. Gopi Arora the Executive Director for India in the IMF participated in all the key policy meetings.

The IMF history says the following:

> The politics of borrowing from the IMF is always complex, but in India it was especially so. On the one hand politicians had long viewed the IMF conditionality with some disdain. As soon as it became know that the government was applying for a stand-by arrangement, its leaders would be attacked in Parliament, and in the press for subjugating the interests to foreign domination. On the other hand, most of the countries' economic and financial officials had good relations with the IMF and an unusually high degree of trust had developed on both sides over the years.
>
> The working relationship was a little unusual, in that the authorities knew full well what they needed to do to qualify for the Fund's seal of approval and financial support. The decision to devalue for example was not made at the insistence of the Fund but on the understanding that the Fund would approve it and that both sides believed that it was necessary and was in India's interest. As had been true for the 1981 negotiations, these discussions were amicable and collegial.

The RBI history says that in financial terms, the IMF's assistance was small compared with the dimensions of the crisis. In 1991-92, the withdrawals from the IMF amounted to US$ 1.2 billion as against India's short term debt of US$ 6.0 billion at the end of 1990-91, with overnight borrowing in international capital markets of the order of US$ 2.0 billion. India's decision to seek assistance from the IMF perhaps came a trifle late. The Governor's letter in late 1989 and early 1990 clearly hinted at the possibility of approaching multinational institutions. However, due to the elections due in November, seemed to be the main reason why the negotiators could not make commitments back then.

Government Seeks IMF Stand-by Arrangement

On August 27, 1991, the Finance Minister addressed the Managing Director IMF for an 18-month stand-by arrangement in an amount equivalent to SDR 1656 million. A memorandum of economic policies setting out the economic program of the Government of India for the period 1991/92 and 1992/93 was also submitted. The Government also requested for an additional purchase under the compensatory and contingency financing facility (CCRF) with respect to any remaining excess in oil import costs or shortfall in merchandise and remittance earnings for the year 1991. The Government indicated its willingness to enter into a comprehensive structural adjustment program, supported by an arrangement under the Extended Fund Facility.

Government agreed for the quarterly performance criteria for 1991/92 with ceilings on overall borrowing requirements of the union government, ceilings on net domestic assets of the RBI, a sub-ceiling on RBI credit to the Government and floors on net official international reserves. Government agreed for 3 reviews of program implementation on March 31, 1992, September 30, 1992 and March 31, 1993. Government agreed to formulate a comprehensive program for tax reform and introduce a detailed tracking system of quarterly expenditure reviews.

The IMF's 1991 Article IV Staff Report said that the fundamental causes of India's external difficulties were excessive fiscal deficits that pre-empted a large share of savings and deep-seated structural rigidities leading to inefficient resource utilization. The Government has made a promising start to addressing these underlying problems while also implementing stabilization measures to cope with immediate difficulties. Substantial financial support for these adjustment efforts has now been committed by multilateral and bilateral donors. Nevertheless, the external reserves position remains very tight, and internal and external confidence is not yet fully restored. In the light of this and the projected continuation of external financing gaps during the next several years, the proposed stand-by arrangement does entail a risk for the Fund, but one that should be acceptable given the strength of the underlying adjustment program and India's record of cooperation.

TABLE 1

INDIA: SCHEDULE OF PURCHASES DURING PERIOD OF STANDBY ARRANGEMENT, OCTOBER 1991-MARCH 1993

Approximate Date of Drawing	Tests/ Reviews	Amount of Purchase (SDR Millions)
October 31, 1991	Executive Board Approval	85
December 15 1991	End October Performance Criteria	185
March 15, 1992	End December Performance Criteria and Completion of First Review	461
May 15, 1992	End March Performance Criteria and completion of Second Review	185
September 15, 1992	End June Performance Criteria and completion of Second review	185
November 15, 1992	End September Performance Criteria	185
March 15, 1993	End December Performance Criteria and completion of Third Review	185
May 15, 1993	End March Performance Criteria	185

Source: India - Staff Report for the 1991 Article IV Consultation, October 8, 1991

The adjustment strategy entailed a set of immediate stabilization measures adopted in July 1991 most notably a 18.7 percent depreciation of the exchange rate and further tightening of monetary policy including increase in interest rates, designed to restore confidence and reverse short term capital outflow. The IMF staff report noted that the implementation began with the final 1991/92 budget, of a comprehensive program built around the twin pillars of fiscal consolidation and a radical structural reform to shift away from the policies of the past. India had also committed to mobilization of substantial exceptional financing to maintain a minimum level of imports so as to avoid a major disruption to the economy. The initial stabilization package was accompanied by a special action to maintain reserves at a minimum working level, including gold backed external borrowing, purchases from the Fund and the provision for quick disbursing aid from the World Bank, the Asian Development Bank and several bilateral donors.

Adjustment Strategy and the Program for 1991/92 and 1992/93

The Fund recommended that the key macroeconomic objectives of the program include an easing of the payments situation and a rebuilding of gross international reserves to over 1½ months by the end of 1992/93; economic growth of 3-3½ percent in 1991/92 followed by a gradual recovery in 1992/93 and a reduction in inflation to no more than 6 percent by end of 1992/93. The current account deficit was targeted at about 2 ½ percent of GDP in 1991/92 and 1992/93.

The structural benchmarks for the program were in the areas of industrial policy, trade liberalization, domestic pricing policies, public enterprises reforms, financial sector reforms, tax reforms and expenditure control. The crisis management measures adopted included utilization of gold to raise foreign exchange resources, liberalization in the policy for import of gold, India development bonds and non-resident deposits, liberalization of import licensing, liberalization of tariffs, industrial deregulation, foreign investment policy and significant steps in the exchange rate policy. In many ways, the IMF program of 1991/92 ensured India's integration into the global economy.

Fiscal Consolidation

A large sustained reduction in the overall public sector deficit was central to the adjustment strategy, both to reduce pressure on the external accounts and to release resources for private sector. The medium term objective was to reduce the public sector deficit from 12½ percent GDP in 1990/91 to 7 percent by mid 1990s. The bulk of the reduction was to take place in the program period, with the deficit reduced to 8½ percent of GDP by 1992/93. The consolidation was to largely reflect in lower Union Government deficit. However, the States and the public enterprise sector was also to share the adjustment burden as their budget constraints are hardened through reduced transfers from the Union Government and restraints on their access to other sources of financing, especially State borrowing through the financial system.

The memorandum of understanding contained a fiscal consolidation path that would address the fiscal imbalances that India faced.

TABLE 2

INDIA: MACROECONOMIC FRAMEWORK AND KEY OBJECTIVES 1990/91 AND 1992/93 (IN PERCENT UNLESS OTHERWISE INDICATED)

	1990/91	1991/92	1992/93
Real GDP Growth	5	3-3 ½	4
Inflation	12.1	9	6
External Current Account/ GDP	3.4	2.7	2.6
Exceptional Financing Need (US $ bn)	1.8	4.0	2.8
Gross Official Reserves (in months of imports)	1.3	1.3	1.7
Official Foreign Exchange Reserves (US $ bn)	2.2	2.2	3.2

Source: India - Staff Report for the 1991 Article IV Consultation and Use of Fund Resources, October 8, 1991

On the revenue side, major tax measures to yield ½ percent of GDP through a 5 percent increase in corporate taxes, a reduction in depreciation allowances, higher excise duties. Sale of public sector enterprises was envisaged to yield revenues of Rs. 25 billion (0.4 percent of GDP). Increase in petroleum product prices by an average of 7 percent to neutralize the impact of the devaluation of the OCC accounts. Specific steps to improve tax compliance were to be introduced.

The key expenditure proposals envisaged sharp reduction in subsidies particularly the cash export subsidies, increases in fertilizer prices by 30 percent and elimination of sugar subsidy. Tight constraints were introduced on defense spending which was budgeted to decline from 3.1 percent GDP in 1990/91 to 2.8 percent of GDP in 1991/92. A cut in transfers to Public Sector Enterprises from 1.5 percent of GDP in 1990/91 to 1.2 percent of GDP in 1991/92 representing a first stage of phased reduction. Tight restraint on all other expenditure items including capital spending was to be enforced. For 1992/93 the fiscal program envisaged continuing deficit reduction while at the same time initiating major tax reform. The IMF also indicated that further substantial expenditure reductions will be needed, items under consideration include curtailment of the Government wage bill, a further cutback in defense spending, a continued reduction in transfers to public enterprises and a further reduction in fertilizer and food subsidies through additional price increases and better targeting.

The IMF said that India's tax system has severe drawbacks including an excessive reliance on import tariffs, a low revenue elasticity, a patchwork of exemptions and tax preferences, a relatively low proportion of revenue generated from direct taxes and endemic tax evasion. The IMF noted that the Government had committed itself to a fundamental tax reform to remedy these deficiencies while at the same time mobilizing additional revenues to compensate the revenue loss from tariff reduction and to support the programmed fiscal adjustment. The report further noted that the Government had constituted a tax reform committee for the first stage reforms that can be introduced into the 1992/93 budget; technical assistance for which was also requested from the Fund.

As the Union Government did not have control over the State borrowings, a statutory liquidity ratio was introduced on commercial banks, in order to ensure that the reduced borrowing by the Central Government does not result in increased borrowings by the State Governments. The interest rates on small savings schemes were kept under close review to ensure that these schemes do not duly draw funds from commercial deposits.

The staff report noted that the performance of central public enterprises has been plagued by mismanagement and inefficiency leading to poor returns and a need for budgetary support. While the petroleum sector enterprises were successful given their monopoly position the performance of other non-petroleum enterprises was weak. The central public enterprises deficit was targeted to decline to 3 percent of GDP in 1991/92 from 3 ½ percent of GDP in 1990/91, partly as a result of reduced capital spending[1].

Monetary Policy

R.N. Malhotra the Governor Reserve Bank of India, had presented the policy dilemmas faced by the Reserve Bank in 1988-89 as follows:

> "Monetary policy has to ensure the twin objectives of maintaining reasonable price stability and meting the genuine credit requirements necessary to support the growth of output. The large and recurring budget deficits have been contributing to strong monetary expansion and over time there has been serious erosion of monetary instruments."

Monetary policy was tightened in response to the external liquidity crisis and build up in inflationary pressures. The tightening was achieved through a combination of indirect instruments that operate through their effect on bank liquidity and interest rates (including the introduction of a special 10 percent incremental cash reserve ratio and several increases in administered interest rates) and more direct instruments (including a reduction in incremental credit to deposit ratios and a tightening of various directed credit and refinance facilities). In addition, the imposition of high cash margin requirements on import letters of credit also contributed to tighter domestic credit conditions.

The IMF said that Monetary policy was expected to play the primary role in defending the external reserves position, and the government had made an explicit commitment to tighten monetary policy further should net international reserves fall below the targeted floors. The broad money growth was targeted to reduce from 13 percent in 1991/92 to 11-12 percent in 1992/93 consistent with output and inflation targets of the program. Interest rates were liberalized and the ceilings on long term loan rates charged by development banks and restrictions on private debenture interest rates were both eliminated in July 1991. This was done to bring

---

1 The RBI history volume 4 part A at page 459 says that the medium term objective was to reduce the public sector deficit from an estimated 12.5 percent of GDP in 1990-91 to 8.5 percent of GDP by 1992-93 and further to 7.0 percent by the mid 1990s.

the borrowing costs of public sector enterprises closer to market rates. The interest rates on deposits and on preferred sector credits (almost half the total credit) remained subject to controls. Deposit rates were increased by 1 percent in July 1991 but rates remained negative in real terms. Thus to implement tight monetary policy, emphasis was placed on selective tightening of credit rather than on further increases in interest rates for deposits. The IMF argued that the level of domestic deposit rates could have a significant influence on external accounts. A readiness to adopt timely and decisive action on all interest rates should therefore be an important element of financial strategy both to make the commitment to exchange rate stability credible and to make the burden of monetary tightness from falling disproportionately on sectors without access to preferential credit.

> Dr C.Rangarajan says:
>
> It must be stated that the policy makers in India in the 1950s and 1960s cannot be blamed for the decisions they took. At that time, there was no clear model available for accelerating growth in developing countries. State intervention on an extensive scale seemed to appropriate. However, by the early 1970s, it was becoming clear that the model we had chosen was not delivering results and that it needed change. But our policy makers refused to recognize this. It was at that time that China made a big change.
>
> The New Economic Policy redefined the role of the State, expanding it in certain areas and reducing it in others. There is a common thread running through all the measures introduced since July 1991. The objective was simple: to improve the efficiency of the system. The regulatory mechanism involving multitudes of controls had fragmented capacity and reduced competition even in the private sector. The thrust of the new economic policy was towards creating a more competitive environment in the economy as a means to improving the productivity of the system. This was to be achieved by removing the barriers to entry as well as the restrictions on the growth

of firms. While the industrial policy sought to bring about a greater competitive environment domestically, the trade policy sought to improve international competitiveness, subject to the protection offered by tariffs which were themselves coming down. The private sector was being given a larger space to operate in, as some areas earlier reserved exclusively for the public sector were now also allowed to the private sector. In these areas, the public sector was to compete with the private sector, even though the public sector was to play a dominant role. What was sought to be achieved, was an improvement in the efficiency of various entities, whether in the private sector or the public sector.

To understand the importance of the changes, we need to go back to the state of the Indian economy in 1990. The sharp increase in crude oil prices as a consequence of the Gulf crisis in the mid 1990 gave a severe jolt to India's balance of payments situation which was already under stress. India's current account deficit had touched 2.7 percent of GDP even in 1988-89. From the middle of 1990, financing the current account deficit became an arduous task. Traditional sources of financing started drying up. It became difficult to roll over short term finance. The danger of default was imminent. Along with the current account deficit, the fiscal deficit was also high. Centre's deficit was hovering in the region of 7 percent of GDP for several years. The growth of the 1980s was supported by a high fiscal and current account deficits. This became untenable and reforms were thus the answer.

On the genesis of reforms, some questions need to be answered. Were reforms of 1991 a continuation of a process that had already begun in the 1980s or did they constitute really a break? How much of the change was influenced by the IMF and other multilateral institutions? As the possibility of default loomed, it became obvious that the "business as usual" would not work. We had to move fast and make fundamental changes in our economic policy. It was true that at that time we were negotiating with the IMF and other multilateral institutions. Obviously they had their own bias. They were in favor of a competitive economy with minimal controls. But the decision that we took to introduce reforms was entirely our own. The credit goes to our leadership.

The Prime Minister also held the portfolio of industry which was directly responsible for initiating the changes that led to the dismantling of various types of controls and licenses relating to the industrial sector. The 8th Five Year Plan, in the writing of which I had a role, spelt out in detail the rationale for reforms. The Prime Minister as Chairman of the Planning Commission had read the draft and approved it fully. However, as a matter of strategy, he couched the reforms in a language that would appeal to the "old guards" of his own party. He used expressions as "middle path" while presiding over a government which initiated far reaching reforms. There is no doubt that reforms could not have moved forward without his support and conviction. The reforms of the 1990s were not a continuation of the 1980s reforms journey. They were a break from the past. The enormity of the crisis was such that business as usual will not do.

The attitude of the IMF was sympathetic. They came to India's help. At the same time the IMF was concerned with the fundamental features of the Indian economy and wanted change. The types of IMF facilities that were available were looked at. The CFF (Contingency Financing Facility) came out from oil price hikes. The CFF was not enough. We needed more financing. Hence the Stand-by Arrangement. I remember Mr. Neiss, the Division Chief very well, he was a friendly man, as also Prabhakar Narvekar the Director Asia-Pacific Department of IMF. The IMF had a philosophy of free trade, and the staff was committed to IMF philosophy. In all negotiations, the IMF staffers brought forward the IMF philosophy of free trade. That said, was it imposed or adopted by us? We had agreed amongst ourselves that these measures would be taken. The IMF was very impressed with the speed of reforms. The IMF recognized that India's intellectual powers in the area of macroeconomics were very high. There were several decisions which were not part of the IMF program. For example, the removal of industrial licensing was not an IMF condition. This was done by the Ministry of Industry.

The conditionality associated with compensatory financial facility was not very tight. Indian policy makers were moving in the same direction which IMF was thinking. The RBI also wrote to Government in 1990 that the bulk of the conditions that the IMF would impose were also conditions that we would ourselves impose. We were moving in the same direction in the late 1980s but that was not enough. India had become non-competitive. The extreme import restriction policy was not helpful at all. Once import restrictions were lifted we could get more competitive in the world.

Following the Stand-by Arrangement, the situation changed rapidly. There was a quick turnaround in the BOP situation. We were in a position to get back the pledged gold. India was on schedule with IMF repayments also.

The Exchange Rates – what we did was very bold. By 1993, we had moved to market driven exchange rates – with RBI intervening when considered necessary. The exchange rate management was a great success. We had a rock solid rupee at Rs. 31.37/ dollar for a long period of time. There were far reaching reforms in the banking system undertaken with the Narasimham committee report's recommendations being implemented with regard to capital adequacy ratio and prudential norms. While many of the changes were regulatory in nature, which could be implemented through executive decision making, the amendment of the Bank Nationalization Act was a significant legislative measure adopted by Government to bring down ownership to 51 percent. The Left Parties asked in our discussions, why capital adequacy, when government is the guarantor? Our reply was that individual institutions have to be strong in themselves.

While we did have a clear idea on the path ahead, all details of the path of economic reforms were not known. We did agree that gradualism was needed on the reform path. The challenge was managing conflicting objectives as part of reforms. The great merit of the Indian reform program of the 1990s was that it was done without disruptions. We made a break with the past and followed it up with gradualism.

The economic reforms India undertook have been on right track. This is vindicated by the performance of the economy since the launch of the reforms. In the post-reform period the economy has grown at an average growth rate of 6.8 percent per annum, a significant improvement over the pre-reform period. Economic growth in the ten year period beginning 2005-06 despite the crisis affected year of 2008-09 was at an average rate of 7.7 percent. Between 2005-06 and 2007-08, the economy grew at an annual rate of 9.4 percent. Economic growth slowed down from 2012-13. However, according to the new methodology adopted by CSO, there was a pickup in growth rate even in 2013-14. For the last few years, the growth rate has been around 7 percent even though there is continued skepticism about the numbers. It is imperative we get back to the high growth rate we had seen in the years following 2005-06. All the same one inescapable fact is that the growth rate in the post-reform period has been distinctly higher. It needs to be added that the balance of payments situation was under control except for a hick-up in 2013.

The Government of India strongly reaffirmed to the IMF their commitment to maintain their unblemished payments record. On the external sector, the IMF program envisaged substantial exchange rate depreciation combined with elimination of cash export subsidies designed to improve and make more uniform export incentives; initiation of fundamental reforms to integrate India more closely with the world economy; and the temporary implementation of a number of special import compression measures.

The IMF felt that tight financial policies were the primary means of maintaining competitiveness. Inflation was expected to be on the higher side as a result of the administered price increases and the lagged effects of the exchange rate depreciation, it was felt that nominal exchange rate stability would be an important part of the strategy to restore internal and external confidence and reduce inflation. This was to be backed by decisive financial policies and in particular active use of interest rate policy.

Export subsidies amounted to 8 percent of exports. The export subsidies were abolished under the IMF program. This was backed by sustained trade liberalization measures. The import compression measures included a sharp increase in large cash margin requirements on payments for imports other than capital goods, prior clearance of import payments above specified amounts as well as for sale of foreign exchange and restrictions on sale of foreign exchange for import of capital goods. These restrictions under Article VIII of the IMF's Articles of Agreement were imposed on temporary basis to alleviate the external cash flow situation.

The IMF program envisaged significant structural reforms to promote economic growth by reducing government intervention, enhancing domestic competition and accelerating India's integration into the world economy. Specific policy actions covered industrial deregulation, trade policy, public enterprise reform, and financial sector reform. The foremost amongst the major initiatives was the virtual abolition of the complex system of industrial licensing, governing the entry, expansion and diversification of firms for all but 18 industries. Second were the measures to enhance competition between private sector and public enterprises, where defacto monopoly power and soft budget constraints have been the root causes of inefficiency. The industries reserved for public sector were narrowed to 8, defense production, atomic energy, minerals and railways, the system of monitoring of public enterprises strengthened, the budget constraint facing the enterprises was hardened through a reduction in transfers and subsidies from union budget; the government announced its intention to sell to mutual funds up to 20 percent of equity in selected public enterprises in 1991/92.

The IMF agreed that the structural reforms measures marked a new beginning. An important benchmark for the first review was the formulation of a list of unviable public sector enterprises to be referred for closure or restructuring and establishing a broad menu of disinvestment options. Foreign Direct Investment was significantly liberalized, from approval on case by case basis (and with foreign equity limited to 40 percent) to automatic approval

The IMF program entailed major trade reforms, in India's trade regime characterized by high nominal tariffs and pervasive non-tariff barriers. There was a complex system of licensing, an actual user policy that restricted imports by intermediaries, canalization of exports and imports to the public sector, phased manufacturing programs that mandate progressive import substitution and government purchase preferences for domestic producers. The IMF staff noted that the Indian authorities intend to significantly dismantle this system over the next 3-5 years moving to a transparent price-based system with moderate protection for domestic industry. In 1991, the cash export subsidies were abolished, peak tariff rates brought down and phased manufacturing programs halted. The World Bank Structural Adjustment program aimed at reducing quantitative restrictions and tariffs.

In the financial sector, the IMF program envisaged a detailed program for strengthening the capital base and supervision procedures of Banks. It also envisaged interest rate liberalization and strengthening of capital markets including term lending of institutions.

The fiscal objectives of the program contained performance criteria on overall borrowing requirement of the union government as well as an indicative benchmark on total bank credit to union government and to the general government sector. The implementation of Rs.20 billion additional revenue and expenditure measures was a performance criterion for December 1991. The monetary objectives of the program entailed performance criteria on net domestic assets of the RBI with a ceiling on RBI credit to the Union Government. The external objectives were monitored through quarterly floors on net international reserves of RBI and performance criteria on exchange and trade system. The program envisaged 3 reviews and structural benchmarks on industrial policy, trade liberalization, domestic pricing policies, public enterprise reform, financial sector reform, tax reform and expenditure control.

The IMF projected an exceptional financing need of US $ 2.8 billion under the program. Of this, purchases from IMF under the stand-by arrangement were to provide US $ 1 billion and the rest was to be financed by other multilateral and bilateral donors. The IMF projected that continued fiscal consolidation and sustained structural reforms would result in gradual build-up of official reserves and the financing gaps would reduce by US $ 2 billion per annum. It was expected that India would be on a sustainable debt path by 1996-97.

The Fund opined that the proposed stand-by arrangement entailed a degree of risk and financing gaps would extend through 1994/95 and India's continued adjustment efforts would necessitate additional support from the Fund beyond the present stand-by arrangement. The IMF also felt that the gross international reserves over the medium term and the reserves relative to imports would remain low by historical standards and in relation to debt service payments.

Thus began the 1991 IMF program with India with a contingency financing facility of SDR 468.9 million on September 12, 1991 which was 22.1 percent of quota and credit tranches of SDR 551.925 million which amounted to 25 percent of quota.

In 1992 the IMF's Article IV Staff Report[2] said that strategy of fiscal consolidation and structural reform pursued over the last year and half has yielded some important early successes. Helped by the timely provision of exceptional financial support from the international community and a marked reversal in capital flight, the external liquidity crisis has been overcome. Inflation has declined, a major output loss avoided, and a moderate recovery in industrial production and private investment was underway. Some of the most egregious structural obstacles to longer-term growth have been removed. Given the magnitude of crisis that India faced in mid-1991, and the stifling over-regulation of the economy until that time, these were impressive developments.

---

2   Staff Report for the 1992 Article IV consultation and Second Review under the Stand-By Arrangement dated November 5, 1992 prepared by the Central Asia Department

The two central elements of the program were the substantial reduction in Government deficit from 9 percent of GDP in 1990/91 to a targeted 5 percent in 1992/93, and significant dismantling of the industrial, trade and financial policies that made India one of the most regulated economies in the world. The 1992 Staff report said that Fund supported program was broadly on track. The end June 1992 overall borrowings requirement of central government and short term external debt were exceeded by small margins, but all performance criteria for the September 1992 review were met and all the structural benchmarks had been observed. Despite the stock market scam, the IMF staff report observed that the reform agenda maintained momentum with the through action on fertilizer subsidies and petroleum product prices, the establishment of a social safety net to facilitate the exit of inefficient firms and cabinet approval for a framework for further financial sector reform.

By end 1992, the real economy had weathered the shock of the 1991 balance of payments crisis. Agriculture sector which was largely insulated from the external crisis benefitted from a good monsoon in 1992. Industrial sector growth reached 4.5 percent in 1992/93, the decline in savings and interest rates during the crisis appeared to have been less severe than originally estimated. Inflation came down from 16 percent in August 1991 to 9 percent in October 1992, despite the increase in administered prices.

The IMF continued to support India's domestic financial policies. The overall public sector deficit was cut by 2 ¼ percentage points of GDP to 10 percent of GDP almost entirely as a result of lower central government deficit. The Nation practiced expenditure restraint with reductions in subsidies and defense budgets but also in capital outlays. The 1992/93 program targeted a further 1 ½ percent reduction in public sector deficit. Further cuts in transfers to States and Public Sector enterprises were carried out. 54 Public Sector Enterprises were identified as chronically sick of which 40 were submitted for Board for Industrial and Financial Restructuring for concrete restructuring plans being drawn up. The most important of these was the National Textiles Corporation where 34 mills were closed and 86000 workers were laid off. The IMF also proposed developing a market for medium and long term government securities with technical assistance from the Fund. Additional safeguards on banking system were to be introduced in the backdrop of the stock market scam.

Indian exports witnessed a 11 percent increase in US dollar terms in the first 5 months of 1992/93 despite the collapse of exports to CIS countries. Higher oil imports also meant that imports were also to rise. There were capital inflows as several foreign owned banks brought in foreign exchange to support their domestic banking operations. The dual exchange rate system continued with a market determined exchange rate for most current and capital transactions and a more appreciated official rate for a few key imports, mainly some petroleum products and fertilizer. The spread between the two rates was a narrow 18 percent. There was also 11 billion of ruble debt outstanding to the former Soviet Union which translated to US $ 13 ½ billion. Negotiations were initiated on the exchange rate for converting this debt. India abolished the 15 percent tax on foreign exchange for foreign travel.

Although the IMF staff pressed hard for a Medium Term Fiscal Strategy, the Indian authorities were not yet in a position to commit themselves to specific fiscal targets. A possible scenario that was projected was to reduce the overall fiscal deficit from 8 ½ percent of GDP in 1992/93 to 6 percent of GDP in 1996/96 and the Central Government deficit to fall from 5 percent to about 2 ½ percent of GDP primarily through additional cuts in current expenditures. After two years of sharp fiscal restraint, India wanted to increase allocations on essential infrastructure investment and core social sector programs which made rapid fiscal adjustment difficult. The IMF staff felt there was additional space for expenditure reduction in subsidies which amounted to 1.2 percent of GDP in the 1992/93 budget, defense and transfers to public enterprises as well as personnel and other administrative expenditures. They also felt that there was scope for additional revenue mobilization.

The IMF teams visited India from October 20- November 2, 1994. Dr. C. Rangarajan was the Governor RBI, Dr. Montek Singh Ahluwalia was the Secretary DEA and Finance Secretary. In 1994 the IMF's Article IV Staff Report said that India's progress of fiscal consolidation and structural reform put in place during 1991/92–1992/93 was effective in restoring external confidence, reducing inflation, and limiting the economic slowdown in the face of a severe initial balance of payments crisis. Exports responded to improved incentives, a major expansion in inflows of private capital has taken place, and a comfortable cushion of external reserves rebuilt. In addition, the process of economic restructuring had begun to make inroads into long standing distortions and rigidities. Nevertheless, much remained to be done, to ensure that the recent stabilization gains were not reversed and that India moved onto a more dynamic growth path that could be sustained over the longer term.

The big achievement over 2 years of program period was reduction of central government deficit by 3 percentage points to 5 ½ percent of GDP. It was still slightly above the program target of 5 percent. The public sector deficit was also reduced to 8 ¾ percent of GDP in 1992/93. This was largely achieved through expenditure cuts, a virtual elimination of export subsidies, lower defense outlays, and sizeable cuts in non-wage expenditure. The cutback in spending contributed to a recession in parts of manufacturing sector particularly steel, cement and construction. Overall GDP growth was raised by a favorable monsoon and rise in agricultural output. The exchange rate was stable and the dual exchange rate system was unified. Inflation fell to 7 percent by end of 1992-93. By 1994, India had made significant progress in bringing changes to the regulatory and economic environment. The most significant steps were the elimination of the complex system of industrial licensing and opening-up of public sector areas to private investment. India had progressed in decontrolling administered prices, the first stage of financial and tax reforms, the freeing up of foreign investment and liberalization of trade and payments systems.

There were fiscal slippages in 1994, with the fiscal deficit widening to over 6 ½ percent of GDP in 1993-94. This was much higher than the budgeted target of 4 ¾ percent and was largely due to a shortfall in customs duties, and greater than anticipated revenue loss from tariff cuts. The expenditure over-runs were largely in food and fertilizer subsidies and some increases in defense spending. The public sector deficit was projected to rise to 10 ½ percent in 1993-94 up from 8 ¾ percent in 1992-93. The IMF kept reiterating that the improvement in the balance of payments situation was no cause for complacency on the fiscal front. The IMF felt that the external position could be eroded if macroeconomic imbalances were allowed to persist. The IMF staff recommended a substantial adjustment in the central government deficit would be needed in 1994-95 to signal a convincing return to the path of medium term fiscal consolidation. They pointed out that to be effective the fiscal correction has to address the fundamental structural weaknesses in both central and State Government budgets. The structural weaknesses included the inefficient tax systems, the high levels of spending and excessive financial support to inefficient public enterprises. Monetary policy accommodated the fiscal slippage and despite low inflation, there were uncertainties expressed by the IMF team on financial sector reform given the large public sector debt. The exchange rate of the rupee was broadly stable since March 1993 and the RBI repaid the short term debt and built foreign exchange reserves. The IMF agreed with the RBI approach on repayments of short term debt.

In 1995, the IMF Article IV Staff report said that the economic recovery was well entrenched and India's performance over the past year had been encouraging. The robust recovery of private investment and continued rapid export growth are evidence of a dynamic response to the reforms initiated in 1991. The external position has strengthened further, with the Indian authorities responding skillfully to a surge of capital inflows with a variety of measures that prevented inflation from getting out of hand or a significant erosion of competitiveness. Further progress was also made on the structural front. The IMF staff agreed with India's cautious approach to capital inflows and supported the anti-inflationary efforts of Government. There were hardly any differences between the Indian authorities positions and the IMF staff recommendations by 1995 and the IMF endorsed and appreciated the policy reforms India had pursued since 1991.

In 1996, the IMF Article IV Staff Report said that strong economic growth propelled by vigorous reforms, modest inflation and stable external positions were visible. India's economic performance had been impressive. There were economic challenges of moving towards VAT, high fiscal deficits and challenges in pushing reforms in an election year in areas like labor reforms, agricultural reforms and better targeting of delivery systems in education, health care and food distribution. There was clear policy consensus between the Fund and Indian authorities which continued over the next 2 decades.

References

1. H.Neiss and T.Leddy. "India-Staff Report for the 1991 Article IV Consultation and Use of Fund Resources – Request for Stand By Arrangement", International Monetary Fund October 8, 1991

2. H.Neiss and T.Leddy. "India-Staff Report for the 1992 Article IV Consultation and the Second Review under the Stand By Arrangement", International Monetary Fund, November 1992

3. B.B.Aghevli and AnupamBasu. "India-Staff Report for the 1993 Article IV Consultation", International Monetary Fund, February 3, 1994

4. H.Neiss and T.Leddy. "India-Staff Report for the 1995 Article IV Consultation", International Monetary Fund, June 16, 1995

5. Chopra, Ajai | Collyns, Charles | Hemming Richard et al. "India Economic Reform and Growth" Occassional Paper No. 134, June 1, 1995

6. IMF Country Report No. 95/87. "India Background Papers" September 14, 1995

7. Interview with Dr. C.Rangarajan

8. IMF Staff Country Report No 85/86. "India – Recent Economic Developments" September 14, 1995

9. D.Goldsbrough and T.Leddy. "India-Staff Report for the 1996 Article IV Consultation", International Monetary Fund, September 11, 1996

10. Press Conference by Michel Camdessus, Managing Director, IMF, 26/9/1996

11. IMF Country Report No: 96/131. "India – Recent Economic Developments", January 23, 1997

12. IMF Staff Country Report No:96/132. "India – Selected Issues", January 23, 1997

13. Press Information Notice: IMF concludes Article IV Consultation with India, June 16, 1997

CHAPTER - VII

EVOLUTIONARY CHANGES IN INDIA - IMF RELATIONS

This chapter presents the salient features made in the statements by the Finance Ministers at the Annual Fund-Bank Meetings held in October every year. The April Spring Meetings of the Fund-Bank are attended only by a limited membership which holds chairs on the IMF and as such do not hold the same level of importance of the Annual October Meetings.

The salient issues flagged by the Indian Finance Ministers and Governors of Reserve Bank of India at the IMFC's Spring and Annual Meetings during the non-program years provide great insights into India's evolutionary relationship with the IMF. India has repeatedly highlighted the critical role of the IMF as a sentinel of global economic stability in a complex world of growing uncertainties and risks to the global financial system. India has reiterated the need to increase the Fund's lending capacity to maintain its mandate of maintaining global financial stability. Further, India has stressed that the IMF needs to realign quota shares to reflect current global economic realities. India has also said that the Fund must sharpen its tools for Surveillance given that several weaknesses in Fund's Surveillance have been exposed by the recent Financial crisis.

India's views on the architecture of global economic cooperation have been presented at the Fund-Bank Annual and Spring Meetings, G-20 Meetings and G-24 meetings. India had 5 Finance Ministers who served as Governors on the IMFC in the period 1997-2017 and spoke from a position of considerable strength in the international policy coordination efforts. In 2010 the Quota increases were duly approved reflecting the reality of the dynamics of the world economy.

The IMFC

The IMFC deliberates the principal policy issues facing the IMF. The outgoing Chairman of the IMFC is Augusten Carstens the Governor of the Central Bank of Mexico. He was preceded by Tharman Shanmugaratnam the Finance Minister of Singapore, Youssef Boutros Ghali the Finance Minister of Egypt and Gordon Brown Chancellor of the Exchequer of the United Kingdom. The IMFC considers the World Economic Outlook and the Global Financial Stability Reports and the work plan presented by the Managing Director on the progress made in key policy areas. The key policy areas include Governance reforms, major Stand-By Arrangements of the IMF, Poverty Alleviation and Growth Facility, and Fund Conditionality. The IMFC is preceded by a breakfast meeting of the Inter-Governmental Group of 20, Finance Ministers and Governors of Central Banks discusses the global economic and financial situation. Meetings of the Inter-Governmental Group of 24 countries are held on the sidelines of the IMFC. India is a member of the G-20 and G-24 and Indian delegations to the IMFC attend both these meetings.

The highlight of the Annual Fund-Bank meetings for India is the statement of the Indian Finance Minister as India's Governor to the IMFC. The Governor of RBI as India's Alternate Governor to the IMF heads the Indian delegation in the absence of the Finance Minister. The IMFC statements offer India's Finance Ministers and Governors of RBI a unique opportunity to present India's role in international policy coordination. The statement is an important milestone for Finance Ministers.

Dr. C. Rangarajan headed the Indian delegation to the IMFC Annual Meetings at Hong Kong in 1997 in the backdrop of crisis in East Asian Countries. India commended the IMF for putting in place a series of rescue packages which helped contain the spillover effects on other countries. Dr. Rangarajan called for a strengthening of the international institutions with a one-time allocation of SDR's and increases in developing countries shares at the IMF. On the domestic front, India expressed happiness with the structural program of economic reforms and commitment to macroeconomic stability which yielded substantial rewards with fiscal deficit declining to 4.5 percent and foreign exchange reserves increasing

US$ 25.5 billion. India's exchange rate was market determined and restrictions on the current account of balance of payments were eliminated. India informed the IMFC that it hoped to sustain 7 percent growth per year which will reduce poverty and provide resources for socio-economic development.

The Finance Ministers who headed the Indian delegations to the IMFC from 1998 to 2002 were Yashwant Sinha and Jaswant Singh. Dr. Y.V. Reddy as Governor Reserve Bank of India led the Indian delegation in 2003 and 2004. During this period India pushed for IMF reforms by increasing the quota shares of developing countries and for house clearing and renovation in Fund facilities. Further India called for streamlining Fund conditionality to ensure that it is consistent with the underlying purpose of the scheme. India called for continuation of the Extended Fund Facility so that structural reforms can be implemented over a longer period of time. India welcomed the headway made in the HIPC initiative and the Poverty Reduction and Growth Strategies.

At the 2001 IMFC meetings, Finance Minister Yashwant Sinha suggested that the first meeting of the 21st century can make a meaningful contribution to the living standards of the global population with the global dialogue on development. India called for the Fund to expand the fund facilities to assist the oil-importing developing countries for managing extraordinary external shocks.

Governor Dr. Y.V. Reddy statement at the 2003 IMFC called for faster global recovery and addressing continued global imbalances. Several emerging market economies were contending with the challenges of rising current account surpluses and pressures on exchange rate to appreciate. To address these challenges, the emerging market economies accumulated large foreign exchange reserves giving necessary flexibility for exchange rate management. Fiscal adjustment would have to weighed carefully against the pace of global recovery. India commended the Fund for even-handed surveillance and emphasized on the Fund's role as a confidential advisor to National Governments. India supported the Fund's efforts for accelerating poverty reduction and strengthening sustainable economic growth in Low Income Countries with the PRSP and HIPC initiative.

In this period, two member countries of the Indian constituency to the IMF – Sri Lanka and Bangladesh availed Fund Programs and witnessed rapid economic recovery following adoption of Fund conditionality.

Finance Minister P. Chidambaram addressed the IMFC in 2004, and his statement reflected the positive economic outlook and policy prospects as world economic growth was expected to peak at its highest levels in 30 years. The only downside risks were from geopolitics and oil market uncertainties, and India called for enhanced investment in exploration of oil resources. India welcomed the Fund's initiative for a debt sustainability framework for Low Income Countries and efforts to streamline the Multilateral and Bilateral Surveillance processes re-emphasizing the Fund's role as a confidential advisor to National Governments. In this period the HIPC Initiative emerged as an important instrument for promoting debt sustainability. India supported the IMF initiative for enhancing international support to Low Income Countries. India maintained that the Fund support to Low Income Countries should be in its core areas of expertise – maintain macroeconomic and financial stability. India did not support the use of Fund's gold stock for financing HIPC debt relief, and felt that debt relief should only come from additional financing commitment from the major donor countries. Finance Minister emphasized on the need to strengthen the voice and representation of developing countries. However, there was little progress on the quota and voice issues.

By April 2005, there were serious concerns on the financial viability of the Fund. Finance Minister in his statement at the 2005 IMFC said that new issues had emerged in the financial situation of the Fund. The new issues were implications of the gradual shift in Fund's portfolio from short term credits to long term lending to a relatively small group of countries to enable structural reforms and resolution of debt crisis; issues relating to the separation of Fund's members into 'debtor' and 'creditor' groups, given the easy access to private finance by developed countries; and the management of contingent risk with the high degree of concentration of Fund's outstanding resources. India further maintained that the high concentration of Fund's resources with the top 3 debtor members had increased its exposure to developments in a few countries thereby raising contingent risks.

The September 2005 IMFC meeting was dominated by HIPC debt relief proposals of the G8 for cancellation of debt stock of all HIPC countries of Africa. India made a strong pitch for all PRGF eligible, IDA-only members including those in Asia, Latin America and Europe. The IMF brought out a Medium Term Strategy and a Medium Term Budgetary Framework. Fund resources were to be directed only for areas of core competence. The Medium Term Strategy focused on stronger surveillance, of regionally and systemically important economies. The Fund made a major pitch for Inflation Targeting to be adopted by Central Banks in the larger context of assigning price stability as the fundamental goal of monetary policy.

IMF's Experience with Inflation Targeting

During the 1980s, global monetary policies were largely devoted to price stability and high employment. In 1997, Swedish economist, Lars Svensson developed the concept of inflation-forecast targeting providing a systematic way to implement the notion of flexible inflation targeting. By mid 2000s, monetary policies of central banks used explicit inflation targets to govern monetary policy, with New Zealand and Canada taking the lead. The United States Federal Reserve gradually adopted an inflation targeting approach under its dual mandate of stabilize prices and maximize employment.

Most advanced economies have adopted an inflation target of 2 percent and others have adopted between 2 and 4 percent. Prior to adopting an inflation target, the nominal anchor for central bank policies was either a fixed exchange rate against a low inflation currency or target growth rate. Emerging Market Economies often adopted the "managed float" which prioritized stabilizing the exchange rate. Advanced economies used setting key short term rates as the policy instrument. Small open economies used exchange rate as a systematic instrument to influence output and inflation. The adoption of inflation-targeting forecasting method was accompanied by considerable transparency in Central Bank's operations, deployment of a team of economists with skills in macroeconomic modeling and forecasting, development of a core macroeconomic model and an updated macroeconomic database.

The macroeconomic model was based on a policy interest rate that systematically responds to bring the inflation rate back to the target within a medium-term horizon. There was always a short-term tradeoff between inflation and output growth. The approach brought down inflation in line with the targets. The IMF argued that monetary policy as a rule should stick to targeting inflation for which it has a strong comparative advantage and prudential policy instruments should be used to deal with financial stability issues. Improved communications in Central Banks' monetary policy operations are marked by press conferences, monetary policy and financial stability reports, and qualitative description of the forecast policy path.

A recent study of 4 countries - Canada, Czech Republic, India and United States – a diverse set of economies presents the universal applicability of the inflation-forecasting targeting regime. Canada, Czech Republic and India have had unstable inflation and widespread skepticism greeted the initial announcements of numerical targets for inflation control. The United States adopted an explicit numerical objective after long-term inflation expectations were anchored at low levels.

Canada adopted inflation targeting in 1991, the Bank of Canada's mandate includes objectives for stabilizing output and inflation. The Bank of Canada developed a model, QPM, well suited for inflation targeting which provided the basis of an efficient forecasting and policy analysis system. The long term inflation expectations were in the range of 1-3 percent. Inflation stabilized at 2 percent in 1995 and by 2017, the Canadian monetary framework has been well tested and without doubt proven sound with inflation varying around 2 percent. Canada adopted a risk-avoidance strategy with heavy penalty on deviation from the inflation target and potential output.

The Czech Republic underwent a transition from a state-run to a market based system. Banking regulation and supervision were at a rudimentary stage, and a banking crisis emerged in 1997 forcing abandonment of the pegged exchange rate. The Czech National Bank decided in favor of inflation targeting for nominal anchor. The announcement made for widespread skepticism given the history of inflation in the country. The Czech National Bank installed a forecasting and policy analysis system with IMF technical assistance and embarked on an open communications policy maintaining that the inflation targeting policy was about returning inflation to target without following any disturbance, taking into account the implications on output. The system worked well and the Czech National Bank has become a leader in central bank transparency.

In India, the Government and the Reserve Bank of India announced an inflation target range of 2-6 percent in 2016. India's monetary policy approach based on multiple indicator approach had failed to stabilize inflation – inflation ranged between 5 and 16 percent in 20 years 1990-2010, and between 8 and 13 percent in the 5 years 2010-15. The Reserve Bank of India faced a difficult legacy of inflation expectations as compared to Bank of Canada and Czech National Bank. Food prices contributed to 50 percent of the basket of goods comprising the consumer price index making it difficult for policy makers to perceive the influence of monetary policy on the inflation rate. The Reserve Bank of India developed macroeconomic models incorporating several special features and India's experience in the early years of adoption of inflation-forecasting targeting seems positive.

> The United States Federal Reserve has not formally adopted inflation targeting, but the Federal Open Market Committee's (FOMC) 2012 clarification of the dual mandate for price stability and maximum employment is tantamount to a statement of inflation-forecasting targeting. The FOMC announced a target of 2 percent inflation rate and non-quantitative commitment to maximize employment. The Federal Reserve has also put in place communications issues with the forward guidance on federal funds rate and quantitative easing.
>
> The IMF has called for further steps in transparency in central bank operations including publication of all macroeconomic variables including the forecast path of the policy rate. The Fund staff have pushed the case for several low-income countries adopting an inflation-forecasting targeting approach with IMF technical assistance in the coming years given the successful experience in implementation. Further, the IMF says that no alternate monetary regime has been as successful or as durable as the inflation-targeting forecasting which can be considered state of the art for monetary policy.

Governor Dr. Y.V. Reddy led the Indian delegation to the IMFC in April 2006. By 2006 inflationary pressures had surfaced with oil prices showing upward trends. International Oil prices were an area of grave concern given the limited spare capacity and continuing geo-political concerns. Although global financial conditions remained largely favorable, the global economic prospects were marked by global imbalances and their changing distribution across nation states. Monetary Policy conditions turned accommodative in Euro Area and Japan. The balance sheets of corporate houses were showing strong improvements.

The Finance Minister led the Indian delegation to the IMFC in September 2006. There were concerns expressed in the Finance Minister's statement at the IMFC on the deepening global imbalances which were proving to be a major risk to global growth and stability. India said that the imbalance is concentrated in the United States current account deficit and mirrored in the current account surpluses of China and Middle East, and that it was necessary to reduce the deficit to minimize the possibility of an adverse reaction from the markets as the US net foreign liabilities position deteriorates. India expressed concerns that abrupt corrections in the US housing market could slow down not only US growth but also global growth. On the issues concerning IMF's Medium Term Strategy – Quota and Voice, Surveillance, Role of the IMF in Emerging Market Countries – India pressed for expediting reforms.

By April 2007, Sustainable Financing of the IMF became an important issue for deliberations of the IMFC. Finance Minister leading the Indian delegation to the IMFC welcomed the Report of the Eminent Persons on the Sustainable Financing of the Fund, and said that the proposals contained therein for investment out of quotas and part sale of gold were far reaching. India did not support the proposal for charging Technical Assistance as it would discourage several needy countries.

The New Income Model and Medium Term Budget continued to be deliberated in the Fund in 2008. The Crockett Committee recommended a New Income Model that involved sale of the post Second Amendment Gold and the creation of an endowment. India said that in implementing an expanded investment authority, the Fund should establish sound policies and transparent procedures and avoid any perception of a potential conflict of interest. The Indian view was that the Fund's unique role as confidential advisor to member Nations with considerable access to privileged information should be preserved. India also welcomed the substantial expenditure reductions proposed by the Managing Director as part of the mid-term strategy of the IMF to ensure it focuses on its core mandate and tackle future financial crisis.

In April 2008, the Fund had completed the General review of Quotas. India said that a degree of credibility in the IMF governance had undoubtedly been restored in realigning quotas and votes. India supported the simple and transparent quota formula that adequately captured the relatively changing economic weights of the countries in the world.

The UPA II Government was in power from 2009-2014. During this period Finance Minister Pranab Mukherji attended the 20th, 22nd and 24th IMFC Annual meetings in 2009, 2010 and 2011. Finance Minister P.

Chidambaram attended the 26th and 28th IMFC Annual Meetings in 2012 and 2013. There was an intrinsic change in the character of the IMF in this period, following the London G20, when members agreed for a 5 percent shift in quota shares in favor of Emerging Market Economies. Further, the G20 also agreed on New Agreements to Borrow as the Fund needed resources to fight the 2008 Global Economic Crisis. There were significant changes in the Fund approach to multilateral and bilateral surveillance in this period.

In April 2009, the IMFC met in extraordinarily complex and challenging times. A global banking crisis, global financial crisis and a global economic crisis had developed post second half of 2008 starting with the sub-prime crisis in the United States. The estimates of the expected write downs were US $ 2.8 trillion on US based assets and US $ 1.4 trillion in Europe and Japan. Global economic activity contracted by 6 percent in last quarter of 2008 and another 6 percent in first quarter of 2009. The sharp deterioration in the global economic and financial situation evoked an unprecedented response with the G20 Leaders' Summits in Washington DC in November 2008 and in London in April 2009 providing a comprehensive multilateral response involving a range of institutions with the Fund in the forefront.

Governor Dr. Duvvuri Subbarao leading the Indian delegation to the IMFC made one of the seminal statements by an Indian head of delegation to the IMFC– His statement focused on Fund Surveillance, Lending Role of the Fund, Augmenting IMF resources and Governance. On surveillance, India reiterated the need for greater focus on systemically important countries, and bridging the gap between bilateral and multilateral surveillance. India called for greater focus on macro-financial sector issues in IMF Surveillance, with the Financial Sector Assessment Programs being made more focused and forward looking and integrated into bilateral surveillance. India stressed the need for developing a framework for early warning system for identifying and mitigating systemic risks. On the lending role of the IMF, India welcomed the two new instruments that were created – Flexible Credit Line (FCL) and the High Access Precautionary Stand-By Arrangements (HAPAs) as timely and progressive steps. India also supported the doubling of access under the Exogenous Shocks Facility (ESF) for Low Income Countries.

On Augmenting Fund Resources, India called for early ratification of the April 2008 Quota and Voice reform by the United States and advancing the 14th General Review of Quotas from January 2013 to January 2011 with the aim of doubling quota resources. In the interregnum period of allocating quotas, India supported the Fund's efforts for securing alternate resources through borrowing, broadly on the basis of quota shares. India called for a front loading of SDRs worth US $ 250 billion which would amount to three-quarters of the present quota size of the Fund, providing a liquidity of US $ 100 billion to developing countries and US $ 19 billion to Low Income Countries. India also called for improvements in the legitimacy, credibility and effectiveness of the Fund by internal Governance reforms through introduction of merit based selections irrespective of nationalities in the senior management of the Fund.

Finance Minister Pranab Mukherji led the Indian delegation to the IMFC meetings of October 2009 in Istanbul. The Finance Minister said that the 2008 Global Economic Crisis revealed the interdependence of economies, and demonstrated that the integration can turn to channels of contagion, and eventually strengthened international coordination. The key lesson of the crisis is that cooperation backed by political consensus can be effective in converting countries' own interests into a robust and resilient global response. India called upon the Fund to play a central role in anchoring the collective resolve of member nations to preserve global financial stability as the key to resumption of strong and sustainable growth.

Governor Dr. Duvvuri Subbarao led the Indian Delegation to the Spring Meeting of the IMFC in April 2010. The Indian statement to the IMFC said that the 2008 Global Economic Crisis had been a turning point in the world view on capital controls. The crisis, saw a rough correlation between the openness of the capital account and the adverse impact of the crisis. The IMF's policy note, of February 2010 referred to certain circumstances in which capital controls can be a legitimate component of the policy response to surges in capital flows. On surveillance, India held the view that multilateral surveillance should be strengthened by innovative instruments like spillover reports, multilateral consultations and enhanced interaction with regional/ country groups. India also pressed for even handed and robust bilateral surveillance and for adequate synergy between bilateral and multilateral surveillance procedures. India welcomed the expansion of the New Arrangements to Borrow to US $ 600 billion given the urgent need for resources as a temporary bridge to quota increase.

Finance Minister P. Chidambaram headed the Indian delegations to the IMFC meetings in 2012 and 2013. It was a period of huge challenges for policy makers in both advanced and emerging market economies. There was an uncertain global macroeconomic environment given the sharp decline in economic activity in the Euro area and the United States. Economic activity in India remained sluggish, impacted by the global economic environment and several domestic constraints. Government tried to tackle the twin deficits of fiscal deficit above 5 percent of GDP and widening Current Account Deficit due to imports of oil and gold.

Finance Minister Arun Jaitley headed the Indian delegations to the the 31st – 35th meetings of the IMFC from April 2015 to April 2017, as India's Governor to the IMF. The Indian delegation to the 30th meeting of the IMFC in October 2014 was attended by Raghuram Rajan, Governor Reserve Bank of India. These were the years when India emerged as amongst the fastest growing economies of the world.

In October 2014, global growth was recovering, but hesitatingly. The US economy had performed better than expected but the recovery in the Euro Area remained extremely fragile. Investment was weak in many advanced economies. Low and falling inflation was witnessed in the euro area. Even as the global recovery was weak, financial stability risks in many advanced economies raised concerns. There were serious risks, with potential to derail the recovery process. The positive developments were that the fiscal situation in the advanced economies was improving, and public debt to GDP ratio had stabilized. At the same time the growth in emerging market economies had also slowed down, and it was worrisome that the potential growth in both advanced economies and emerging market economies had declined significantly. A strong, sustainable global growth had eluded till then, and 2 major challenges had emerged – financial stability in the wake of prolonged use of low interest rates, and secondly the uncertainty about the smooth exit from the unconventional monetary policies pursued by the central banks in advanced economies.

India said that the process of exit from unconventional monetary policy has to be predictable and well communicated. Central Banks in

Advanced Economies have to take into account the spillovers of their policies on other economies. EMEs also need to take measures to address the financial stability risks and adverse impact that the withdrawal of accommodative monetary policy by managing domestic liquidity to ensure credit flows are not hampered. EMEs would also need to build reserves, strengthen fundamentals, address domestic vulnerabilities and prepare contingency plans if the exit from unconventional monetary policies is bumpy. India said that despite some improvement, fragilities persist in the Euro area affecting corporate and bank balance sheets resulting in credit contraction and financial fragmentation.

On the IMF's role in the architecture of global cooperation, India expressed great disappointment that the 2010 Quota and Governance reform has not become effective in spite of strong support from the global community for the reform. Moreover, it was not clear how the quota reform would be effective. India called upon the members to extend their fullest cooperation for completing the quota reform process.

Finance Minister Arun Jaitley said that the performance of the global economy is a matter of concern. Global growth was declining, with a slight pickup in growth rates of advanced economies and decline in growth rates of EMEs as also the LDCs. The uneven recovery had become even more uneven. Global financial stability risks had heightened. The economic transition underway in the Chinese economy, the sharp slowdown in Brazil and Russia and weaker growth in Sub-Saharan Africa all added to substantial decline in growth in EMEs'. Although the April 2015 IMFC Communique had committed itself to "take further measures to lift actual and potential growth' and support the goal of a more robust, balanced and job rich global economy" the global economic developments had belied such hopes. The IMF's near term assessment of EMEs and LICs had worsened sharply in the period April – October 2015.

India pointed out that the recent global economic developments had implications for IMF's operations and called upon the Fund to exercise closer surveillance to give timely warning of crisis, and be prepared for greater lending support. There was greater possibility of newer demands emerging for use of Fund resources. India sought closer international cooperation and coordination with each other's economic policies. An orderly exit from the unconventional monetary policies had become even more complicated. There was no clear communication about the exit. India further said that difficult structural reforms were required to lift growth in addition to strengthening fiscal and monetary policies.

India's economic growth continued to be robust with a growth rate of 7 percent in first quarter of 2015-16, low levels of inflation around 5 percent enabling the RBI to cut interest rates by 50 basis points, and foreign exchange reserves rising to US $ 355 billion. The gross fiscal deficit was expected to decline further to 1.1 percent of GDP by 2015-16.

Global economic recovery remained sluggish and was marked by increasing macroeconomic uncertainties, including those arising out of the UK vote in favor of exiting the European Union. Weak confidence indicators and financial sector conditions hamper the outlook for advanced economies while prospects for most emerging markets are subdued by diverse factors such as commodity price uncertainty and structural reform challenges. The unfolding of the political and economic developments in Europe has potential macroeconomic repercussions around the world. The persistence of ultra-accommodative monetary policies could result in spillovers in the form of large and volatile capital movements, thus endangering financial stability. There is growing consensus that monetary policies are near the limits of their effectiveness and need to be supported by fiscal policies and structural reforms that can boost actual and potential growth.

India has emerged as the fastest growing major economy globally. GDP growth stood at 7.6 percent in 2015-16. In 2016-17, the growth rate continues to exhibit strength. Inflation has eased to 5.05 percent, the RBI has reduced the policy rate by 25 bps and foreign exchange reserves have risen to US $ 372 billion. The Government had formulated an institutional framework for monetary policy and the bankruptcy code notified for recovery of bad debts. Government remained committed to reduction in fiscal deficit and structural reforms including early roll out of the GST.

References

1. Statement by the Hon. Chakravarthy Rangarajan, Alternate Governor of the IMF for India at the Joint Annual Discussion, September 24, 1997

2. Statement by Hon. Yashwant Sinha, Governor of the IMF and the World Bank at the Joint Annual Discussion, October 7, 1998

3. Statement by Hon. Yashwant Sinha, Governor of the World Bank and the Fund for India at the Joint Annual Discussion, September 29, 1999

4. Statement by Hon. Mr Yashwant Sinha, Finance Minister at the International Monetary and Financial Committee Meeting on April 16, 2000

5. Statement by Carlos Saito, G-24 Chairman to the Second Meeting of International Monetary and Finance Committee, September 24, 2000

6. Statement by Hon. Yashwant Sinha Governor of the IMF and World Bank for India at the Joint Annual Discussion, September 27, 2000

7. IMFC Statement by Hon. Jaswantsingh, Finance Minister India, September 29, 2002

8. IMFC Statement by Hon P.Chidambaram, Finance Minister India, October 2, 2004

9. IMFC Statement by Hon. P.Chidambaram, Minister of Finance India, April 16, 2005

10. IMFC Statement by Hon. P.Chidambaram, Finance Minister India, Sept 24, 2005

11. IMFC Statement by Dr. Yaga V Reddy Governor RBI, April 22, 2006

12. IMFC Statement by Hon. P.Chidambaram, Finance Minister for India, Sept 17, 2006

13. IMFC Statement by Hon. P.Chidambaram Finance Minister for India, Oct 22, 2007

14. IMFC Statement by Hon. P.Chidambaram Minister of Finance, India, April 12, 2008

15. IMFC Statement by Mr. DuvvuriSubbarao, Alt Governor India, April 25, 2009

16. IMFC Statement by Hon. Pranab Mukherjee, Finance Minister India, Oct 4, 2009

17. IMFC Statement by Pranab Mukherjee, Minister of Finance, India April 21, 2012

18. IMFC Statement by Hon. P.Chidambaram Finance Minister India, October 12, 2012

19. IMFC Statement by P.Chidambaram Minister of Finance for India, October 13, 2012

20. IMFC Statement by Hon. P.Chidambaram, Finance Minister, India" Oct 12 2013

21. IMFC Statement by Dr. RaghuramRajan, Alt Governor India" October 11, 2014

22. IMFC Statement by ArunJaitley, Minister of Finance, India October 9-10, 2015

23. IMFC Statement by Hon. ArunJaitley, Minister of Finance, India October 8, 2016

CHAPTER - VIII

THE IMF'S ARTICLE IV CONSULTATIONS 1997 – 2016

It is important to understand the key recommendations made by the IMF to the Indian authorities as part of the annual Article IV Consultations as part of IMF's surveillance mandate. As such the India-IMF relations were marked by co-evolution in collaborative approaches to fostering economic growth and development.

As a non-program country on a regular 12-month consultation cycle, Indian authorities were not bound to implement many of the recommendations of the Fund's economists. A study of the recommendations made the IMF as part of Article IV consultations are largely laudatory in nature, consistent with the IMF's recommendations for emerging market economies, in that they pushed for fiscal consolidation, trade reforms, banking sector regulations and capital account liberalization. The Indian experience has enabled the IMF policy in several emerging market economies too.

The United Front Government assumed office in June 1996. The IMF supported the new Government's policy initiatives and impetus given to structural reforms. The 1997-98 union budget provided for substantial tax cuts, liberalization of investment regulations, trade regulations along with tougher banking regulations. Reform measures were also pursued in industrial and infrastructural policies. The IMF said that India's overall economic performance had remained broadly favorable, despite a slowdown in industrial production and exports. The reform momentum of early 1990s continued to produce strong results. The IMF recommended continued fiscal consolidation path given the large public sector deficit.

Public sector deficit was around 9 percent and the Government had adopted a fiscal deficit target of 3 percent of GDP by the turn of the century. In this backdrop the IMF advised for improvements in composition of expenditure and improved public enterprise performance. The IMF considered the gains for India from capital account liberalization. The roadmap was laid down by the Tarapore Committee on Capital Account Convertibility for establishment of transparent guidelines for foreign direct and portfolio investment were welcomed.

As the Asian financial crisis unfolded in East Asia, India's growth in 1998, moderated to 5 percent, there were inflationary pressures and decline in export growth. Foreign exchange reserves stood at USD 26 ½ billion in 1998. There was an increase in Central and State deficits with a major shortfall in tax collections. Public sector deficits increased to 9 ½ percent. The balance of payments situation remained comfortable.

The IMF said that contagion from Asian crisis contributed to the slowdown in the Indian economy. The IMF felt that India could consider adopting a medium term fiscal adjustment program, and there was considerable scope for tax enforcement by eliminating tax exemptions. The IMF also highlighted the need for curtailing subsidies and reducing public sector deficits. The Narasimham committee report recommended financial sector reforms including adoption of internationally accepted standards, full independence of Reserve Bank of India, phased opening of the capital account and further liberalization of the foreign direct investment and portfolio equity flows. All these measures were fully supported by the IMF in their Article IV consultations.

The NDA government took office in 1998 and after elections again in 1999 and ruled for 6 years. The Indian economy had weathered the Asian crisis well. GDP growth rate moderated to 6 percent in 1999-2000, 5 ½ percent in 2001-02 and 4 ½ percent in 2002-03. India witnessed one of the worst drought years in 2002-03. Inflation moderated in the initial year due to good performance of agriculture sector but reached 6 ¾ percent in 2003 largely due to higher global oil prices and drought. India's GDP growth rate rebounded to 8 ½ percent in 2003-04 the highest level in over a decade. Foreign exchange reserves increased to USD 83 billion by end July 2003 and further increased to USD 129 billion by mid-January 2004. The fiscal position remained an area of concern – consolidated public sector deficit – comprising of central and state governments debt, central public enterprises and oil pool – was 10 percent of GDP. The slippages from budget numbers was significant, central government deficits touching 6 percent of GDP, with the Kargil war situation resulting in a significant increase in defense outlays. Government took important steps for introduction of VAT, by reducing the number of tariff bands. However, the rock solid rupee depreciated against the US dollar necessitating RBI to intervene in the foreign exchange markets directly. By early 2004, the deterioration of Government finances reversed and for the first time since mid 1990's the Central Government budget came in below target at 5.1 percent of GDP reflecting strong revenues and economic growth.

India outlined a draft fiscal responsibility bill, a securitization bill and a blueprint for second generation structural reforms in financial sector, petroleum sector and power sector. The Expenditure Reforms Commission recommended cutting fiscal subsidies, improving the delivery and targeting of poverty alleviation programs, downsizing government and increasing the efficiency of public spending. Fiscal reforms at State level were promoted through value added tax and fiscal responsibility legislations at State level. The Government introduced a debt-buy back scheme from Banks for rolling over the high cost debt of State Governments. The rupee was broadly in line with the macroeconomic fundamentals. Financial sector reform was necessary in the aftermath of the stock market scandal as also supervisory and regulatory systems.

The IMF outlined that India's large fiscal deficits and public debt were exacting an economic cost in terms of forgone growth despite the apparent ease with which India financed the deficits. The Fund welcomed the Fiscal Responsibility and Budget Management Act as one that would bring important discipline and transparency to the central government budget process and enable return fiscal sustainability. It was felt that fiscal adjustment needs to focus on revenue mobilization through widening the tax net and narrowing the range of tax exemptions. The Fund also supported the easy monetary conditions as appropriate with inflationary pressures under control. The Fund encouraged deeper capital account liberalization and trade reform as also enhanced risk supervision of the financial sector. They supported the steps taken up for strengthening the banking sector including reducing government ownership and improving the commercial orientation of public owned banks.

The UPA government was elected in 2004 and stayed in office till 2014. The 2 phases of UPA government are dealt with separately in terms of Article IV consultations with IMF.

India's GDP growth rate was 7 ½ percent in 2005, 8 percent in 2006, 8 ½ percent in 2007. India was the second fastest growing economy in the world surpassed only by China. The key challenge was to sustain the rapid and inclusive growth, foster job creation and maintain macroeconomic stability given the large capital inflows. The rupee appreciated against the dollar given the strong fundamentals of the Indian economy. There was buoyancy in India's tax revenues. Public expenditures and public debt were still high and it was felt that expenditure reforms were needed. Most States enacted fiscal responsibility laws. India's overall economic performance was outstanding reflected in strong growth, enhanced resilience to shocks and increasing integration to the world economy.

Then the global economic crisis happened.

India's Response to the Global Economic Crisis

By 2009, India had arrived on the international economic scene. The Indian economy had grown at 8.6 percent for 5 years, and it was opined that if the rate of growth kept up, India would be transformed like China with US $ 1 trillion economy doubling in 8 ½ years. It was projected that poverty would be reduced at an unimaginable speed and the 11th Five Year Plan had projected an annual growth rate of 9 percent rising to 10 percent by 2011. Indian policy makers had reckoned that India may not be severely affected from the 2008 Global Financial Crisis largely because of public ownership of banks, strict prudential rules laid down by RBI and limits on external commercial borrowings. That said, Indian stock markets witnessed a 60 percent loss in values, foreign portfolio investment slowed down and rupee lost 20 percent value against the dollar reaching Rs. 50/ dollar, with the global financial freeze accelerating the currency depreciation. Government borrowing rose sharply and abruptly in the crisis years of 2008-09 and 2009-10. The Reserve Bank of India managed the borrowing program by maintaining easy liquidity conditions. The growth forecast was revised from 9 percent to 7.1 percent and even that proved optimistic, although India remained the second fastest growing economy in the world after China.

Expectations that the Indian economy is 'decoupled' from the West were completely belied. The stock markets' sharp decline in response to global crisis were the first indications of global developments retaining their hold over Indian markets. Foreign institutional investors were pulling out. The current account deficit widened. Remittances and earnings from software exports that had propped up the current account in the past showed signs of declining. Software exports to the U.S. were under strain.

India's corporate sector was increasingly integrated with the world. India's IT companies which derived 85 percent of their revenues from exports to United States and Britain, employing 2 million workers witnessed job losses.

An analysis by the IMF suggested that the global crisis could have a serious impact on the Indian corporate sector and near-term growth. The significant volatility in the exchange rate, equity prices, and interest rates triggered by the global crisis, together with the decline in global economic activity and capital flows were to weigh on India's firms. The IMF estimated that the economic growth impact could be over four percentage points; with GDP growth rate in 2007/08 at 9 percent, the IMF estimates implied a deceleration to around 5 percent. As capital flows to India declined in the immediate aftermath of the crisis, the IMF suggested that India could prepare for the return of capital flows to Emerging Markets by continuing with capital account liberalization and pro-growth reforms. On the sharp decline of the rupee, the IMF said that an exchange rate depreciation is likely to be less inflationary when output was slowing.

In the G-20 meeting in October 2008, Governor RBI, Duvvuri Subbarao urged advance economies to keep the emerging market central banks in the loop on financial market developments as they viewed them and also on their proposed policy responses. The US Treasury and the Federal Reserve had conducted regular briefings for select emerging market economies including India. The advanced economies had to resort to unconventional monetary policies and quantitative easing and large scale asset purchases to flood the system with liquidity. The lowest policy rate India reached during the crisis was 3.25 percent while several advanced economies had reached near zero percent policy rates.

On February 16, 2009 the Union Finance Minister appraised the Parliament of the Global Financial Crisis. In his budget speech, Finance Minister, Pranab Mukherji said:

> "The global financial crisis which began in 2007 took a turn for the worse in September 2008 with the collapse of several international financial institutions, including investment banks, mortgage lenders and insurance companies. There has been a severe choking of credit since then and a global crash in financial markets. The slowdown intensified with the US, Europe and Japan sliding into recession. Current indicators of the global situation are not encouraging. Forecasts indicate that the world economy in 2009 may fare worse than in 2008.
>
> A crisis of such magnitude in developed countries is bound to have an impact around the world. Most emerging market economies have slowed down significantly. India too has been affected. For the first time in 9 months of the current year, the growth rate of exports has come down to 17.1 percent. ..Industrial production has fallen by 2 percent...In these difficult times, when most economies are struggling to stay afloat, a healthy 7.1 percent rate of GDP growth still makes India the second fastest growing economy in the world."

The Government decided to relax the Fiscal Responsibility and Budget Management Act targets in order to provide for much needed demand boost to counter the situation created by the global financial meltdown. The Fiscal Responsibility and Budget Management Act (FRBM) requires the government to commit up-front to a fiscal policy strategy over a multiyear period. The FRBM lays down the following: (i) reduction of the current deficit by at least 0.5 per cent of GDP in each financial year beginning with 2004/05; (ii) reduction of the overall deficit by at least 0.3 percent of GDP in each financial year; (iii) limit of 0.5 percent of GDP on the incremental amount of guarantees given by the central government; (iv) initial annual limit on debt accumulation of 9 percent of GDP, to be progressively reduced by at least one percentage point of GDP each year.

A substantial fiscal stimulus was provided through two packages announced by the Government on December 7, 2008 and January 2, 2009 to provide tax relief to boost demand and aim at increasing expenditure on public projects to create employment and public assets. The Government renewed its efforts to increase infrastructure investments by approving several infrastructure projects. The Reserve Bank of India took a number of monetary easing and liquidity enhancing measures including the reduction in the cash reserve ratio, statutory liquidity ratio and key policy rates. The objective was to facilitate funds from the financial system to meet the needs of productive sectors.

The First Stimulus dated December 7, 2008

The government effected an across-the-board 4 per cent cut in Cenvat to bring down the prices of cars, cement, textiles and other products, and earmarked an additional Rs. 20,000 crore for infrastructure, industry and export sectors for the current fiscal. In what may be dubbed as a mini-budget of sorts to lessen the impact of the global slowdown and recession in the West on the Indian economy, the package, while entailing a revenue loss of Rs 8,700 crore in the remaining four months of 2008-09, sought to revive various crucial sectors such as housing, exports, automobile, textiles and small and medium enterprises (SMEs).

In an all-encompassing measure, the Cenvat on all products — barring non-petroleum goods — was reduced from 14, 12 and 8 per cent to 10, eight and 4 per cent for various categories. Full exemption from basic customs duty was effected on naphtha to provide relief to the power sector. While the export duty on iron ore fines was withdrawn, the levy on export of iron lumps was cut from 15 to 5 per cent. Apparently, the package, drawn up at the instance of Prime Minister Manmohan Singh, who also held the Finance portfolio, sought to boost power, exports, housing, auto, SMEs and infrastructure sectors through additional funding.

The 10-point package, with significant incentives for the sectors affected by the slowdown, permitted India Infrastructure Finance Company Ltd. to raise Rs.10,000 crore through tax-free bonds by March as part of the exercise to support the Rs.1,00,000-crore highways development program.

> An official statement said: "The government has been concerned about the impact of the global financial crisis on the Indian economy and a number of steps have been taken to deal with this problem." It also noted that monetary measures effected by the Reserve Bank of India were being "supplemented by fiscal measures designed to stimulate the economy. In recognition of the need for a fiscal stimulus the government had consciously allowed the fiscal deficit to expand beyond the originally targeted level." "The economy will continue to need stimulus in 2009-2010 also and this can be achieved by ensuring a substantial increase in Plan expenditure as part of the budget for next year," the statement said.

The size of India's fiscal stimulus package of Rs. 30,000 crores was considered as modest in comparison with those of most other countries. It was termed a feeble response given the lack of fiscal space considering the budget had provided for salary hikes, oil and fertilizer subsidies and fiscal deficit was projected around 10 percent. The RBI had taken the lead in reduction of policy interest rates, the repo and reverse repo rates to increase bank lending. That said, the transmission mechanism from policy rates to interest rates charged by banks was weak to avert a sharp slowdown. This necessitated the second stimulus package dated January 2, 2009.

> ### The Second Stimulus dated January 2, 2009
>
> The government, in tandem with the Reserve Bank of India (RBI), on Friday announced the much-awaited second stimulus package aimed at reversing the economic slowdown through higher public spending, providing additional liquidity for onward lending at lower interest rates, boosting sagging sale of commercial vehicles and making easier credit availability for the export sector, housing and small industries. The package — the second within a month and last for this fiscal — marks

a clear shift from reining in inflation to spurring growth in the grim scenario of a crumbling financial system and recession in the West so as to minimize the slowdown impact, even as the government's total revenue loss in 2008-09 was officially expected to be Rs. 40,000 crore with a fiscal deficit of about 6 per cent of the GDP (gross domestic product), as per Planning Commission estimates. While the RBI slashed its key policy rates yet again to inject an additional Rs. 20,000 crore into the banking system, the government asked the public sector banks (PSBs) to hike their credit targets for the fiscal so as to ensure optimal disbursal of funds at least cost. The RBI has pumped over Rs.3,20,000 crore into the monetary system to usher in a low interest regime, especially when inflation was coming down in the wake of the fall in the prices of fuel, metals and farm commodities.

The interim budget did not enthuse the media, who felt that despite the Rs. 30,000 crores allocation to NREGS, the issues of generating employment of non-rural workers were not addressed.

The Hindu said:

"..India is among countries that have a high exposure to increased risk of poverty due to the global economic downturn. As the sectors that fueled the high annual economic growth rates brace themselves for hard times, job creation in these areas has also weakened. Specific measures to facilitate employment are called for in segments that are badly affected by the economic slowdown, such as Information Technology (IT), IT enabled services, textiles, gems and jewelry, and retail trade. ... the entire issue of addressing the urgent issue of urban employment has been left to the successor government that will be formulating the full budget."

On February 19, 2009 the rupee hit 50/ dollar in a jittery market. The RBI's holding of US T bills rose by US $ 6.9 billion to US $ 23.1 billion in December 2008 as India's forex reserves rose from US $ 247.8 billion in November 2008 to US $254 billion in December 2008. Monetary authorities in China, Russia, Hong Kong, Norway, Ireland and Israel also added the lower yielding dollar asset to their foreign exchange reserves. China had added US $ 218 billion in 2008 while India added US $ 8.2 billion.

The Economic Times said

> On Wednesday, the rupee briefly breached the 50-mark against the dollar to end Rs. 49.97, with the market beginning to price in political risk, fiscal slippages and decline in interest of foreign fund houses in emerging market assets. What's pushing up the dollar in the international market is the pervasive interest even among central banks, in US Treasury bills. Despite the US slowdown and abysmal return in US T bills, funds, banks and sovereigns are buying these bonds, which are still perceived as safe haven.
>
> In the face of these forces, the domestic currency market largely ignored RBI Governor D. Subbarao's sentiment that lower inflation and current account deficit in coming months could create the possibility of a rate cut. Some state owned banks sold dollars to prevent the rupee from dropping further, but this did not help."

India's 2008 Article IV Consultations with the IMF were concluded on February 6, 2009. The IMF projected India's growth to moderate to 6 ¼ percent in 2008-09 and further to 5 ¼ percent in 2009-10. Headline inflation came down from 13 percent to 4.4 percent in January 2009 and was projected to further drop to 3 percent by March 2009 and to 2 percent on average in 2009-10. Current account deficit was projected at 3 percent of GDP primarily due to oil import bill and deterioration in exports. For 2009-10 the IMF forecast that the current account deficit will narrow to 1 ½ percent of GDP. Capital inflows were expected to decline, with portfolio investment recording US $ 11 billion outflow and external commercial borrowing slowing down considerably. The foreign exchange reserves declined from a historic peak of US $ 315 billion in May 2008 to US $ 252 billion in February 2009. The stock market declined by 50 percent and the rupee declined by 23 percent. The RBI's measures had eased the domestic liquidity pressures and brought down interbank rates significantly. India's spending prior to the onset of crisis had risen significantly with the agricultural debt forgiveness, expansion of the rural employment guarantee scheme and 21 percent civil service wage hike.

The IMF recommended that India faced spillovers from the global crisis. The key short term policy objective was to sustain liquidity and credit flows. The monetary and structural policies had to bear the burden of adjustment given the high public debt – GDP ratio. The IMF felt that rising credit risk and liquidity pressures could put the financial system under strain. It was important that India took note of the potential bank recapitalization needs and measures to promote early loss recognition, full disclosure of bad assets and filling of information gaps. The IMF supported India's gradual approach to capital account liberalization. It was felt that the sizeable fiscal stimulus should support economic growth in 2008-09. There remained concerns about fiscal sustainability given the high ratio of public debt to GDP. The fiscal space available was to be used for infrastructure and poverty related spending and for bank recapitalization if needed. The IMF reiterated that medium term fiscal consolidation remained a priority and should be anchored in the fiscal rules framework.

The 2009 Article IV consultations of the IMF with India were concluded in January 2010. India's economy was one of the first in the world to recover after the global crisis. Prompt fiscal and monetary policy easing combined with a fiscal stimulus had brought growth to pre-crisis levels. Capital inflows were back on the rise and financial markets regained ground. Growth was projected to rise from 6 ¾ percent in 2009-10 to 8 percent in 2010-11. The IMF commended the Reserve Bank of India for commencing the first phase of exit from monetary accommodation and generally considered that conditions were right for a progressive normalization of monetary stance. The withdrawal of the monetary stimulus was to be done in a gradual manner to soften the impact on long term interest rates and help anchor inflation expectations. India faced challenges in managing capital flows and the IMF recommended sterilized intervention to help reduce exchange rate volatility. The RBI's approach to use prudential measures in case of asset bubbles was also supported by IMF and tightening of capital controls was to be an instrument of last resort.

The financial system had weathered the global crisis well. The strengthening of capital of public sector banks and financial regulation, the higher provisioning arrangements introduced had all proven successful. There were issues of distressed assets and the insolvency framework.

Infrastructure investment remained a priority and public institutions had an important role to establishing the framework for infrastructure financing.

By 2013, India's growth had slowed markedly to 4.7 percent and inflation was stubbornly high, well above the RBI's comfort zone. Current account deficit widened to 4.2 percent in 2011-12, causing the rupee to depreciate sharply. The growth slowdown reflected global developments and domestic constraints. The financial positions of banks and corporates deteriorated. India started the direct benefits transfer and the unique identification number for improved targeting of subsidies. The RBI projected a modest growth-pick up in 2014-15, but the overall macroeconomic situation was one where growth risks were on the downside.

The NDA government came to office in 2014 and there was increased political certainty, improved business confidence and an overall positive outlook. The new government adopted a pro-cyclical fiscal and monetary policy stance resulting in an improved growth outlook. Growth picked up from 5.6 percent in 2014-15 to 7.3 percent in 2015-16 to 7.5 percent in 2016-17. The RBI achieved its inflation target and inflation came down below 6 percent. There was a significant improvement in India's economic performance. This was followed up with efforts to improve targeted delivery of subsidies by creation of a digital economy across India's villages, the transformation of India's villages with the Jan Dhan – Aadhar – BHIM applications was the most striking feature of Rural India's economic transformation.

The external situation was favorable with adequate foreign exchange reserves. After almost a decade there is good news on economic growth in April 2017. The World Economic Outlook has said that global growth is projected to increase from 3.1 percent in 2016 to 3.5 percent in 2017 and 3.6 percent in 2018. Growth picked up in the United States, has remained solid in the United Kingdom despite Brexit. Japan and Euro Area countries of Germany and Spain were also witnessing strong growth.

The IMF noted India's strong economic performance and commended the Indian authorities for their strong policy actions including fiscal consolidation and anti-inflationary monetary policy.

References

1. Public Information Notice: IMF Concludes Article IV Consultation with India, September 22, 1998www.imf.org

2. IMF Staff Country Report No. 98/ 112. "India – Selected Issues" November 4, 1998www.imf.org

3. IMF Staff Country Report No 98/120. "India – Recent Economic Developments", November 4, 1998www.imf.org

4. Public Information Notice: IMF concludes Article IV Consultation with India, June 30, 2000www.imf.org

5. IMF Staff Country Report No: 00/155. "India: Recent Economic Developments" December 07, 2000www.imf.org

6. Public Information Notice: IMF Concludes 2001 Article IV Consultation with India, August 14, 2001www.imf.org

7. IMF Country Report No 01/ 181. "India: Recent Economic Developments and Selected Issues", October 16, 2001www.imf.org

8. IMF Country Report No: 01/181. "India: Recent Economic Developments and Selected Issues", October 16, 2001www.imf.org

9. Public Information Notice: IMF Concludes 2002 Article IV Consultation with India, August 29, 2002www.imf.org

10. Public Information Notice: IMF Concludes 2003 Article IV consultation with India, August 21, 2003www.imf.org

11. IMF Conference on Fiscal Policy in India, New Delhi. "The Rewards of Virtue", Address by Anne O.Krueger, First Deputy Managing Director of the IMF, January 16, 2004 www.imf.org

12. Purfield, Catriona | Hausman Ricardo. "The Challenge of Fiscal Adjustment in a Democracy: The Case of India" IMF Working Paper 04/168, September 01, 2004www.imf.org

13. Dani Rodrick and Arvind Subramanian. "Why India can grow at 7 percent a Year or More: Projections and Reflections", IMF Working Paper WP/04/118, July 2004www.imf.org

14. IMF Country Paper No. 05/86. "India: 2004 Article IV Consultation – Staff Report; Staff statement; Public Information Notice on the Executive Board Discussion" March 10, 2005www.imf.org

15. IMF Country Paper No. 06/55. "India: Article IV Consultation – Staff Report; Staff statement; Public Information Notice on the Executive Board Discussion" Feb 21, 2006www.imf.org

16. KalpanaKochhar, Utsav Kumar, RaghuramRajan et al. "India's Pattern of Development: What Happened, What Follows", IMF Working Paper WP/06/22, January 2006www.imf.org

17. Remarks by John Lipsky, First Deputy Managing Director IMF at the Joint India-IMF Training Program in Pune India, January 24, 2007www.imf.org

18. IMF Country Report No 08/51. "India: 2007 Article IV Consultation: Staff Report; Staff Statement and Supplements; Public Information Notice on the Executive Board Discussions and Statement of the Executive Director for India" February 04, 2008www.imf.org

19. The Hindu., "Government unveils stimulus package"., dated December 8, 2008

20. The Hindu., "The Second Stimulus Package" dated January 03, 2008

21. India Selected Issues., International Monetary Fund, January 23, 2009www.imf.org

22. Interim Budget 2009-10, Speech of Pranab Mukherji, Minister of Finance February 16, 2009

23. DuvvuriSubbarao., India and the Global Financial Crisis – Transcending from Recovery to Growth., Comments of Dr. D. Subbarao, Governor RBI at the Peterson Institute for International Economics, Washington DC, April 26, 2010., RBI Speecheswww.rbi.org

24. IMF Country Report No 09/187. "India: 2008 Article IV Consultation: Staff Report; Staff Statement and Supplements; Public Information Notice on the Executive Board Discussions and Statement of the Executive Director for India" March 09, 2009www.imf.org

25. The Hindu., "Addressing Urban Job Losses"., dated February 20, 2009

26. The Economic Times., Rupee hits 50 in jittery market., dated February 19, 2009

27. India 2009 Article IV consultations., International Monetary Fund., January 25, 2010 www.imf.org

28. IMF Country Report No 10/73. "India: 2009 Article IV Consultation: Staff Report; Staff Statement and Supplements; Public Information Notice on the Executive Board Discussions and Statement of the Executive Director for India" May 16, 2010 www.imf.org

29. IMF Country Report No 11/50. "India: 2010 Article IV Consultation: Staff Report; Staff Statement and Supplements; Public Information Notice on the Executive Board Discussions and Statement of the Executive Director for India" February 1, 2011 www.imf.org

30. IMF Country Report No: 12/96 "India: 2011 Article IV Consultation – Staff Report; Staff Statement and Supplements; Public Information Notice on the Executive Board Discussions and Statement of the Executive Director for India" April 18, 2012 www.imf.org

31. Arvind Virmani. "Accelerating and Sustaining Growth: Economic and Political Lessons" IMF Working Paper No 12/185 www.imf.org

32. IMF Country Report No: 13/37. "India: 2013 Article IV Consultation" February 06, 2013 www.imf.org

33. IMF Country Report No: 14/57. "India: Staff Report for 2014 Article IV Consultation" February 20, 2014 www.imf.org

34. Press Release: IMF Executive Board concludes 2014 Article IV Consultation, February 2-, 2014 www.imf.org

35. IMF Country Report No:16/75 "India:2016 Article IV Consultation – Press Release: Staff Report and Statement by Executive Director for India" March 02, 2016 www.imf.org

36. Press Release: Statement by IMF Managing Director Christine Lagarde at the conclusion of the Conference on "Advancing Asia: Investing for the Future" March 13, 2016 www.imf.org

37. IMF Survey: Conference Highlights Asia's Advancing Role in the Global Economy, March 15, 2016www.imf.org

38. Seizing India's Moment, by Christine Lagarde MD IMF, March 16, 2015www.imf.org

39. Gaining Momentum, The World Economic Outlook, The International Monetary Fund, April 2017

40. DuvvuriSubbarao., Who Moved My Interest Rate., 2016 pp 21-45

CHAPTER - IX

FINANCE SECRETARIES, GOVERNORS OF RBI, CHIEF ECONOMIC ADVISORS AND EXECUTIVE DIRECTORS

This chapter presents the views of Institution Builders in the India-IMF relations following discussions with the author.

India-IMF relations have remained constructive and cordial for several decades. The men who contributed to strong India-IMF relations were visionary civil servants who were willing to accept the principles of economic liberalism and macroeconomic stability placing the Nation of a high growth path amidst the fastest growing economies in the world.

The Finance Secretaries

Dr. Montek Singh Ahluwalia, a seminal figure in Indian economic policy making served as Secretary Department of Economic Affairs, Founder Director Independent Evaluation Office of IMF and Deputy Chairman Planning Commission. His imprint on the economic governance of India has been significant.

On his years in IEO

The Vajpayee government was willing to offer my services to the IMF for the post of Director IEO. It was a new job, and I could recruit professionals from scratch. We produced the first few evaluation reports. The experience convinced me that every organization needs an IEO on how to conduct evaluations. I replicated it in the Planning Commission with the IEO being headed by an official in the rank of a member, who would get expert views and place it in Parliament. In the Fund, once the Director signs off on the report, it goes to top management. The Directors of the Department concerned can comment and the Board had a clear sense of what was happening. The new Government did not want a Planning Commission. The Director IEO of Planning Commission shot off a report in 2 weeks without consulting anyone that Planning Commission should be shut down. Even the NITI Aayog as an independent organization needs an IEO.

On being part of the Government in 2004-2009 years when Indian growth rates had peaked.

There was a global bump up in 2004-09 period. The growth was a result of lagged effort by several Government. India's time had come. India achieved 8.5 percent to 9 percent over longer time period. Anything above 7 percent was a new India. Contrary to other perceptions, poverty was coming down too. Literacy levels also went up significantly. I also felt that high growth rate cannot be taken for granted. The 11th and 12th Plan documents brought out the underlying risks to the Indian growth story.

On the policy responses to the 2008 global financial crisis.

The global mood was for fiscal expansion. Most Governments liked the fiscal stimulus, reducing tax rates, additional liquidity in the system. The IMF perhaps said that while the world needed a fiscal expansion, India may not need a fiscal expansion. It would have been better if the one or 2 year bonanza was spent on infrastructure financing.

On his critical role as India's Sherpa at the G-20 meetings.

After the initial crisis, I am not sure what the G-20 achieved. The major countries met periodically. The composition of the G-20 is not very comprehensive. Argentina for example, is a member. The French wanted a G-15. Its good for India to be at the high table, but more important is what do we do once we are at the high table. Prime Minister Modi on the issue of climate change said that India would accept the challenge of cutting emissions. Climate change is one area where pressures of being part of elite group worked. There were occasions when the MOEF objected to 12th Plan targets citing international obligations.

On the changes in the IMF after the 2008 Global Financial Crisis and how he sees the IMF in the decade 2020-2030.

The Fund is a good international organization. The Fund has changed over time with received wisdom. The western world wants the Fund as an organization that will predict crisis in major countries, formulate technical papers and surveillance. For smaller countries it will be a good institution for lending. If India were to have a crisis, the Fund will not be empowered to finance India. An International Monetary Fund with US $ 360 billion is not much. If India were to go to Fund today, it would need about US $ 50 billion financing. It is very unlikely that the Fund's Executive Board would part that much moneys.

For decades, the multilateral governance institutions were led by the United States. It is difficult to envisage an American leadership for multilateralism in the current context when protectionist forces are gathering momentum. Although the United States is unlikely to say that the IMF should be abolished, it may not support the Institution too much in the coming years. The Fund itself may think of its future, 5 years from now. I would refer to the Michael Camdessus report on the Future of the Fund.

The IMF faces a problem of mission creep. Fiscal professionalism is the need of the hour. No one has given the Fund a license to look at other issues. The Fund has to look at short term measures to tighten the belt – that's what is Fund's role. The Fund has to prescribe that the fiscal deficit is unsustainable and leave it to Governments to achieve the fiscal targets. The Fund is getting into issues that it has no role.

On Financial Stability, the IMF is not doing much. The Financial Stability Forum and the BIS are doing far more. Unfortunately, no one in the west is looking at the Fund for financial stability.

Today, India is a moderately open economy. In 5 years, we will be better. Government needs to be aware that the Indian financial system is integrating rapidly with the global economy. Subsequent to the global financial crisis, India's financial sector integration has progressed well, although I am not sure if the dollar exposure of some of the Indian corporates have been well thought out.

On his memories of the 1991-93 years. On the convergence in ideas between Dr. Montek Singh Ahluwalia and Mr. Hubert Neiss led to the success of the 1991 reforms program with IMF.

History will remember us well. Even the IMF history says that Indian officials knew what we needed to do. It must also be borne in mind that at the political level there was deep understanding of the IMF program which ensured political support for the economic reforms.

India is a poster child for the Fund. Each of their 3 programs were terminated earlier than projected. Post program growth rates were always higher than pre-program growth rates. The repayments were always on schedule.

The 1981 program the IMF said we don't need the money. M. Narasimham networked with the IMF management at a time when we were not doing too well. Prior to the 1991 crisis, there were a lot of internal papers in the Indian government on the reform process. Indian policy makers were aware of the way we had to go. There is no doubt that the 1991 crisis triggered the economic reforms. Only the Left parties were opposed to the 1991 economic reforms. History has proved that the Left was wrong and the Government was right on the economic reforms of 1991.

The Fund staff knew how to deal with large countries like India. Their relations with us were always cordial and constructive.

When I look back, I wonder what would the then Secretary DEA Shukla and CEA Deepak Nayyar would have done. During discussions on trade policy, they were opposed to trade reform at that stage.

On the 1985 Long Term Fiscal Policy Document. On the fiscal expansion of the 1985-89 period creating an unsustainable fiscal policy.

The LTFP was a Finance Ministry document. It was unfortunate that the Finance Ministry eroded it. Indian Finance Ministers are not judged by fiscal prudence. There was a massive expansion of defense expenditure in those years. The Government felt that the capacity to do more in Defense was necessary for India to be taken seriously. Subsequent experience proved that it we want to be taken seriously, the best way is to raise GDP.

We underestimate the fact that how much China has achieved by staying under the radar in terms of economic growth.

On his Memories of the 1997 East Asian Crisis and the impact on India.

The East Asian crisis did not alter the world. It was quickly brought under control. Korea recovered quickly, Indonesia suffered, Thailand and Malaysia which faced the crisis also came recovered. The RBI did convey the impression of a professional organization. The NDA government wanted a strong rupee. That said, the Governor RBI, Jalan convinced the Prime Minister on the benefits of a weaker rupee. Both the RBI and the MOF gave the impression that eyes were open during the 1997 crisis.

On how he sees the economic reforms progressing 2014 onwards.

The reforms process is a continuation of the previous Government. There have been 2 important steps – the GST and the Bankruptcy code. For GST both Government and the Opposition can take credit. The Bankruptcy code is an important step to handle the challenges of non-performing assets and the multiplicity of interest rates. It could also consider to identify bad banks and staff them with RBI officials to tackle the NPAs. There are issues of consortium lending where a lot of responsibility is left to the Lead Bank most of the time. I have often asked "Who is suffering with NPAs? The truth is nobody is suffering except the Banks."

On his 30 year legacy in economic policy making at the highest levels of Government.

The leader was Dr. Manmohan Singh. Around him there was a lot of collegiality in economic policy making. We could build teams of officials to work together. It was always said that the United States was one country that could put a team together. The Indian growth story reveals the success that we have had in working in teams.

Shri Shaktikanta Das

Shaktikanta Das, IAS served as Joint Secretary/ Additional Secretary in the Department of Economic Affairs, as Secretary Department of Revenue and Secretary Department of Economic Affairs for the years 2008-2017. During his long tenure in the Department of Economic Affairs he was closely associated with India's economic reforms and global financial sector integration. He has been a dominant force in the 2014-17 period in major economic reforms in India. Shri Shaktikanta Das was appointed Governor of the Reserve Bank of India on December 12, 2018.

On the changing role of the IMF.

Till 2008, the IMF's role was largely bilateral surveillance. After 2008, the IMF strengthened multilateral surveillance. The IMF's role got a further boost with G-20 becoming an active forum. The G-20 summit meetings and the OECD meetings provided the IMF with a forum to present its analysis of the situation. This brought about a quantitative shift in the IMF's role in the global arena.

The IMF kept advocating a 3 pronged approach to deal with the global crisis and restore economic growth - use the additional fiscal space available, monetary policy expansion and structural reforms.

On the Challenges in dealing with capital flows into India.

There was a huge surge in capital flows post the global economic crisis. Long term flows are always in India's interest. There was a lot of capital in a world witnessing slow growth and slow appetite for investment, and money was flowing to markets with better returns, India was seen as a robust economy, markets were giving good returns and structural reforms were strong.

Post 2014, the Government initiated a number of steps to ensure inflow of stable long term capital into India – focus on make in India, focus on improving the ease of doing business including removal of licenses and FIPB abolition. Another very important step was the introduction of easier customs clearances and building permissions. On the taxation side, GST was the single big step forward. While the GST bill was introduced in 2011, it could move forward only in 2014 in consultation with the State Governments. The flexibility shown by the Union Government helped in breaking the deadlock between the States and Centre. The compensation period to States was increased to 5 years for revenue losses. The reduction of corporate income tax from 30 percent to 25 percent in the 2015-16 budget was a big step forward.

On structural reforms, the Government addressed the hibernation of FDI policy by initiating major FDI reforms. The major FDI liberalization of November 2015 and March 2016 provided for significant sectoral easing of FDI caps including the introduction of FDI in real estate. Following the sectoral easing it was seen that 90 percent of FDI was coming on automatic route and only 10 percent was coming on FIPB route. This made abolition of FIPB much simpler.

In your tenure as Secretary DEA, India had emerged as the Fastest Growing Major Economy in the world. The transformation causes.

The transformation was built on fiscal prudence and rigid adherence to FRBM's long term fiscal targets. The SEBI initiatives for reforms of capital markets and reforms of stock markets including the introduction of online trading enabled greater financial sector integration. The introduction of Masala Bonds which were rupee denominated bonds enabled internationalization of the Indian rupee. Several PSEs like the NTPC, NHAI and Private sector companies like HDFC used the Masala Bonds for raising foreign capital. There was simplification of the external commercial borrowings regime and G-secs markets both of which could follow the KYC norms. India's participation in the Financial Action Task Force (FATF) enabled the simplification in external commercial borrowings reforms.

Views on the Fund's bilateral surveillance. Usefulness of recommendations from the Article IV consultations.

The Article IV consultations provided Government with an outsider's view of the Indian economy. We were not bound by the recommendations. We were autonomous in economic policy making. There was considerable convergence of thoughts with regard to adoption of inflation targeting and subsidy reforms. We also accepted IMF advise on the manner in which we were calculating our fiscal deficit, by agreeing to reflect bonds in the fiscal deficit. The Finance Minister subsequently announced that the Government would not release subsidy payments to oil PSUs by way of issuance of bonds. Subsidy payments would be in cash form in fiscal accounting of Government.

On the way forward for India-IMF relations.

Going forward perhaps it is time for MD IMF to be from outside Europe. It is Asia's economic decade and our strengths should be reflected in the IMF quota reforms. The IMF has used bilateral windows of funding for raising resources to finance the programs following the 2008 global crisis – the New Arrangements to Borrow and the Note Purchase Agreements could have been incorporated into quotas for raising additional resources. Further quota reforms are necessary to reflect the actual economic strengths of Asian Nations.

On the technical assistance side, India and IMF have signed the MOU for establishing the SARTAC, the South Asia Regional Training Center for capacity building of central government and state government officials.

There has been a continuity in India-IMF relations. From the major structural and taxation reforms of 1991, till the bilateral surveillance of 2017 under Article IV, the India-IMF relations have been marked by strong national ownership and convergence of ideas.

The Central Bank Governors

Dr. Y.V. Reddy, IAS has been one of India's most seminal civil servants who served as Technical Assistant to the Executive Director (India) in the World Bank, as Joint Secretary in the Department of Economic Affairs during the 1991 crisis, as Deputy Governor RBI, as Executive Director (India) in the IMF and as Governor Reserve Bank of India and Alternate Governor to the IMF (2003-08).

On the Bretton Woods Institutions

In the Bretton Woods Conference that took place towards the end of World War II, 44 countries were represented, India was an active participant. It accepted the idea of a provision of resources to a country from the general pool to get over its temporary balance of payments problems, and this is the basis for the creation of the International Monetary Fund (IMF). The basic structural characteristics of BWIs remain somewhat unchanged. Their membership, open only to Governments, is voluntary. They are cooperative in character, though the voting power is weighted by 'quota' in the IMF, reflecting uneven strength partly due to historical reasons and partly due to emerging economic and trading strengths.

On India's relationship with the IMF

India has always been represented by an Executive Director on the Board of IMF and its contribution in the conduct of business of the IMF is generally valued. India has been a responsible and prudent borrower of resources from the IMF. In times of crises, the IMF extended support to India in a timely manner. The IMF acknowledged the valuable contribution made by Indian policy-makers to their policies and procedures - though there are many differences.

On IMF Reforms

There have been several suggestions for reform of IMF, and a few of the more serious ones are (a) Eichengreen's Proposal: Eichengreen has argued for making the IMF more independent. According to Eichengreen, "international standards" must form the basis for future IMF multilateral surveillance. He recommends giving IMF more independence by prohibiting its Executive Director from taking instructions from national Governments and by giving them an explicit mandate to foster policies that "maximize stability, prosperity and growth". (b) Lawrence Summers: Mr. Summers, former Treasury Secretary in the USA, argued that the IMF needs to be more transparent and open in its agreements with countries. In designing its programs, he indicated that the IMF needs to take better account of the broader structural and institutional environment with which they are to be implemented.

On India's economic integration with the world economy.

India's economic integration with the global economy will continue to take place through sound public policies. Pragmatic policies in the management of capital account and exchange rate, have served us well by contributing to growth, resilience to shocks and an overall stability. Enhanced competition among diverse players, including from branches of foreign banks, has been encouraged.

On the fiscal front, the ratio of public-debt to GDP is high in our country, but the structure of public-debt displays characteristics that make us less vulnerable than other countries with similar debt magnitudes. There is advantage in continuing the progress in public debt management keeping structural aspects in view. Furthermore, an effective and qualitative fiscal adjustment would enhance the scope for a more successful integration with the global economy. In matters relating to trade, significant liberalization of external trade has taken place smoothly, which has imparted competitive efficiency to the domestic sector.

On Global Macroeconomic Imbalances.

Global macroeconomic imbalances were a feature of the global economic governance agenda in the years 2004-2007 and there were many meetings at the IMFC, G-20 and BIS on the subject. India by itself hardly ever contributes to global financial imbalances, any large and rapid adjustments in major currencies and related interest rates or current accounts of trading partners could indirectly impact the Indian economy. That said, the Impact on India depended on the pace and extent of currency and current account readjustments, and changes in global interest rates. It was also clear that readjustment of the currencies and rise in interest rates would impact India. India faced added risks increasing global financial and economic integration, but through sound macroeconomic management and by adopting appropriate prudential measures is better prepared against the risks of financial globalization.

On India's financial sector liberalization.

India has made significant progress in financial liberalization since the institution of financial sector reforms in 1992. India's commitment to fiscal consolidation in the medium term is laid down by the Fiscal Responsibility and Budget Management Act, 2003. India is better prepared to deal with surges of capital flows, large reversals and associated fluctuations in financial prices that become inevitable with accelerated liberalization of financial sector. The adequacy of foreign exchange reserves has enabled faster financial liberalization.

On major banking sector reforms India has witnessed.

One of the major objectives of banking sector reforms has been to enhance efficiency and productivity through competition. New private sector banks have been set up and private shareholding in public sector banks is permitted upto 49 percent. Foreign direct investment in the private sector banks is now allowed up to 74 per cent. The consolidation in the banking sector has been another feature of the reform process. Interest rate deregulation imparted greater efficiency to resource allocation. The process has been gradual. The infusion of funds by the Government into the public sector banks for the purpose of recapitalization on a cumulative basis amounted to less than one per cent of India's GDP.

The RBI has undertaken seminal work in this regard, the Report of the Committee on the Financial System (Chairman: Shri M. Narasimham), in 1991, the Report of the High Level Committee on Balance of Payments (Chairman: Dr. C. Rangarajan) in 1992; and the Report of the Committee on Banking Sector Reforms (Chairman: Shri M. Narasimham) in 1998 outline the banking sector reforms roadmap for India.

On India's exchange rate management policies since reforms.

The devaluation of the rupee in July 1991 was part of the reform program. There was a move in March 1992 to a regime of partial convertibility. In March 1993 the regime changed to a uniform exchange rate of the rupee which was market-determined – a system which remains in place to date. In August 1994, India moved over to current account convertibility. From the latter part of 1997, India moved to a cautious and well calibrated move towards capital account convertibility. These developments tested the exchange rate regime which proved conducive to growth while maintaining stability.

On the role of IMF staff on India's reform program.

One of the major reasons for the seamless implementation of the 1991 program was the synergy between the India's top bureaucracy and the IMF Staff. The intellectual convergence of ideas was a major reason for the seamless implementation.

On the international policy coordination in the aftermath of the global crisis of 2008

The Global Financial Crisis compelled coordinated fiscal-monetary actions in all countries. Coordination was inevitable under the circumstances. In reality, the monetary authorities had to take unconventional measures which had large quasi-fiscal implications. Coordination of policies at global level was also required in the light of the `agreement in the meeting of G20. Both fiscal and monetary stimulus in India were undertaken and supplemented by regulatory forbearance by RBI. After some time, it became evident to RBI that withdrawal of stimulus should be commenced. The fiscal authorities, however, did not seem to be on board. The uncoordinated responses could be witnessed during the period of withdrawal of stimulus. This proved to be stressful. However, it must be recognized that coordination becomes difficult during extraordinary situations and this was no exception. These developments led to questioning the monetary policy frame work that was in place.

On the contours of India's new monetary policy framework.

The conduct of monetary policy in India underwent a transformation since 2014, transiting to a flexible inflation targeting framework. During 2014-15, a formal architecture for flexible inflation targeting was put in place through an agreement between the RBI and Government. Amendments to the RBI Act, 1934 were made with the primary objective "to maintain price stability while keeping in mind the objective of growth". Constitution of MPC was mandated and entrusted with the responsibility to determine the policy rate required to achieve inflation target. We now have a rule-based fiscal policy mandated by FRBM Act and a rule-based monetary policy through the amended RBI Act.

On your memories as Executive Director IMF and Governor RBI.

IMF (2002 – 2003): I moved out of RBI to become an Executive Director in IMF. I was now on the Board of IMF as an important member in managing the IMF. This is a cooperative institution. However, it was a cooperative with unequal membership. We could command respect because we became a lender in 2002-03, in ten years, from being a borrower after pledging gold.

On close quarters, I understood the Fund's program in Turkey, Brazil, Argentina and Mexico. The most important lesson was very clear. All systemic risks that arise out of globalization will have to be borne by the government of the country concerned. The only exception may be USA because U.S. Dollar is virtually the world currency. Major sources of risk for a country are government's borrowing in foreign currencies from non-residents and banking system.

Governor (2003-2008): On the basis of the lessons learnt from the IMF, we from the RBI took a highly nuanced position in regard to external sector. We differentiated the balance sheets of households, corporates, government and financial intermediaries. We were fairly liberal in regard to households and corporates, but tight with regard to foreign currency exposure in regard to government and finance. Further, we were not willing to take any chances with global imbalances. Despite all the precautions taken, our economy was affected to some extent, that is because the channels of contagion are several, viz., trade channel, finance channel and sentiment channel. We increased global integration in a dramatic manner while building a war chest of reserves.

On the Global Perspective of Globalization.

The limitations of the present global financial architecture comprising IMF, World Bank, WTO, and possibly G20, are well-known. Improvements in their resources as well as governance have been made, but by all accounts they are marginal. There are signs of diminishing returns from G20, though there is promise of greater role in future. These considerations give rise to a strong possibility of lack of substantial improvement in global monetary and financial systems, and possibility greater uncertainties and tensions in the global monetary system and financial architecture.

Finally, there is an increasing recognition that global power balances would shift from West to the East, and in particular, to Asia. There is considerable consensus that incremental economic activity in the global economy and incremental trade will shift considerably to the developing economies, in particular, Asia. It is not very clear whether financial intermediation will undergo a corresponding shift. More important, in terms of institutional capital and human capital, the advanced economies are way ahead of the developing economies. The shift of global power balances is also influenced by the social and cultural factors.

India will inevitably be an important part of the shift in power balances.

Dr. Duvvuri Subbarao Governor Reserve Bank of India and Alternate Governor to the IMF (2008-2013)

Duvvuri Subbarao, IAS Governor Reserve Bank of India and India's Alternate Governor to the IMF for the period 2008-2013 and led a number of Indian delegations to the IMFC. His statements at the IMFC reflect his depth of knowledge and thinking on India-IMF relations. His handling of the Indian economy at the time of 2008 Global Economic Crisis will be long remembered in the annals of Indian economic history.

On India's external sector liberalization.

Before 1991, India was one of the most closed economies in the world. Today we are much more integrated, indeed more integrated than we tend to acknowledge. Since 1991, India has shifted from an administered to a largely market determined exchange rate, the rupee is convertible on the current account, there has been a sharp reduction in tariffs, QRs have been removed, export incentives have been phased out and there is a deeper, more vibrant forex market.

There was dismay in India that we were affected by the global financial crisis. They ask 'how come we were not affected by the Asian crisis of 1997/98 but were affected by the global financial crisis of 2007/08?'. The reason is that in the decade between the Asian crisis and the global crisis, India had integrated into the world. Our two-way trade as a proportion of GDP doubled while the two way financial flows nearly tripled. It is because of this deepening globalization that we were affected by the global financial crisis although we were relatively unscathed by the Asian crisis.

The lesson from this is not to withdraw from globalization; that will be exactly the wrong response. The lesson from this is to learn to manage globalization to our best advantage. Globalization is a double edged sword. It comes with benefits and costs. The challenge is to implement policies so as to minimize the costs and maximize the benefits.

On India-IMF relations as a non-program country.

Sure, we are not a program country. But that does not mean the IMF is irrelevant to us. India's economic prospects depend on global growth and global welfare more than ever before. We missed out on the first wave of globalization of the 70s and 80s when many countries, especially those in Asia opened up and prospered on the back of exporting to the rich world. We should not miss out again. For India to benefit from globalization, we need a global regime of trade and financial flows that is free, fair and equitable. It is the responsibility of the IMF to ensure that. Let me also add that despite all the criticism it gets, the IMF is still a very credible institution and its voice is heard and heeded.

The IMF's ability to sustain global linkages.

Global interlinkages have become stronger, more complex and potentially more disruptive. The IMF needs to be ahead of the intellectual curve in understanding these linkages. The models used by IMF could not predict spillovers before the crisis. Research within and outside IMF has focused on trying to understand linkages through trade, finance and confidence channels.

It is not clear that we have a clear understanding of the spillovers through these channels. The spillovers predicted by the models that we use are small relative to the reality of the large and pervasive spillovers that we saw during the global financial crisis and are seeing through the ongoing euro zone crisis. This clearly suggests that the assumptions underlying these models are incomplete if not flawed. Greece, Cyprus, Spain have had much greater impact on EMEs than we thought possible.

To the IMF's credit, I must add that learning from the lessons of the crisis, it has since started publishing a 'global spillover report' periodically so as to enhance our collective understanding of a critical issue in global economy.

On the IMF's post-crisis revised view on capital account liberalization.

The crisis challenged many conventional policy perspectives, pushed policy making into uncharted territory and changed our worldview on several aspects of macroeconomic management. Nowhere is the intellectual shift more remarkable than in the broad area of capital account management.

The pre-crisis orthodoxy that countries benefit from capital account liberalization just as they do from trade liberalization has rich intellectual origins. When John Maynard Keynes and Harry Dexter White were negotiating the Bretton Woods agreement, they clashed on many issues, but one issue on which they both agreed was on 'the desirability of encouraging the flow of productive capital to areas where it can be most profitably employed'. They recognized that failure to manage flows could lead to serious economic disruption, but that caveat got lost in translation. Consequently, evangelizing to emerging markets on capital account liberalization, almost as an article of faith, became an integral part of the IMF policy toolkit.

The crisis broke that faith. The post crisis view, more guarded, more nuanced and evidently more sympathetic is that capital account liberalization carries costs and benefits, and the challenge for emerging markets is to negotiate their way forward by trying to minimize the costs and maximize the benefits.

The IMF's revised post-crisis position is that capital flow liberalization is generally more beneficial and less risky if countries have reached certain levels or - thresholds of financial and institutional development. However, liberalization needs to be well planned, timed, and sequenced in order to ensure that its benefits outweigh the costs, as it could have significant domestic and multilateral effects.

This post crisis position of the IMF which sees capital account liberalization more as a journey rather than a destination will hopefully form the nucleus of a new consensus.

On Fund Surveillance.

In the current context, as a non-program country, IMF Surveillance is an important aspect of India's engagement with the IMF. The IMF needs to put in greater effort at being even handed in both its policy advice and in working towards its acceptance.

How far is IMF advice based on country-specific factors? Second, is the Fund's surveillance even handed? Viewed from these two standpoints, there is a lot of scope for improvement. According to the IEO survey, authorities of many large emerging market economies found that the surveillance process added little value and offered very limited perspectives and that their advice failed to take into account country-specific factors. Advice by the Fund should stem from a complete understanding of not only macroeconomic, but also social and political settings of a country. Advice should be founded on hard evidence and driven by facts. Ideology should not play any role in analysis of facts. The Fund also needs to exercise extreme caution when it gives advice based on models. This is because in many cases even small changes in model specifications, definitions of variables used, and time periods used in estimation can lead to significant differences in the results. At times, models are also not amenable to country-specific factors.

The impact of IMF surveillance works primarily through debate with country authorities and public dissemination of its findings that is expected to condition market and public response to IMF advice, and thereby work indirectly on policy making. More transparent and wider dissemination of balanced surveillance analysis may be an important means to enhance the effectiveness of surveillance. The IMF must be open to criticism and advice.

On the issue of even handedness, I believe, it is necessary to enhance the IMF's legitimacy in its role as a trusted advisor. Surveillance is often believed to have less impact on large member countries relative to smaller ones. There is a perception that the IMF is dominated by the interests of its largest shareholders. Surveys have shown that about a third of country authorities and half of the mission chiefs did not believe that the IMF has become more even handed since the between these two objectives which will give a boost to the IMF's credibility.

On the evolution of the G20.

The rise of the G20 is a significant development in the global economic horizon. The G 20 is an informal club with 19 member countries and the European Union which together represent 90 per cent of global GDP, 80 per cent of global trade and two-thirds of the global population. The G 20, has been in the forefront of battling the financial crises - the global financial crisis of 2008/09 and the Eurozone crisis since 2010 - that have taken a devastating toll on global growth and welfare. Indeed when the history of this crisis is written, the London G 20 Summit in April 2009 will be acknowledged as the clear turning point when world leaders showed extraordinary determination and unity. Sure, there were differences, but they were debated and discussed, and compromises were made so as to reach the final goal - of ending the crisis. This resulted in an agreed package of measures having both domestic and international components but all of them to be implemented in coordination, and indeed in synchronization where necessary. The entire range of crisis response measures - accommodative monetary stance, fiscal stimulus, debt and deposit guarantees, capital injection, asset purchases, currency swaps, keeping markets open - all derived in varying degrees from the G 20 package.

On the lessons from Fed and ECB's handling of the 2008 Global Economic Crisis

It's interesting that the same historical experience can lead to different interpretation and therefore different lessons. There has, in fact, been some recent writing on how the US Fed and the ECB viewed the crisis differently. The Fed saw potential deflation, on account of the deleveraging under way, as the bigger threat, rapidly responded with zero lower bound interest rate and followed it up with several variants of quantitative easing. The ECB under former President Trichet, on the other hand, inferred that in most cases, it is an unbridled rise in credit growth prior to a crisis that causes the eventual crisis. And importantly, the economy fully recovers only after the pre-crisis excesses are worked out. This means significant capital destruction. The quicker the process of capital destruction, the faster and stronger the recovery. And liquidity support in the aftermath of the crisis only slows this process of creative destruction. We have all witnessed how this differing perception has guided differing policy approaches to crisis management. There are similarities and differences between the Great Depression and the Great Recession. As Liaquat Ahmed says in his very thoughtful book, Lords of Finance, "More than anything else, the Great Depression was caused by a failure of intellectual will, a lack of understanding about how the economy operated. No one struggled harder in the lead-up to the Great Depression, and during it, to make sense of the forces at work than John Maynard Keynes. He believed that if only we could eliminate 'muddled' thinking, then society could manage its material welfare".

The Executive Directors –

Dr. Arvind Virmani served as Executive Director of India in the IMF from 2009-2012

On his experience as Executive Director, India on the IMF Executive Board.

I was the only Economist Executive Director on the IMF Board, the other Executive Directors were either Central Bankers or Civil Servants from the Ministries of Finance. The key issues that we faced in my tenure were the reform of the IMF, the Greece debt crisis and IMF response, capital flows and capital markets and IMF response and lastly the establishment of the BRICS bank i.e. the New Development Bank. I was very confident on the IMF Executive Board given the strength of the Indian economy and was not deferential to anybody. By 2009, India had 6 years of rapid growth, and I had the independence and authority to look at issues in a neutral manner.

On the IMF Governance Reforms happened in your tenure as Executive Director IMF.

On IMF reforms, regular meetings were held both in the Executive Board and amongst the G-24 countries. The IMF Board was clearly dominated by the EU, through a European Managing Director and the Europeans large equity and voting share, representation on the Board along with influence acquired through bilateral foreign aid. The influence was strengthened by US support on key issues. China gained in confidence and was increasingly assertive on the IMF Board. The meetings of G-24 countries on quota and related issues did not evince support from China. It was obvious that China was increasingly charting its own path. They were negotiating directly with the Managing Director. This was visible in several instances.

The United States in their media statements often said that the Chinese currency the RMB was undervalued and several American politicians called China a currency manipulator. However, the IMF staff papers said the RMB was valued right. Efforts to get the RMB into the SDR basket had commenced. Closed doors discussions were often held between Management, Americans and Chinese on the issue.

On Quotas, I often said that the Implications for IMF Quota Reform were significant for Global Economic Governance. There was a large gap between economic reality and IMF quotas. Dissatisfaction among global public opinion can only be reduced or eliminated if Quota shares were changed to reflect the fast changing economic reality. This required a much greater role for the relative size/power of economies, an element that is not adequately captured by the existing formula. Unless fully taken into account, dissatisfaction would persist after 2013, the year in which the next quota reform was to be completed. The gap is likely to widen every year unless the formula is modified appropriately. The end result of the

Quota review in 2013 resulted in an increase in India's quota following. China became the 3rd largest shareholder of the IMF.

On India's position on the Greece debt crisis.

I felt that the Greece debt was too high and GDP growth projections in IMF staff reports too ambitious and not achievable, necessitating a greater fiscal correction to attain macroeconomic stability. I told the Executive Board that I had dealt with 3 capital crisis in recent years. The Europeans were the ones with equity and were supported by the Americans and Japanese on the Executive Board. The Brazilians, the Russians and several Asian countries that had experienced debt crisis were more supportive. The Chinese were ambiguous – they had no real interests in the Greece program.

On his contribution as ED IMF.

I could contribute to the IMF's ongoing work on Capital Flows and Capital Markets through a series of interventions on the IMF Board and informal consultations subsequent to Board meetings.

The creation of the BRICS bank was significant initiative. Infrastructure financing was a felt need, and while we could convince the Brazilians and South Africans, it took a very long time to convince the Russians and Chinese. The BRICS bank was set up in Shanghai as the New Development Bank.

On the future of India and IMF.

Looking to the future, the emergence of the G20 is a very important development. The G20 which was a grouping of Finance Ministers and Central Bank Governors was elevated to an annual meeting of Heads of Government to address the challenges of the 2008 global economic crisis. India needs a strong and powerful IMF where it has a strong voice to pursue a global economic agenda. Given its growth rate, it is possible that India emerges as the 3rd largest economy in the world by 2035.

Dr. Rakesh Mohan served as Deputy Governor Reserve Bank of India, Secretary Department of Economic Affairs and Executive Director (India) IMF (2012-2015).

On his IMF years.

The IMF regained a role on the global high table of crisis management following the North Atlantic Financial crisis with global economic impact. I call it the North Atlantic Financial Crisis as no institution other than the American and European Institutions were affected by the crisis. The IMF failed to see the crisis and one of the systemic improvements was surveillance became more active following the crisis. Both multilateral and bilateral surveillance was strengthened particularly the surveillance over the systemically important advanced economies. The IMF also raised additional resources through the new agreements to borrow and the note purchase agreements. The IMF programs following the 2008 crisis were much larger and IMF lending was much bigger as compared with the Asian crisis or the Latin American Crisis. There were questions on how much independence the IMF had on program funding. The European response for the crisis was the setting up of the European Stability Mechanism (ESM). The ESM raises questions on the future of IMF as a crisis manager.

On the changes in IMF management.

Christine Lagarde was successful in restoring the credibility of the IMF. In her tenure as Managing Director one hardly hears any criticism of the IMF despite the Greece program causing distress and Ukraine program giving huge moneys for a political cause. China has made strides in the IMF with a post of Deputy Managing Director and the RMB being added to the SDR basket. Further, the DMD's in Lagarde's administration were low key as compared to Stan Fischer or Anne Krueger. The Lagarde years also saw the IMF working on income distribution models, gender issues and responses to the Ebola virus, which took the critics by surprise. The IMF further moderated its views on capital account convertibility.

Dr. Subir Gokaran currently serves as Executive Director (India) at the IMF. He has served as Deputy Governor Reserve Bank of India.

On the Managing Director – Executive Director (India) IMF relationship? Your predecessors Dr. M.Narasimham, Dr. Y.V. Reddy had close relations with the Managing Directors of their tenure.

It is not a particularly close relationship as India is not a program country. In our constituency, there is an ongoing IMF program with Sri Lanka. I do get to interact closely with the Deputy Managing Director in-charge of Sri Lanka. I was associated with the visit of the Managing Director's to India in 2016 for a conference and the Deputy Managing Director's visit to India in 2017 for the inauguration of the SARTAC center. On a routine basis there is no interaction. The Executive Director maintains a working relationship with the Managing Director. The Departmental heads have grown stronger and the Asian Department interacts closely with the Executive Director.

On the points of friction between you and the IMF in your tenure as Executive Director.

There have been only 2 areas of friction – there were times when we felt that the Fund was not reflecting India's views on the exchange rate policy. The most recent differences arose in our views on demonetization. Other than these there have been no are issues between India and IMF in recent years. The Managing Director has called India a bright spot in the world economy during her 2016 visit.

On the several changes in the Fund itself. For several years from 2002, the Fund faced several protests seeking its closure from NGOs and Civil Society.

The Managing Director's espousal of non-traditional issues has helped shape public perceptions. The Fund has become sensitive to subjects like gender and climate change. These issues have been filtering into the work program of the Fund. In-house capacity building programs have been developed for sensitizing Fund staff. For example, in the Selected Issues paper of India the IMF staffers did a gender study which is unconventional.

There have been changes in the Fund's views on capital flow management and fiscal policy. The Fund view now promotes social safety nets in Fund programs. The quality of expenditure has become very important in Fund programs.

There has also been a 3rd dimension to enhance engagement with civil society. Civil Society engagement during Fund-Bank annual meetings has been incorporated. The Executive Board of IMF also meets the civil society and the number of Directors participating in these discussions has increased dramatically. In these meetings with civil society, the Fund's views were discussed at length.

This 3 pronged approach of espousing non-traditional issues, promotion of social safety nets in Fund programs and civil society engagement during Fund-Bank annual meetings have changed the perceptions of the Fund programs as those which cause immense hardship with deep cuts in social sector spending.

On the changes in the Fund management. It seems to have moved away from the Polak years. The American First Deputy Managing Director was a very visible global personality like Stan Fischer or Anne Krueger. The Fund seems a more centralized organization dominated by Christine Lagarde.

The Fund had become irrelevant in the mid 2000s, with several countries building reserves. Private capital flows had become larger. Fund had to reinvent themselves. There was significant downsizing. The Fund reinvented themselves. Strauss-Kahn was willing to accept the changes necessary in the Fund's ideology. The Fund's engagement with member countries in terms of Technical Assistance was enlarged to 28 percent of Fund's budget. This completely changed the Fund's perception in member countries as Fund's visibility had increased. Even in the Indian constituency, technical assistance is used by Bhutan, Sri Lanka, Bangladesh use technical assistance extensively.

The Fund has also become more sophisticated, there is a realization that macroeconomic policy entails more measures than fiscal deficit reduction and exchange rate devaluation. Even in the research department there have some changes. RaghuramRajan and Olivier Blanchard have brought in a new culture. Blanchard has given some new thoughts like enhanced spending in crisis countries.

In the management, the past 2 Managing Directors Dominique Strauss-Kahn and Christine Lagarde have been very high profile personalities and they have played an unchallenged role in becoming the face of the organization.

On the revision of Quotas benefitted India in improving its voice on the Fund. On the rise of China on the IMF Board.

The 14th Quota review took 5 years. The 15th Quota review has been postponed by 2 years. The review really rests on the positions taken by the United States. It appears that the United States will not be supportive of a further Quota increase. The current US administration is not very favorable to multilateralism.

The current quotas are very much in the backdrop of economic reality. China is still 18 percent below its Quota in the current formulation. Having got the 4th Deputy Managing Director's position, China has a more very strong voice in the management, with the potential to influence Fund's policies. They are not yet doing it to their full potential.

On India's interactions with China, in the IMF, the BRICS group meets quite regularly. We have issued collective gray statements on some of the smaller issues. On the bigger issues, we coordinate. The BRICS group, of Executive Directors meets every few weeks.

On the India-IMF relations in the 2020-2030 decade. The Executive Director's position has been a high visibility position for Indian Government for over 50 years.

India's comfort levels with its external positions has changed the relationship. We are not in a balance of payments stress. The IMF does not say too many negative things about India's policies in Article IV consultations. The IMF – India cooperation resulted in the establishment of the SARTAC, a training center for South Asia.

In the Board itself my role has been to participate in the more substantial discussions in Fund's policy making. As a multilateral institution, the Fund takes note of the fact that India is out of the zone of vulnerability.

Looking ahead, in the 2020-2030 years, the Fund's relationship with India would not be very different. India will get more Quota and the BRICS countries collectively will exceed 15 percent Quota. We have tended to be individualistic in our views. We need to place far more emphasis on collective activity. There is a reason why the ED and his staff get diplomatic visas to the United States. Robust alliances with other countries are needed to effective presence in the Board. We need to work closely with the BRICS and the Constituency members to speak for a larger community.

There are not enough resources in the Indian back office to handle international relations. The Secretary Department of Economic Affairs handles IMF along with a host of issues. We need to restructure the back office. Instead of having a post retirement person as ED (India) IMF, a younger Executive Director can be sent to the IMF, as placements in these Institutions are being increasingly seen as trainings for Secretary postings.

The Chief Economic Advisors

Dr. Shankar Acharya served as Chief Economic Advisor from 1993 to 2001and Economic Adviser, Ministry of Finance from early 1985 to end 1990.

On the role of the IMF.

First a caveat, not having ever been either a staff member or an Executive Director of the IMF my views are those of an outsider, who had observed the Fund from the World Bank (as a young post-Ph.D staffer) in the 1970s and the Government of India from 1985 to 2001. My understanding is that the IMF has had to rediscover its role in the international monetary system a number of times. The first was in 1971 when the US under President Nixon ended gold convertibility of the US dollar. That was death knell for the earlier "adjustable peg" regime of exchange rates that the IMF oversaw. After that, and the resurgence of private international capital markets, flexible exchange rates gradually became the norm. The UK in the mid 1970s was the last major developed country to borrow from the Fund and have an associated program of policy undertakings. After that the IMF had to justify its role in the international monetary system solely with respect to developing countries facing temporary balance of payments problems. Hence its focus in the 1980s on the debt crises which affected a number of Latin American countries at that time. This was a period of substantial soul-searching within the IMF.

The IMF's role received a major boost in the 1990s following the collapse of Soviet Union and the spate of new members from the former Soviet "bloc", seeking both IMF programs and technical assistance in transiting to market economies. Throughout the 1990s, the IMF was heavily involved with the East European and Central Asian economies. Third, following the 2008 global financial crisis, and the ensuing banking and fiscal crises in southern Europe, notably Greece, the IMF became deeply involved in these nations, in concert with the European Union, in crafting stabilization programs for Greece and other small European nations. The central point is that the IMF has searched for a role several times in the past 70 years. It was not always the all-powerful international monetary institution with a global mandate as the Lender of Last Resort.

On India-IMF relations.

The normal rule of thumb is that India –IMF relations have generally remained cordial and professional, even during the programs of 1981-83 and 1991-93. Of course the engagement has been much more during program periods and fairly routine outside them.

The 1981-83 IMF program, following India's external financing pressures after the "second oil shock" of 1979-80, was not a "tough" program in terms of mutually agreed policy content. Very little economic policy reform was sought or agreed. We remained a very closed economy subject to widespread licensing and controls. In effect, the Sixth Plan public investment program and policy aspirations outlined in the Plan were the main basis justifying IMF lending. The "success" of the program was probably more due to the surge in Bombay High oil revenues (and associated diminution of balance of payments pressures) than anything in the agreed Fund program.

The 1991 program policy changes were far more significant and real, including overhaul of the exchange rate regime, reduction of quantitative controls on trade and industry, reduction of customs tariffs, some reform of banking and finance, some reduction in the fiscal deficit and so forth. The key point here is that all these far-reaching policy changes were very much "home grown" and "owned" by the Government. They had been recommended by a large number of high level Government Expert Committees during the 1980s, such as those chaired by Narasimhan, Abid Hussain, Dagli and P C Alexander. The IMF funding support was helpful, but not critical. Since the policy reforms were real, so were their fruits in terms of a resurrection of growth in major sectors and the economy as a whole, as well as the surge in exports and the restoration of BoP viability.

My impression is that the IMF staff worked well with the Indian authorities in both the early 1980s and the early 1990s. They were generally sensitive to our political economy.

Dr. Ashok Lahiri served as Chief Economic Advisor in the Government of India from 2002-2005. He had also served as an Economist in the IMF in the early years of his career in 1991-95 period.

On his IMF years as a staff member.

I have very fond memories of working as an Economist in the European II department of the IMF. I worked on Latvia. In the 1990s, Latvian independence had been recognized by the European Nations and United States. I had to undertake 9-10 visits to Latvia. The Rouble was being replaced by the Lat. The country went from Central Planning to a market economy. The Latvian program required a lot of IMF handholding in terms of technical assistance particularly for strengthening their banking and financial sectors. The World Bank was also supportive of the power sector reforms in Latvia.

On the status of reforms in India in 1996.

When I return from the IMF, I was appointed as an Economic Advisor in the Ministry of Finance. In 1996, there was vulnerability in the Indian economy. From independence to 1991, India had been through multiple crisis. In 1996, the jury was still out whether India's reforms were driven by the crisis, whether the Indian authorities had no option but to adopt reforms, because there was a slow-down in reforms once the political realities crept in. For an Economic Advisor the pace of reforms can always be faster. The rupee had begun to depreciate after being rock solid at Rs. 31/ US Dollar for a number of years. There was political instability from 1996 which continued till 2001. Despite political instability there was no BOP crisis. In retrospect we did alright, ofcourse we could have done better. In a way some of the reforms were reforms by stealth.

1996-2001 in retrospect were lost years for reforms. If there was political stability a more concerted reform program could have been undertaken. But as a democracy, populist policies have to be implemented.

On the major reforms he was associated with.

The hydrocarbon reforms, I was associated with, were a major success. The administered pricing mechanism was dismantled to a market driven process. That said, liberalization was easy when international oil prices were low. Once Oil prices started rising the pressures for protectionism and subsidies returned. The other major reform I was associated with was the urea price liberalization.

On being a member of several Indian delegations to the IMFC and the positions taken.

By 2002, the importance of IMF in terms of financial resources has become less important to India. We no longer felt the need for IMF assistance. The engagement was largely in the form of Article IV consultations which were in the nature of health checkups. The relationship was one of friendly ambience. At the IMFC, India was consistently talking of Quota reforms. The Quota Reform is reflective of economic performance. China's economic performance has been better than us since 1979. The relative weights of quota between India and China has changed after the 2015 quota reform. China has a quota of 6.14 percent against India's 2.66 percent. In my view, India should press for the next quota reform after economic performance gains greater momentum.

On the extent to which the IMF influences India's economic policy.

The IMF has a classical approach to balance of payments issues. India averted a major balance of payments of crisis in 1991 and never defaulted on repayments. India – IMF relations were characterized by a lot of convergence in terms of diagnostics. In terms of prescription, the quantum of adjustment and change, Indian positions were quite divergent from the IMF views.

On the IMF's future.

The IMF has undertaken significant reforms in the past decade. Conditionality reforms, Quota reforms, surveillance reforms, financing arrangements have strengthened the IMF's interactions with member countries. The Quota reform is unlikely to go far.

A new international architecture has emerged in terms of BRICS. India and China and to an extent even Russia may not require contingency financing. The Contingency Financing Facility established by BRICS thus represents an insurance facility and may not actually be used.

The G-20 has emerged as a body with a global agenda. In 2017, the G-20 may not have a major policy coordination role. It does have a policy agenda as and when the situation demands.

Senior Officials

Dr. Rahul Khullar, IAS served as Deputy Secretary/Director in the Prime Minister's Office from 1985-90 and Private Secretary to Finance Minister from 1991-93 and was closely associated with India's 1991 reforms program. He went on to serve as India's longest serving Commerce Secretary pioneering India's integration into the global economy and subsequently as Chairman Telecom Regulatory Authority of India emerging as one of India's leading voices in economic governance over the past 30 years.

On his years in Prime Minister's office in the run-up to the crisis. On why the Government did not approach the IMF in 1988.

One has to start with the 1981-83 IMF program. It is quite surprising that India went through the 1981 IMF program without major reforms. Mr. Narasimham, the Executive Director IMF, who negotiated the IMF program, did not yield much ground on the reform front. He assured the Prime Minister Mrs. Gandhi that he had succeeded in persuading the IMF to permit flexibility to develop a fully home-grown program. In the 1981-84 period, the Government did start changes e.g. Export Oriented Units and SEZs were established. But the pace of reforms was slow. Following the 1984 elections, the reforms continued. But there were no major overhauling reforms. Gradualism ruled.

By 1988 the Rajiv Gandhi government lost control of expenditure. In pursuit of higher growth, Government expenditures zoomed which were monetized by the RBI. The Government took the view that the resultant inflation could be handled. However, as later observed famously, India could not spend itself to prosperity. In 1988/89 serious efforts were made to bring the fiscal situation under control.

By 1989/90, it was clear that India's fiscal situation was out of control. The Government authorized J.L.Bajaj, the Joint Secretary Fund-Bank Division of Department of Economic Affairs, to visit Washington DC for initiating discussions with the IMF for a possible Stand-by Arrangement.

In 1989, the V.P.Singh Government was told that an economic crisis was on hand. The political situation was fluid and the decision on a Fund program was placed at the next Government's desk. By the first quarter of 1991, it was clear that things were going horribly wrong. India's credit ratings were sinking, forex reserves declining rapidly and the Government fell. Creditors were at our door and India had to maintain its reputation of never defaulting on an external commitment. The Government then had to pledge gold; but they had to shift gold physically to London to unlike in the past when gold was pledged in a paper pledge.

Memories of his appointment as Private Secretary to Finance in 1991-93 years.

It was July 1991. I had just returned from leave from USA when I was informed at the airport that the Finance Minister (FM) wanted to see me. I went to North Block and apprised the FM that my Government of India tenure had ended, and I had reported to the State cadre for placement. FM heard me out and simply said : "Go and take charge of the files".

On the events that unfolded in July 1991 after he joined.

When I joined the FM's office, the IMF mission had just left. The Government had just carried through two successive devaluations in July 1991 – the first one was as per expectations and the second one was for a fuller correction in the exchange rate and to convince the world that India was serious about addressing the crisis. The next 3 months were highly stressful.

The Finance Ministry's core team to handle the crisis comprised K.P.Geethakrishnan as Finance Secretary and Dr. Montek Singh Ahluwalia as Secretary DEA. They were supported by Ms Janaki Kathpalia, Additional Secretary (Budget), N.K.Singh the Joint Secretary Fund-Bank and, to some extent, Dr. Y.V.Reddy the Joint Secretary Capital Markets.

The lead from the IMF was Hubert Neiss, then Director of the Asia Pacific Department in the IMF. He was supported by, among others, a young economist from IMF, Urijit Patel. Neiss was an Austrian-German in the classical Fund staff mold viz. an ardent adherent of the Polak model. The model's all-time remedy was to reduce government expenditure (reducing domestic absorption), increase exports and adjust exchange rates to make exports more competitive (simultaneously cutting back imports by making them more expensive).

Most meetings with Hubert Neiss were held in the Finance Secretary's office. In official level meetings, MrNeiss always drove a very hard bargain e.g. on expenditure cuts. The Managing Director IMF, Michel Camdessus visited India in September – October 1991 and was, in general, very supportive of India's planned reform program. The second tranche of IMF loan negotiations were contingent on successful conclusion of the performance criteria of the first tranche.

The second tranche negotiations involved certain tough decisions (a) expenditure cuts of 1991-92, (b) identifying the levels of export performance, (c) what further reforms to cut deficits beyond what has already been done. The discussions centered on increasing tax revenues. In April 1992 when the Finance Minister visited Washington DC for the Spring Meetings of the IMF the second tranche discussions were concluded in a meeting between Finance Minister and Managing Director IMF. After FM's meeting with Managing Director, Neiss was brought around to accept the Indian proposals. The World Bank Structural Adjustment Loan which India sought was contingent on India fulfilling the performance criteria on the IMF program. The approach was that the Fund and the Bank move together. The World Bank team was led by Heinz Vergin; Neiss and Vergin worked in tandem.

India adhered to the program guidelines and met the performance criteria. In May 1992, the Harshad Mehta scam broke out. Government appointed a new Governor RBI, Dr. C.Rangarajan.

On the fierce opposition to 1991 reforms program.

The Finance Minister undertook a major outreach program to convince the nation about the 1991 economic reforms. He would speak at several national fora including Universities. The recurrent theme was threefold: the devaluation had altered terms of trade in favor of agriculture; inviting industry to avail of the new opportunities created by the reforms; calling on exporters, old and new (especially industry), to make the most of the reforms. A general overarching message was that India had to compete and become more competitive. (With the reduction in tariffs, Indian industry which thrived in the license raj suddenly faced competition.) At the political level, the Finance Minister reached out to MPs with same message e.g. agriculture would benefit from the economic reforms, new industry would rise to the occasion and avail of the new opportunities.

On how much was the 1991 IMF program a home grown program.

Many of the 1991 economic reforms were largely driven by Indian self-interest. That is to say that a reform was in India's self-interest and that was the rationale for its adoption and implementation. For instance, making the expenditure correction was in our own interest. And, this is true of a swathe of other reforms.

The IMF advice was a simple product of the Polak model: reduce domestic absorption (cut fiscal deficits), exchange rate adjustment to keep exports competitive and imports expensive, reduce Government expenditure. The add-ons were the sector reforms (where the World Bank had a greater say). The Government recognized that reducing the fiscal deficit was in India's own interest; hence, the drastic expenditure reduction. Tighter monetary policy was inescapable to rein inflation in. The Government's big reforms were in the fiscal/ industrial/ trade sectors. The rapid reduction in customs duties ensured integration of the Indian economy with the world economy in less than 10 years after the 1991 reforms.

Trade reforms formed a major part of the 1991 reforms. The dismantling of the export subsidy regime was the first step (abolition of the Cash Compensatory Support scheme). The transition to TRQ, reduction of duties and steady reduction in applied tariff rates were the key features. The dismantling of the quota regime and the import licensing was a significant step. India shifted to a WTO compatible trade regime, including the legally permissible TRQs which was a move away from quota to duty based trade. By 2003 the customs duty reductions were largely completed.

The integration of the financial sector with the global economy was a significant step forward. India successfully recapitalized banks, created market instruments, strengthened bond markets particularly the government securities markets. Soon global markets started trusting the Indian market and investments kept coming in.

Shri Kanagasabapathy Kuppuswamy

Kanagasabapathy served as Senior Advisor to Executive Director (India) in the IMF from November 2001 to September 2005. During this period, he served with 3 Executive Directors, Vijay Kelkar, Y.V.Reddy and B.P.Misra. He headed the RBI's Monetary Policy Department and was Secretary to the Y.V.Reddy Committee on India's assessment of Financial Standards and Codes in 2000 and then on return from IMF served as Secretary to the Rakesh Mohan Committee on India's Financial Sector Assessment. Before joining the IMF, he was closely associated with the IMF through Article IV consultations.

On his memories of his years in the IMF.

From 2001 to 2005, India was not an IMF program country. India became a creditor country in IMF Financial Transactions Plan, which was a major step forward. Vijay Kelkar, BhaskarVenkatramany and I worked closely on the IMF Board and with the RBI and Ministry of Finance to enable India to join the IMF's Financial Transactions Plan. The IMF Executive Board according creditor country status to India based on its foreign exchange reserves position and financial stability enhanced the image of the country.

There was a lot of collegiality in the ED's office and amongst all 24 EDs' offices. There was also high cordiality and collegiality in the IMF's internal meetings during the G-11, G-20, G-24 discussions which I participated in. I also witnessed collegiality amongst IMF staff. The ED's office coordinated with considerable success with the RBI and the Fund-Bank division of Department of Economic Affairs.

A unique feature of the Executive Director's office is that the officials are part of IMF staff and also country representatives. They have a considerable role in coordination between country authorities and IMF in addition to working on the IMF Executive Board. They also had a role in coordinating with other countries.

The IMF staff on the other hand were international staffers. Anoop Singh Director Western Hemisphere, IMF during the IMF's Argentina program had visited Buenos Aires 26 times and the Argentine authorities did not like his involvement in their policies. One of the Argentine newspapers reported that "one Indian in the IMF was opposing Argentina in their reforms program" and I had received a call from the Indian Embassy in Argentina that the country's image would be affected by this media reporting. It was clarified to the MEA and the Indian Embassy in Buenos Aires that Anoop Singh was a Fund Staffer and the Indian Authorities in the IMF were very much in support of the Argentine reforms programs.

On the IMF's global role.

The IMF remains the only global institution which maintains economic data bases across countries over long periods. It's a repository of valuable information for research work, understanding political economy and global economic governance.

I also found that IMF Surveillance was effective more in program countries. There was some bias in favor of creditor countries during Article IV consultations. However, following the Asian crisis, the IMF became more conducive for capital controls and financial stability issues. The bias in favor of creditor countries is largely because of the voting shares on the Executive Board. The G-7 dominance has come down slightly and the G-20 countries have a greater role in the IMF's decision making following the quota revision and after the global financial turmoil.

For Advanced Economies, the Article IV consultation papers provided a wealth of information. The quality of research and analysis were always appreciated even if we did not agree with the recommendations.

On the IMF's programs with India.

The 1983 IMF program was an opportunity missed to undertake major economic reforms.

The 1991 IMF program was highly reform oriented because of the confluence of circumstances. Dr. C.Rangarajan was posted in the RBI, Dr. Montek Singh Ahluwalia was in the DEA, Dr. Manmohan Singh was Finance Minister and Shri P.V.Narasimha Rao was Prime Minister. A critical role was played by the economic monitoring group since mid-1980's led by Dr. BimalJalan, Dr. Rakesh Mohan and Dr. ShankarAcharya. Even MichealCamdessus, former Managing Director IMF at a later stage mentioned that the IMF's India program of 1991 was more of India than IMF, it was totally home grown.

On the RBI relations with the IMF.

The RBI has been led by progressive and visionary Governors in Dr. Bimal Jalan, Dr. Y.V. Reddy, Dr. Duvvuri Subbaroao. In the years 1997-2008, the Jalan/ Reddy years at the RBI, policies were initiated for India's external sector management, reserves management and exchange rate management which acted as a trend setter for other EME's. Neither Jalan nor Reddy went for Capital Account Convertibility despite two reports from the Tarapore Committee. Their gradual approach towards capital account convertibility has now been accepted by the IMF.

Y.V. Reddy played a critical role in combining RBI's prudential measures with monetary policy to address asset bubbles. He took a pioneering step in fixing higher margins for real estate loans and introduced prudential norms for banks while ensuring a credit growth of around 30 percent. Y.V. Reddy protected the banking system from entering capital markets which insulated Indian banks during the 2008 global crisis. His actions have ensured that India attained a position to address the Financial Stability Board from a position of considerable strength and stature and play a guiding role. There was policy continuity in the DuvvuriSubbarao years at the helm of RBI.

On the major issues India sought IMF advise in Article IV Consultations.

The Article IV consultations offered India an opportunity to seek IMF policy advise on critical global issues. The impact of the oil economy in the world was a common issue that featured in many Article IV discussions. As a major oil importing country, India had an important stake in stabilization of world oil markets. The other issue that featured prominently was the inflation targeting approach. India did not favor the IMF's policy advise on Inflation targeting in the Jalan/ Reddy/ Subbarao years. The Governors addressed the trilemma of balancing interest rate, exchange rate and capital account management policies rather than adopt an inflation targeting approach. Post Duvvuri Subbarao years India has moved forward to inflation targeting.

CHAPTER - X

MY YEARS WITH THE IMF

This chapter presents my memories of the greatest financial institution in the world, the nuances of the functioning of the Executive Board, the various Fund programs implemented in the years 2003-2006.

I served as Advisor to Executive Director in the International Monetary Fund from September 8, 2003 to October 5, 2006. I represented India on the Executive Board of the IMF in about 500 meetings. Not only did I learn the intricacies of the IMF's role as a confidential advisor to member countries, but also understood the functioning of the Executive Board, the functioning of the IMFC, the drafting of communiques, Departmental workings in the Fund and above all leadership skills of individuals who had the courage and determination to address financial crisis.

In the Executive Director's Office, I was assigned several policy issues to handle - the work of Poverty Reduction and Growth Facility (PRGF), Heavily Indebted Poor Countries Initiative (HIPC), the Multilateral Debt Relief Initiative (MDRI), Fund Conditionality Technical Assistance and Capacity Development and Independent Evaluation Office. In the program countries, I was assigned Turkey, Ukraine and Serbia & Montenegro which were under Fund Stand-By Arrangements and the Sub-Saharan African Countries as also the Eastern European Countries which had PRGF programs. As part of Fund Surveillance, I handled the executive board agenda on Article IV consultations for 56 countries including the Russian Federation and South Africa. In our constituency of 4 Nations, I was assigned the work of Bhutan and coordinated with the Royal Bhutan authorities for their Article IV consultations on a 24-month annual cycle. I was also assigned the coordination of the Finance Minister's visits to Washington DC for the Annual Fund-Bank meetings and the Spring Meetings.

At the end of 3 years, I knew most of the senior staff of the Fund and also almost all officials in the Executive Directors offices. Representing India on the Executive Board of the IMF was a unique experience – it was multilateral, multicultural, multiethnic and above all highly professional. The Executive Directors from 24 countries were largely Central Bankers or Ministry of Finance officials. There were several officials who had served in the Finance Minister's offices – Tom Scholar the United Kingdom Executive Director had served as Private Secretary to Chancellor of Exchequer, Olivier Cuny, the Senior Advisor in the French Executive Director's Office had served as Private Secretary to Finance Minister of France, GuiseppeCippolone, Senior Advisor in the Italian Executive Director's Office had served as Private Secretary to Finance Minister of Italy. Having served as Private Secretary to Finance Minister of India, I felt at home interacting with officials from the Ministries of Finance who were serving on the Executive Board. Inter-personal relations were a key to successful presence on the IMF board.

The Reserve Bank of India provided inputs for formulation of position papers on IMF Policy matters. In cases where the Reserve Bank of India did not have any specific views, discretion was available with the Indian Executive Director office to firm up our own positions based on National policies. It took many hours of work and research to prepare gray statements. I worked meticulously preparing my Gray Statements to be submitted to the Secretary's Department for discussions in the Executive Board. I always believed that not only were big policy issues important, but work on smaller member countries was equally important. I participated in the Executive Board discussions energetically through carefully thought out interventions based on several days of research. Board meetings would commence at 10 am, followed by a second meeting at 1130 am and then post lunch there would be 2 more meetings. The IMF Executive Board met 3 days in a week and every day there would be 3-4 meetings. There were days when I attended 4 Executive Board meetings in a day, sitting in the Indian chair of the Executive Board for several hours. I can look back with pride and say that I was a valiant voice for India's support to developing countries on the IMF Board.

There was much about the IMF policies and articles of agreement which required on-the-job learning, I would visit Rodney Ramcharan, Senior Economist in the Research Department to help me with the econometric analysis in staff papers. I often met Prabhakar Narvekar, the only Indian to have served as Deputy Managing Director IMF, and he explained to me the Fund's involvement in resolving major financial crisis and working in the Departments. I worked in the IMF library, reading over 300 books, working papers, occasional papers, staff discussion notes and research bulletins. The potential for learning was enormous. The institutional ideals of economic liberalism and democracy were deep rooted both in IMF staff and Executive Directors offices. A positive energy to assimilate the Fund ideals and their benefits to national economies greatly enthused my long work hours in the IMF.

Executive Directors on the IMF Board were men of vast experience, having spent decades working on IMF policies. There was Abbas Mirakhor, the Executive Director representing Iran and the Dean of the Executive Board who had spent over 20 years on the Board, Shoukur Shaalan, the Executive Director representing Egypt who had spent almost his entire career of 35 years in the IMF, Willy Kiekens the Executive Director representing Belgium who had spent 12 years on the Board, Aleksi Mozhin the Executive Director representing Russia who had spent 16 years on the Board. However most countries rotated their Executive Directors on a 3 year cycle, amongst those were India, China, Germany, Italy, the Netherlands, United Kingdom, United States; and several constituencies rotated their Executive Directors on a 2 year cycle like Malaysia-Indonesia constituency, Korea-Australia constituency, the 2 African chairs and the Nordic countries chair. Several Executive Directors in the IMF in my years with the IMF went on reach great heights – Murilo Portugal became the Deputy Managing Director of the IMF, Sri Mulyani Indrawati became the long-standing Finance Minister of Indonesia, Miranda Xafa became the Central Bank Governor of Greece and Tom Scholar became the Cabinet Secretary of United Kingdom. The Indian Executive Directors to the IMF, Dr. Y.V.Reddy went onto become one of the most celebrated Governors of the Reserve Bank of India and Dr. Vijay Kelkar served as Advisor to Finance Minister in the rank of Minister of State.

The Managing Directors

In my tenure at the IMF, the Fund had 2 Managing Directors – Horst Kohler and Rodrigo De Rato.

Horst Kohler was a very pleasant and affable Managing Director. He had served as Deputy Minister of Finance for Germany and President of the European Bank for Reconstruction and Development. Horst Kohler resigned as Managing Director in March 2004 following his nomination to the position of President of Germany. I vividly remember the rushed farewell speech that Horst Kohler gave to the IMF Executive Board in a meeting convened at short notice, in which he informed the Board that he had received a telephone call from the Chancellor of Germany requesting him to contest for the post of President of Germany. In his farewell address, Horst Kohler said that his tenure was marked by significant progress toward better crisis prevention, transparency in Fund publications, deepening of the Fund's role in financial sector and international capital markets. He had also given the IMF an active role in the global fight against poverty.

Horst Kohler served as Managing Director when the anti-globalization protests were at their peak, and the Fund was the principal proponent of free trade and economic liberalism. The Fund program in Argentina was received with vociferous street protests and debt default. Kohler's speeches reflected the need to make globalization work better for all, he acknowledged that the disparities between the world's richest and poorest nations had grown and far too many of the world's people had been left behind. Poverty he said was not only the greatest challenge to peace and stability for 21st century but was also the greatest moral challenge.

Horst Kohler took steps to streamline Fund Conditionality to make room for actual national ownership and reform programs. While he believed that Fund Conditionality was essential to enforce good policies for stability and growth, sustained progress of programs would require countries taking responsibility for them. He tried to convert the Fund into an institution that listens and learns and not just from member countries.

After Horst Kohler's resignation from the post of Managing Director there was a period of 3 months when Anne Krueger was Acting Managing Director.

Anne Krueger

Almost all the key Board meetings were chaired by the First Deputy Managing Director, Anne Krueger, who served as First Deputy Managing Director from September 2001 to August 2006. She was a towering presence on the IMF Executive Board, allowing discussions in a democratic manner, giving adequate time and voice to all member countries and trying to accommodate their views in the Chairman's Summing Up at the end of the discussions. A Professor from the Department of Economics at Stanford University, she had published extensively on policy reform in developing countries, role of multilateral institutions in the international economy and political economy of trade policy. She was an avid supporter of India's economic policies and had written a book Economic Reform and the Indian Economy (2003).

Anne Krueger's views represented the thinking in the IMF management in that period. Her tenure was a period of absence of international financial crisis with the exception of Argentina and Turkey. It was also a period when anti-globalization protests were witnessed on a large scale. Anne Krueger often addressed the issues of economic reform in 21st century even in economies whose performances were termed as enviable by the Fund staff. Economic reforms are intended to promote growth and improve citizen's well-being. Reforms that deliver low inflation make it possible for countries to grow more rapidly. Respect for law, property rights, well-functioning public institutions, an economic environment that fosters competition and enterprise and enables actors to participate in the global economy were essential part of economic reforms. Sound policies bring considerable rewards, as evidenced in the increased living standards of industrial countries.

Anne Krueger was of the view that capital account crises can occur rapidly because the holders of a country's debt lose confidence in its ability to service that debt. A macroeconomic crisis can occur even if a country's macroeconomic policies are sound if the creditors believe that such policies cannot be sustained. The only effective response to a full-blown crisis in her view was to restore the creditors confidence that a country will be able to meet its debt obligations in full. Anne Krueger shifted the focus of work in the IMF to detecting crisis and how to respond to warning signals. The IMF's Article IV consultations hitherto had always examined the economies and economic policies of member countries. Anne Krueger ensured that greater attention was paid to debt sustainability and also focused on the Financial Sector Assessment Program aimed at closely looking at the Banks and other financial institutions. She felt globalization's benefits were so evident that the anti-globalization protests were simply misguided and always presented a powerful case for globalization.

Anne Krueger visited India a number of times, and commended the progress of economic reforms in India particularly the Fiscal Responsibility and Budget Management Act. That said, she flagged the issue of mounting fiscal deficit as an area of concern which needs to be addressed to reduce government's reliance on borrowing and free up resources for private sector and so contribute to growth and poverty reduction. She also flagged strengthening infrastructure, labor market reform and encouragement to foreign investors as key issues for India's progress.

Rodrigo de Rato y Figaredo

Rodrigo de Rato assumed office as Managing Director on July7, 2004 and stepped down from office on October 31, 2007. Rodrigo de Rato had served as Minister of Economy for Spain prior to his appointment to the IMF. Shortly after assuming charge of the post of Managing Director, Rodrigo de Rato initiated a strategic review aimed at determining whether the Fund is fully prepared to meet the challenges and crisis of today and future. The review suggested a more focused approach to Fund's work particularly on Low Income Countries, Financial Sector Assessments and Standards and Codes as also a reduction in documentation work. The review further suggested that the IMF deepen the analysis of globalization and broaden research into dynamics of capital account liberalization. Rodrigo de Rato also called for reassessing IMF governance by reallocation of quotas.

Rodrigo de Rato was part of the consultations to reduce global imbalances. The IMF joined the discussions between the United States, the Euro Zone, Japan, China and Saudi Arabia aimed at coordinating economic policies. They were linked to global imbalances in different ways – either by carrying substantial current account surplus or deficit or because they were having a large percentage of world output. The countries agreed that reducing global imbalances was a multilateral challenge and shared responsibility. China planned to boost domestic demand, Euro Zone aimed to implement a series of structural reforms, Japan planned to strengthen its fiscal sector, Saudi Arabia aimed to increase investment in the oil sector infrastructure and the United States aimed to take steps to balance its budget and jump start savings.

The Deputy Managing Directors

In addition to the Managing Director and the First Deputy Managing Director, the IMF also had 2 other Deputy Managing Directors. One post of Deputy Managing Director was for Japan and the other was for Latin America. Takatoshi Kato was the Deputy Managing Director from Japan and Agusten Carstens was the Deputy Managing Director from Mexico. Currently the IMF has 3 Deputy Managing Directors with one post of Deputy Managing Director from China.

Takatoshi Kato had served as Vice Minister of Finance and Executive Director of Japan at the Asian Development Bank before he joined the IMF. He chaired a number of Executive Board meetings for most Asian member-countries and also the Caribbean countries, and played a prominent role in the Extractive Industries Transparency Initiative. Takatoshi Kato supported the Managing Director's views in the Medium Term Strategy for the IMF and said it was motivated by the central insight that the world is changing fast and that the IMF needs to adapt accordingly to help member countries deal with the 21st century challenges.

Agustin Carstens served as Deputy Managing Director IMF from August 1, 2003 to October 2006. He had served as Deputy Secretary Finance Mexico and Executive Director representing the Spain-Mexico constituency from 1999-2000. As Governor of the Banco De Mexico Agustin Carstens headed the IMFC from March 2015 to December 2017. He was only 44 years old when he was appointed as Deputy Managing Director and was the youngest Deputy Managing Director the IMF has ever had. Agustin Carstens handled the capacity building and technical assistance activities of the IMF. He headed the Africa-Capacity Building Initiative to help train government officials and thus improve the institutional capacity of countries to design and implement their own development strategies. The IMF operationalized 2 African Technical Assistance Centres (AFRITACS) in Mali and Tanzania as a key part of this strategy. Agusten Carstens was also part of the Fund outreach to explain its policies about Low Income Countries to African member countries.

The Executive Directors, Senior Advisors and Advisors

The Fund's Executive Board is a very interactive and closely knit group of officials. Each of the 24 Executive Directors was supported by an Alternate Executive Director, an Advisor/ Senior Advisor for each member country in the Constituency. The Advisors were young civil servants mostly in their thirties and forties who were the foot soldiers in the Executive Board. We would often interact in small groups or individually to firm up positions on specific Board agenda.

The Indian Executive Director's office is located on the 13th floor of the IMF. It has a beautiful view of the George Washington University and Constitution Avenue. On the same floor were located the Executive Director offices of United States, Germany, the Netherlands, Francofone Africa, China, Argentina, the Russian Federation, Malaysia, Canada, Norway and Italy. The 12th Floor had the Executive Board room with statues of Johan Maynard Keynes and Harry Dexter White as also the Managing Director and Deputy Managing Director Offices. The 11th floor had offices of 12 Executive Directors including Saudi Arabia, Egypt, Belgium, Japan, Sub-Saharan Africa, Brazil, Iran, Egypt, France, Korea-Australia, Brazil and Switzerland. It was easy to walk across and talk to colleagues or meet in the corridors or in the Fund cafeteria for discussions. Most of the advisors particularly those from single constituencies or with few members like ours had to attend Board meetings of the Executive Board for long hours every alternate day, and in workshops or seminars on Tuesdays and Thursdays. The work ethic was very high, Advisors would complement each other on the quality of their statements in the Executive Board or email or in lunch hour cafeteria discussions. There was a lot of camaraderie, inter-personal relations were very strong and the policy interactions were often fascinating.

As the Advisor in the Indian constituency working on Low Income Countries, Poverty Reduction and Growth Strategy and Multilateral Debt Initiative, I had the opportunity to interact extensively with the Executive Director representing the Sub-Saharan Group of Countries – Peter Ngumbullu the Executive Director representing Tanzania and his Deputy, Peter Gakunu the Alternate Executive Director representing Kenya. Ngumbullu headed a 19-member country constituency including South Africa, Nigeria, Tanzania, Kenya, Uganda, Ethiopia and Zimbabwe.

Ngumbullu and Gakunu had both served as Finance Secretaries in their countries and were very aware of the importance of the IMF's PRGF programs for their countries. They often sought India's support for defending their positions on the Board particularly in cases where conditions could not be implemented.

The Indian Executive Director B.P. Misra was extremely supportive of African positions on the Board. On behalf of the Indian constituency, I submitted gray statements in support of the policy measures and country programs in each of the 19 member countries of the Sub-Saharan African constituency. Several of the program countries were on quarterly/half-yearly review and were placed before the Executive Board very often. India always stood up for Sub-Saharan Africa on the Executive Board. During Annual / Spring Meetings several African Ministers met the Indian Executive Director to thank us for the support extended during Executive Board discussions.

I must mention my interactions with Willy Kiekens the Executive Director representing Belgium and his Deputy Johan Prader, a Central Banker from Austria. I worked on Turkey which was part of the Belgian constituency and was a major program country in the period 2003-06 and its economy had just started recovering from the economic crisis. Prader headed the EU group meetings in the Board and had a deep insight into the Eurozone economies. Kiekens had an in-depth knowledge about the IMF and his insights into the legal issues of Fund governance were often fascinating.

I interacted closely with the Netherlands Executive Director Jeroen Kremerswho headed a 11-member constituency, most of which were program countries on which I worked on, Georgia, Romania, Ukraine, Bulgaria, Bosnia and Herzgovina, Croatia, Macedonia and Armenia and also Israel which was a non-program country. The challenges of poverty and institution building in Eastern European countries was quite visible particularly in Romania and Bulgaria. Georgia had just witnessed an important political transition and Fund management wanted to support the Georgian transition. The Dutch officials in the Executive Board came to work by bicycles in summer, it was only when I visited Amsterdam a few years later that I discovered their Nation's huge love for bicycle riding.

Amongst the other Executive Directors of that period, I interacted closely with Ms. Phang Hoo Eng the Executive Director from Malaysia, Richard Murray the Alternate Executive Director from Australia and Miranda Xafa the Alternate Executive Director from Greece.

Every country had its own set of challenges in dealing with the Fund Management. The Fund Conditionality was never easy to implement and structural benchmarks necessitated strong country ownership.

Work on Major Non-Program/ Program Countries

The important non-program countries that I worked on were Russian Federation, and South Africa. I had an opportunity to visit each of these countries a number of times heading Government of India delegations subsequently. I was fascinated by how close to reality the assessments in the Article IV consultations were. The quantum of in-depth research conducted by the IMF staff in formulating the Article IV reports and selected issues papers was highly commendable even in non-program countries.

The economic outlook for the Russian Federation in the years 2004-06 was robust real GDP growth, strong external and fiscal positions and an economy running close to full potential. The Russian policy of taxing and saving oil revenues had served the country well. There was a windfall of oil revenues. Russia started loosening its expenditure and this was witnessed in higher wages and tax cuts. There were no major structural reforms that Russia pursued in that period.

South Africa was witnessing 4.5 percent growth per annum in the 2004-06 period but was faced with the challenge of accelerating the growth further and reducing unemployment. One of the main initiatives to reduce wealth disparities that were the legacy of the apartheid era was land reform and Black Economic Empowerment, both initiatives were supported by the IMF. However, the IMF cautioned South African authorities against influencing the real exchange rate through monetary policy to promote growth as it would undermine the inflation targeting regime.

The important program countries that I worked on were Turkey which had a borrowing of US $ 13.1 billion, Ukraine which had a borrowing of

US $ 1.1 billion and Serbia and Montenegro which had a borrowing of US $ 965 million. The Turkey program was a successful program for the IMF while the other 2 programs did not perform well.

Work on Low Income Countries

When I look back at my years in the IMF, my work on Low Income Countries is a matter of immense pride for me. HIPC Initiative, PRGF programs, MDRI debt relief were buzzwords in the IMF in the 2003-06 period.

The Fund advocated to the Low Income Countries the need for a sustainable borrowing strategy to achieve development goals. Low Income Countries faced significant challenges in meeting their development objectives while at the same time ensuring their external debt remained sustainable. The IMF felt that the concept of debt sustainability in low income countries should be based on 2 pillars – indicative country specific external debt-burden thresholds that depend on the quality of the country's policies and institutions and an analysis and careful interpretation of actual and projected debt-burden indicators under a baseline scenario and in the face of plausible shocks. The Fund urged the Low Income Countries that the primary responsibility to achieve debt sustainability was that of Low Income Countries themselves and the binding thresholds that it recommended were necessary for managing debt prudently and accelerating growth.

Work on Debt Relief for Heavily Indebted Poor Countries (HIPCs) and the Multilateral Debt Relief Initiative Assistance (MDRI)

The Heavily Indebted Poor Countries (HIPC) Initiative was designed as a debt reduction mechanism to end repeated debt rescheduling and provide a solid platform for Low Income Countries to achieve debt sustainability. The HIPC represented a strong commitment of the international community to reduce the external debt burden of the heavily indebted poor countries. The HIPC initiative had a significant impact in reducing debt stocks and debt services and enabled redirecting the debt service payments to poverty alleviation. The debt stocks reduced by 2/3rds and the HIPC initiative freed billions of dollars for poverty alleviation.

The IMF provided debt relief assistance of US $ 3.1 billion to 19 countries that met all criteria and reached completion point of the total cost of debt relief of US $ 41.3 billion that was provided by the G7 member countries.

The Multilateral Debt Relief Initiative (MDRI) was adopted by the IMF in later 2005. The G8 in June 2005 put into action the debt relief proposal that called for cancellation of 100 percent debts of IMF, World Bank and African Development Bank of HIPC countries that had reached or eventually would reach the HIPC completion point. The decision was implemented in an even handed manner across the IMF membership after discussions in the IMF Executive Board that all member countries at or below the per capital income threshold of US $ 380 should be eligible. The MDRI debt relief was thus provided to 18 countries that had reached HIPC completion point and also to two non-HIPC countries namely Cambodia and Tajikistan that were below the US $ 380 income threshold for eligibility and had debt outstanding to the IMF.

The Fund thus provided Multilateral Debt Relief Assistance of US $ 136.2 billion from General Resources Account and an amount of US $ 3.7 billion from the PRGF-ESF credit outstanding to 20 countries as part of MDRI. The MDRI was an initiative driven entirely by G8 and the IMFC Chairman Gordon Brown played a critical leadership role in the decision.

Work on Independent Evaluation Office (IEO) Reports

Dr. Montek Singh Ahluwalia was the Director of the Independent Evaluation Office in the years 2003-06. Dr. Montek Singh Ahluwalia visited the Indian Executive Director's office quite frequently, he knew B.P.Misra personally for a number of years. Dr. Montek was a role model for Fund's economists who were astounded by his rapid rise in the Indian Government and his contribution to India's economic reforms. He successfully led the nascent Independent Evaluation Office to conduct a number of important evaluation studies. I worked on 3 papers presented by the IEO during this period – The Effectiveness of Poverty Reduction Strategy and the Poverty Reduction Growth Facility (PRGF), IMF Technical Assistance and the IMF Assistance to Jordan. I was also associated with the formulation of terms of reference for another evaluation study taken up by the IEO on IMF Structural Conditionality.

References

1. Horst Kohler, Managing Director IMF., "Working for a Better Globalization" Remarks at the Conference on Humanizing the Global Economy, Washington DC, dated January 28, 2002 www.imf.org

2. Horst Kohler, Former Managing Director IMF., "Farewell Remarks" at IMF Headquarters Washington DC, dated April 14, 2004. www.imf.org

3. Anne O. Krueger, Acting Managing Director, IMF., "Economic Growth in a Shrinking World: The IMF and Globalization" Address to the Pacific Council on International Policy., San Diego, June 2, 2004. www.imf.org

4. Anne O. Krueger, First Deputy Managing Director, IMF, "Bismarck's Warning: The Challenge of Economic Policy Reform in the 21st Century", Lecture at the University Philosophical Society, Trinity College Dublin, dated April 5, 2005. www.imf.org

5. Anne O. Kruege, First Deputy Managing Director, IMF, "Heeding Hippocrates: The IMF and the Reform Process", Address to the Council on Foreign Relations, New York, November 22, 2004. www.imf.org

6. Anne O. Krueger, Acting Managing Director, IMF., "Letting Future In: India's Continuing Reform Agenda", Keynote Speech to Stanford India Conference, June 4, 2004. www.imf.org

7. Rodrigo de Rato, Managing Director IMF., "The World's Lender Must Redefine its Role to Stay Relevant"., Financial Times, September 14, 2005 www.imf.org

8. Rodrigo de Rato, Managing Director IMF., "Is the IMF's Mandate Still Relevent?" Global Agenda January 2005 www.imf.org

9. Rodrigo de Rato, Managing Director IMF., "Consultation to Reduce Global Imbalance", Le Monde March 15, 2007 www.imf.org

10. Takatoshi Kato, Deputy Managing Director IMF., "Enhancing Macroeconomics through Communications" Remarks at the Regional

Media Seminar on Middle East and IMF: Cooperation for Development, Dubai, United Arab Emirates December 18, 2004 www.imf.org

11. Agusten Carstens, Deputy Managing Director IMF., "Role of the IMF in Low Income Countries", Dar es Salaam, Tanzania February 3, 2004 www.imf.org

LOOKING FORWARD

CHAPTER - XI

G20 – A DECADE IN MULTILATERALISM

This chapter presents the progress achieved in the G-20 Summit meetings, documenting the specific milestones achieved and the consensus on globalization efforts.

The rise of the G-20 is a significant development on the global economic horizon. The G-20 is the leading forum of world's major economies that seek to develop global policies to address today's most pressing challenges. The G-20 has 19 member countries and the European Union, which represent 90 percent of global GDP and 80 percent of global trade and 2/3rds of the global population. The G-20 was born out of a meeting of G-7 Finance Ministers and Central Bank Governors who saw the need for a more inclusive body with broader representation in addressing the world's financial challenges.

The G-20 has been at the forefront of battling financial crisis – the Global Financial Crisis 2008-09 and the Eurozone Crisis in 2010 – that have taken a devastating toll on global growth and welfare. In the annals history of financial crisis, the London G-20 summit of April 2009 will be acknowledged as the clear turning point when world leaders showed extraordinary determination and unity. There were sharp differences but they were debated and discussed and compromises were made so as to reach the final goal – of ending the crisis. This resulted in an agreed package of measures having both domestic and international components but all of them to be implemented in coordination and in synchronization where necessary. The entire range of crisis response measures – accommodative monetary stance, fiscal stimulus, debt and deposit guarantees, capital injection, asset purchases, currency swaps, keeping markets open were all derived from the G-20 package. G-20 Leaders summits are attended by the Heads of State and Government.

G-20: Navigating the Global Recovery

The G-20 designated as the premier forum for international economic cooperation, has over the past decade, formulated an agenda for strong, sustainable and balanced growth; strengthened international financial regulatory system; reformed the mandate, mission and governance of the International Monetary Fund; deliberated on Energy Security and Climate Change; strengthened the support for the most vulnerable countries and placed quality jobs at the heart of the recovery. The G-20 established the Financial Stability Board (FSB) to include major emerging market economies to coordinate and monitor efforts in strengthening financial regulation. The G-20 was at the forefront of the efforts for shifting 5 percent quota shares in the International Monetary Fund to dynamic emerging markets and developing countries from over represented countries.

Over the past decade the G-20's agenda has expanded to include additional issues affecting the financial markets, trade and development. The G-20 offers India a place at the High Table to influence and participate in the global decision making processes. Climate change is one area where the pressures of being part of an elite group worked and India accepted the challenge of cutting emissions.

The G-20 Heads of Government and State summit meetings have been held at Washington DC (2008), London and Pittsburgh (2009), Toronto and Seoul (2010) Cannes (2011), Mexico City (2012), Rome (2013), Brisbane (2014), Antalya (2015), Hangzhou (2016) and Hamburg (2017). The real power of the G-20 is multilateralism. A diverse group of stakeholders and international institutions came together to make globalization work better for all.

G-20 Shared Benefits of Globalization

In 2016, the G-20 committed itself to the Action Plan on the 2030 Agenda for Sustainable Development including the Sustainable Development Goals (SDGs) and the Addis Ababa Action Agenda on Financing for Development (AAAA). The 2030 Action Plan envisaged bold transformative steps through both collective and individual concrete actions at international and domestic levels. The G-20 further sought to improve sustainable livelihoods with its endeavors in energy and climate despite the United States Plan to withdraw from the Paris Agreement. The G-20 assumed the responsibility for launching the Africa Partnership in recognition of its goal for fostering sustainable and inclusive economic development.

The G-20 meetings have enlarged in scope and number over the past decade. The G20 Meetings comprise of Meeting of Finance Ministers and Central Bank Governors (twice a year), Meeting of G20 Deputies, G20 Ministerial Meeting on Development and the Summit Meeting

The G20 has further diversified to include Climate Change, Energy, Skill Development, Science and Technology, Agriculture and Labor Ministers meetings. The G-20 meetings in Argentina in 2018, will have Working Group Meetings, Finance Meetings, Sherpa Meetings, Engagement Group Meetings and the Leaders' Summit. The G-20 today represents the world's foremost facet of multilateralism.

The Washington DC Summit: November 2008

In 2008, Global Output was contracting at a pace not seen since 1930s. Trade was plummeting, jobs disappearing rapidly. The world was on the edge of a depression. The Summit on Financial Markets and the World Economy was held on November 15, 2008 in Washington DC amid serious challenges to the world economy and financial markets. The Leaders of the Group of Twenty expressed determination to enhance cooperation and work together to restore global growth and achieve needed reforms in the world's financial systems. The root causes of the 2008 crisis were inadequate appreciation of the risks building up in financial markets by policy makers, regulators and supervisors in advanced countries. They also felt that inconsistent and insufficiently coordinated macroeconomic policies, inadequate structural reforms led to unsustainable global macroeconomic outcomes, and severe market disruptions.

The Common Principles for Reform of Financial Markets were the most significant decision of the Summit. The Leaders of the G-20 formulated an Action Plan to Implement the Principles of Reform by the Finance Ministers and Experts. The common principles for reform were (a) Strengthening Transparency and Accountability; (b) Enhancing Sound

Regulation; (c) Promoting Integrity in Financial Markets; (d) Reinforcing International Cooperation and (e) Reforming International Financial Institutions

While Regulation was the first and foremost responsibility of the National Regulators, the G-20 decided on intensified international cooperation amongst regulators and strengthening of international standards affecting international financial stability. Effectively the Leaders of the G-20 pledged to bolster investor protection, prevent illegal market manipulation, to strengthen financial market transparency. They further sought to reform the Bretton Woods Institutions to adequately reflect changing economic strengths to increase their legitimacy and expand the Financial Stability Forum by including emerging market countries.

The Action Plan to Implement the Principles of Reform contained Immediate Actions by March 31, 2009 and Medium Term Actions. The Immediate Actions envisaged that the IMF with its focus on surveillance and the expanded FSF with its focus on standard setting should strengthen their collaboration. The adequacy of resources of IMF and World Bank was to be reviewed and the Institutions were asked to restore emerging and developing countries access to credit and resume private capital flows essential for sustainable growth.

The maximum emphasis was on enhancing sound regulation. All G-20 members were to review and report on the structure and principles of their regulatory systems to ensure compatibility with global financial systems. As part of prudential oversight, the G-20 agreed that financial institutions shall maintain adequate capital amounts to sustain confidence. The Regulators were asked to strengthen banks risk management practices in line with international best practices.

The Leaders of the G-20 confronted with a massive Global Financial Crisis, reiterated their commitment to an Open Global Economy. They felt that increasing financial sector regulation was necessary but nothing should be done to contract capital flows and reforms should be grounded in a commitment to free market principles. Continued partnership, cooperation and multilateralism was the clarion call given the Leaders of the G-20 in Washington DC in November 2008.

The London Summit April 2009

At the London Summit of April 2009, the Leaders of the Group of Twenty faced the greatest challenge to the world economy in modern times. Global economic activity was falling and turning around the global growth depended critically on concerted policy actions and concerted policy support. The crisis had deepened since November 2008, and the global crisis required a global solution. It was in this backdrop that the Leaders of the Group of Twenty adopted 3 major declarations - the Global Plan for Recovery and Reform, the Declaration on Strengthening the Financial System and the Declaration on Delivering resources through International Financial Institutions.

The Global Plan pledged to (a) restore confidence, growth and jobs; (b) repair the financial system to restore lending; (c) strengthen financial regulation to rebuild trust; (d) fund and reform international financial institutions to overcome the crisis; (e) to promote global trade and invest to underpin prosperity and (f) build an inclusive green and sustainable recovery.

To restore growth and jobs, the Central Banks of the G-20 took exceptional action. In line with the G-20 framework for restoring lending and repairing the financial sector, Central Banks cut interest rates, Governments put together the largest fiscal and monetary policy stimulus and agreed to put in place credible exit strategies from expansionary policies.

For strengthening financial supervision and regulation, the Financial Stability Board (FSB) with a strengthened mandate was established including all G-20 countries, Spain, and the European Union. The FSB was to coordinate with the IMF to provide early warning systems. To strengthen the global financial institutions, the G-20 committed to implementing the package of IMF quota and voice reforms agreed in April 2008 and called on the IMF to complete the review of quotas by January 2011. The G-20 at London, reiterated the commitment made in Washington DC to refrain from raising new barriers to investment or trade or new export restrictions or implementing the WTO – a pledge extended to end of 2010. The G-20 recognized the human dimension of the crisis, and agreed to create employment opportunities, income generating measures for those who lost jobs. The G-20 agreed to make the best possible use of investment funded by fiscal stimulus programs towards building a sustainable recovery.

The Global Plan for Recovery and Reform was accompanied by the Declaration on Delivering Resources through International Financial Institutions and Declaration on Strengthening the Financial System. The resources to the IMF were trebled to US $ 750 billion, a new SDR allocation of US $ 250 billion and additional resources from IMF gold sales for a US $ 1.1 trillion program lending. The IMF introduced a new Flexible Credit Line (FCL) as part of its reformed and more flexible lending. The scope of regulation brought careful oversight to large and complex financial institutions given their systemic importance. FSB was mandated to coordinate with IMF and BIS to develop macro-prudential tools for regulation. The G-20 also agreed to improve accounting standards and for effective oversight of credit rating agencies. Tax havens were also to be subjected to international prudential and supervisory standards.

The Pittsburgh Summit: September 2009

"It Worked" - was what the Leaders of the Group of Twenty said on September 25, 2009. The G-20 economies had implemented wide reaching policy measures that helped stabilize the confidence, limit the threat of financial stability, provided impetus to economic growth. Considerable fiscal stimulus remained in pipeline through 2010 for the G-20 as a whole, and there was a positive impact on growth and employment.

The global economy was beginning to grow again, but the recovery was sluggish and policy support required to be sustained for the expansion to be firmly established. Financial conditions continued to improve but markets remained dependent on public support. The Banking systems were undercapitalized and saddled with impaired assets. The biggest risk was a premature exit from accommodative macroeconomic policies.

The G-20 faced the key challenge to map a course between unwinding public interventions in a time-bound manner and maintaining market confidence for sustainability of public finances. They also needed to evolve clear communication of exit strategies. Central Banks needed to unwind their extraordinary liquidity and credit support and start tightening their monetary stance.

The path from Pittsburgh in September 2009 was to Canada in June 2010 and then to Korea in November 2010.

Toronto Summit – June 2010

The G-20 noted that global recovery was moving at different paces in different countries, and individual countries needed to tailor their responses to their own circumstances. The Toronto Summit Communique said that "Those countries with serious fiscal challenges need to accelerate the pace of consolidation. This should be combined with efforts to rebalance global demand to help ensure global economic growth continues on a sustainable path".

The Leaders Summit developed the G-20 Framework for Strong Sustainable and Balanced Growth. The G-20 sought to build on its achievement of addressing the global economic crisis by ensuring a full return to growth with quality jobs, to reform and strengthen financial systems and to create a strong and balanced global growth. The IMF released it assessment of scenarios for improving growth through the Mutual Assessment Process designed to enhance the synergy of country economic programs to achieve stronger growth worldwide. The G-20 Mutual Assessment Process was the mechanism through which the growth challenge was to be addressed.

The G-20 Mutual Assessment Process showed that appropriate collective action could increase the global GDP by 2.5 percent over medium term, creating tens of millions of jobs and lifting tens of millions out of poverty. The G-20 Mutual Assessment Program envisaged action in 3 areas – first, fiscal consolidation in advanced economies with credible fiscal plans starting in 2011; second, economies with surpluses to boost internal demand by spending on infrastructure, social safety nets and allowing exchange rate flexibility; third, structural reforms in advanced economies – encompassing changes in labor markets that will lift growth and financial reforms on a sustainable basis.

The G-20 Leaders' Summit also made progress towards a comprehensive set of new standards to enhance strength and stability of the Financial Sector. A healthier and safer Financial Sector could play a significant role in government interventions to repair the financial system. The Financial Sector reform rested on four pillars – a strong regulatory framework, effective supervision, resolution of financial institutions in distress and transparent international assessment and peer review. Banks were required to hold significantly more and higher quality capital, the Financial Stability Board in consultation with IMF was to make recommendations on improved supervision, and there would be greater commitment to the IMF/ World Bank Financial Sector Assessment Program.

The Leaders of the G-20 supported the IMF quota reforms and to deliver in parallel the other governance reforms in line with the Pittsburgh summit commitments to enhance the IMF legitimacy and credibility.

The Seoul Summit 2010

In November 2010, the Leaders of the G-20 met in Seoul, Korea in a meeting aimed at strengthening the international policy framework to help sustain the global economic recovery.

The Communique said "Cohesion and cooperation defined the G-20 during the crisis. This allowed decisive policy action to help avert a second Great Depression. Now the challenge is to secure the recovery and to create the growth and jobs the world needs. We all recognize that much remains to be done, but the Seoul Action Plan is a step in the right direction."

The G20 leaders agreed that the Mutual Assessment Program should be continued and country specific commitments should be spelt out in key policy areas. A set of indicative guidelines to help identify large imbalances that require preventive corrective actions to be taken were to be formulated by the IMF and Financial Stability Board. Based on these guidelines the progress towards external sustainability and global consistency of national economic policies. The Fund's modernized surveillance mandate and instruments – including new country specific spillover reports on the wider impact of systemic economic policies would support this effort. With the objective of strengthening global financial stability the G20 called upon the IMF to deepen its work on capital flow volatility.

The G20 adopted the Seoul Development Consensus for Shared Growth that sets out the G20's commitment to work in partnership and complement efforts to achieve Millennium Development Goals. The

Multi-Year Action Plan on Development to make a tangible and significant difference in people's lives, including in particular the development of infrastructure in developing countries.

Cannes Summit 2011

On the eve of the Cannes Summit 2011, the IMF submitted a report titled "The G20 Mutual Assessment Process: From Pittsburgh to Cannes – IMF Umbrella Report" to take stock of the progress made in delivering upon the policy commitments made in the Seoul Action Plan, an updated assessment of G20 macroeconomic frameworks and a sustainability report of the nature of large imbalances (key imbalances being public debt & fiscal deficits; private savings and private debt; external position – trade balance). The IMF said that the G20 economies had been making progress toward the policy commitments made at the Toronto and Seoul Summits. At the same time, however, the global environment had become much more challenging, as growth in advanced economies had slowed sharply and financial stress had increased. The IMF recommended swift and decisive action to secure the agreed objectives. Major advanced economies needed to articulate medium-term fiscal objectives and further financial sector reforms to resolve underlying problems and weaknesses that led to the crisis. Key emerging surplus economies needed to address impediments to rebalancing and allow greater exchange rate appreciation. All of them needed to focus on reforms including in the financial sector aimed at alleviating key impediments to higher growth.

The Cannes Summit 2011, the G20 faced another major challenge in handling the European crisis. The global strategy for growth and jobs was built around endorsing the decisions of the European Leaders to restore debt sustainability to Greece, strengthen European Banks, build firewalls to avoid contagion and lay the foundation for robust economic recovery in Europe. They once again focused on efforts towards a more stable and resilient International Monetary System. The big decision was the SDR basket composition should reflect the role of currencies in the global trading and financial system and the SDR basket was to be reviewed in 2015. The G20 further agreed that the resources of the IMF should be mobilized to implementing the euro area's comprehensive restructuring plan including country reforms.

The Washington Summit of 2008 had agreed that all financial markets, products and participants would be regulated or subject to oversight. The Financial Stability Board started publishing the list of Global Systemically Important Financial Institutions (G-SIFIs). The G-SIFIs would be subjected to strengthened supervision, a new international standard for resolution regimes as well as from 2016 additional capital requirements. Similarly the systemically important non-bank financial institutions were to be identified. The Financial Stability Board was mandated to coordinate and monitor the G20's financial regulation agenda.

The other issues that were taken up by the Leaders of the G20 included addressing commodity price volatility and promoting agriculture, improving energy markets and pursuing the fight against climate change, avoiding protectionism and strengthening the multilateral trading system, addressing the challenges of development, intensifying the fight against corruption and reforming the global governance for the 21st century. The G20 pursued dialogue and cooperation amongst the major international organizations especially the UN, WTO, the ILO, the WB and the IMF.

Los Cabos Summit 2012

The Los Cabos Summit of 2012 of the G20, was held amidst political impasse in dealing with large imbalances in the United States and Japan. The economic activity in the major emerging market economies had decelerated on the back of spillovers from advanced economies. The outlook for growth remained weak with huge downside risks. The euro area crisis required timely and resolute policy implementation. Financial conditions remained fragile.

The Leaders of the G20 agreed that they would do everything necessary to strengthen the overall health and growth of the world economy. Their focus was to rebuild the confidence in global financial markets. They felt that the reduction in global imbalances had not been sufficient, and the policy commitments for fiscal tightening in the United States, Japan and Europe remained critical to reduce risks and secure a durable and strong recovery. In this backdrop, the G20 adopted the Los Cobos Growth and Jobs Action Plan.

The European crisis necessitated stronger supervision and direct bank recapitalization. Public finances were to be brought back to a sustainable path. The G20 agreed to move rapidly to a more market determined exchange rate system and exchange rate flexibility and avoid persistent exchange rate misalignments. The enormous focus on exchange rate misalignment was to bring greater flexibility in the renminbi. The G20 also pledged additional resources to the IMF for crisis resolution – an amount of US $ 461 billion pledges were received and US $ 286 billion borrowing agreements were finalized. The G20 also pledged to move faster on the financial sector regulation agenda. They also agreed for faster implementation of the Basel II, 2.5 and III measures and endorsed the charter for the Regulatory Oversight Committee.

In the backdrop of the Global Economic Crisis and the European Crisis, the G20's focus was on enhanced surveillance of the world economy through the IMF and stronger financial sector regulation through the Financial Stability Board. The Surveillance Framework was strengthened through the Integrated Surveillance Decision and Mutual Assessment Framework. The Financial Stability Board started publication of an updated list of systemically important banks, and the framework for dealing with systemically important domestic banks. The G-SIFI supervision was intensified and greater transparency of financial institutions encouraged.

Further the G20 promoted Sustainable Development Policies and incorporated green growth into their agenda. They resolved to phase out medium term inefficient fossil fuel subsidies that encouraged wasteful consumption. A G20 Climate Finance Study Group was constituted to effectively mobilize resources for climate finance.

Saint Petersburg Summit 2013

The agenda for the Saint Petersburg Summit of the Leaders of G20 covered a diverse range of issues. The financial issues discussed were Financial Regulation, International Financial Architecture, Financial Inclusion, Financial Education, Consumer Protection, Tackling Tax Avoidance, Promoting Tax Transparency and Automatic Exchange of Information. The developmental issues deliberated included Growth through Quality Jobs, Promoting Development for All, Sustainable Energy Policy & Resilience in Commodity Market and Intensifying the Fight Against Corruption.

The G20's coordinated action had done much to stabilize the world economy and the financial system. Yet there was much to be done to get the world economy work better. Global growth remained subdued, with persisting market volatility and stability risks. While the advanced economies were gathering some momentum, the emerging markets were showing a slowdown. The Saint Petersburg Action Plan stressed the importance of cooperation as countries addressed the challenges of promoting global growth, jobs and financial stability. The action plan recognized the need for fiscal consolidation to reflect economic conditions, the need to push forward on financial oversight and regulation, and the importance of comprehensive structural reforms to support growth.

The Saint Petersburg Action Plan recognized the need for supportive monetary policy and the need to ensure an orderly exit from the unconventional monetary policies, effectively managing spillovers. The G20 made progress on tax evasion and tax avoidance and recognized that international taxation was an important area of multilateral discussions. The G20 also continued support for IMF's 2010 quota reform and the urgent need to ratify the agreement.

Brisbane Summit November 2014

The Brisbane Summit meeting of the Leaders of G20 accorded highest priority to deliver better living standards and quality jobs for people across the world. Global recovery was slow and not delivering the jobs needed. There was a shortfall in demand and risks persisted in financial markets. The G20 set itself an ambitious goal to lift the G20's GDP by atleast an additional 2.1 percent which will add US $ 2 trillion to the global economy and create millions of jobs.

To promote infrastructure investment, the G20 agreed to create a Global Infrastructure Hub with a 4-year mandate. The G20's actions to deliver quality jobs were to increase investment, trade and competition. For generating quality jobs, the G20 set up an Employment Working Group to submit its report by 2015.

The G20 had delivered on strengthening the resilience of the global economy and stability of the financial system. The Financial Stability Board proposed that systemically important banks hold additional loss absorbing capacity to protect taxpayers if the banks fail which was accepted by the G20. The G20 made further progress in the areas of international taxation. They further reiterated that the IMF Quota and Governance reforms and the 15th General Review of Quotas agreed in 2010 remains the G20's highest priority and urged the United States to ratify them.

The G20 agreed on several developmental issues with special emphasis on climate change. They agreed to support mobilizing finance for the Green Climate Fund. They also sought to have a coordinated approach for Ebola.

Anatalya Summit November 2015

The G20's comprehensive agenda for Anatalya Summit included decisive implementation of past commitments, boosting investments as a powerful driver of growth and promoting inclusiveness so that benefits of growth are shared. The G20 remained committed to lift their collective GDP by an additional 2 percent by implementation of growth strategies that include measures to support demand and structural reforms. The Anatalya Action Plan reflected the growth priorities of the G20 along with implementation schedules for key commitments. To provide strong impetus to boost investment, country specific investment strategies were estimated to increase the G20 investment to GDP ratio by 1 percent.

The G20 remained committed to strengthening resilience of financial institutions and enhancing the stability of the financial system. The G20 finalized common international standard on total loss absorbing capacity for systemically important banks. They agreed to strengthen the oversight and regulation of the shadow banking system to ensure resilience of market-based finance. To reach a globally fair and modern international tax system, a package of measures developed under the G20/ OECD Base Erosion and Profit Sharing Project were adopted, in particular the exchange of information on cross-border tax rulings. A G20 Anti-Corruption Plan and the G20 High Level Principles on Integrity and Transparency in Private Sector were also adopted to bring transparency in private sector. To bring transparency in public sector, the G20 Principles for Promoting Integrity in Public Procurement were adopted.

The G20's developmental agenda included adoption of the G20 and Low Income Developing Countries Framework to strengthen the dialogue on development. The 2030 Agenda including Sustainable Developmental Goals (SDGs) remained the basic framework for the G20's developmental agenda. The G20 continued its work on Global Partnership for Financial

Inclusion and on the G20 Principles for Energy Collaboration. On Climate Change the G20 reaffirmed its commitment to the below 2 degrees C goal and to contribute to the UNFCCC ahead of the Paris Conference on Climate Change.

Anatalya witnessed the diversification the G20 Agenda to cover Energy Sector issues and greater commitment to multilateral collaboration for Climate Change initiatives.

Hangzhou Summit September 2016

The Hangzhou consensus of the Leaders of the G20 was based on a vision to strengthen the G20's growth agenda; forging synergy in fiscal, monetary and structural policies; promoting global trade through greater openness and inclusive growth. The global economic recovery was progressing and new sources of growth were emerging. There were profound shifts in the configuration of the global economic landscape.

The growth strategy was to strive to reduce excessive imbalances and promote greater inclusiveness. That said, the G20 felt that excess volatility and disorderly movements in exchange rates can have adverse implications for economic and financial stability. A new path for growth was to be charted with the 2016 G20 Innovation Action Plan which sought to pursue pro-innovation policies, investments in science, technology and innovation (STI), support skills training for STI, and mobility of human resources. They also delivered the G20 New Industrial Revolution Action Plan to strengthen SME's and address workforce skill challenges. Further the G20 Digital Economy Development Cooperation Initiative was formulated to unleash the potential of digital economy. An Enhanced Structural Reforms Agenda was adopted consistent with country specific choices.

The G20 welcomed the entry into effect of the 2010 IMF Quota and Governance reform and sought early completion of the 15th Quota review to reflect the shares of dynamic economies in line with their relative positions in the world economy. Paris Club the principal international forum for restructuring official bilateral debt was expanded to include Korea, Brazil and China. The G20 remained committed to a resilient financial system through the Financial Stability Board.

The Hangzhou Communique laid emphasis on robust international trade and investment as also inclusive and interconnected development. The Hangzhou Comprehensive Accountability Report on G20 Development Commitments reflected the progress made over the period 2014-16. The G20 Labor Ministers, G20 Agriculture Ministers meetings were also included in the Developmental Agenda.

Further the G20 took note of Brexit, and the uncertainty it brought to the global economy. The G20 felt its members were well positioned to address the potential economic and financial consequences of Brexit. The G20 reiterated its support for Climate Change and supported the Green Climate Fund.

The Hangzhou summit reaffirmed the G20's founding spirit to bring together the major economies on an equal footing to catalyze action. The G20 had expanded into several new areas in its developmental agenda.

Hamburg Summit July 2017

The Hamburg Summit decided to take concrete actions on the three aims of building resilience, improving sustainability and assuming responsibility. Highest priority was accorded to strong sustainable, balanced and inclusive growth. Further the G20 recognized that globalization and technological change had raised living standards across the globe, but its benefits had not been shared widely enough. The Hamburg summit also resolved to tackle the common challenges to the global community including terrorism, displacement, poverty, hunger and health threats, job creation, climate change, energy security and gender inequality as a basis for sustainable development and stability.

The Leaders of the G20 took note of the decision of the United States to withdraw from the Paris Agreement. The United States had announced that it would cease the implementation of its nationally determined contribution and adopted an approach that lowers emissions while supporting economic growth. Despite the United States withdrawal, the Leaders of the G20 stated that the Paris Agreement was irreversible. "Investing in Climate, Investing in Growth" was the line of the G20 as it adopted the Hamburg G20 Climate and Energy Action Plan for Growth.

Conclusion

The G20 has emerged as the world's premier forum for international economic cooperation and for forging a comprehensive and integrated narrative for strong, sustainable and balanced growth. The G20 was successful in avoiding a second Great Depression in 2009 by putting together the largest taxpayer funded bailout of the global financial system. Since then there has been a massive regulatory oversight of financial institutions and banks. The major institutional reform that has been carried out by the G20, has been the governance reforms in the IMF and the emergence of the Financial Stability Board as the major forum for a strong regulatory framework in the financial sector.

The G20 has diversified into climate change, energy security, agriculture, sustainable development initiatives and skill development. A G20 summit meeting is preceded by meetings of working groups, Sherpa meetings, Finance meetings, Engagement Group meetings and then finally the Leaders Summit meeting. There is a B20 (for business), C20 (for civil society), L20 (for labor groups and unions), S20 (for scientific and academic community), T20 (for think tanks and research institutions), W20 (for women's groups) and Y20 (for youth leaders). There is a high level of deliberative democracy at work in the G20 meetings.

The last G20 summit cost Germany 130 million euros, marked by violent protests against globalization on a daily basis causing an upheaval in the daily lives of citizens. The landmark event of the Hamburg G20 Summit Meeting was that it had to deal with the United States distancing itself from global governance, poor performance of the WTO with the slow death of the Doha Round of Trade negotiations of WTO, and the rise of China and Germany in the G20. The G20 remains committed to the principles of "strong, sustainable, balanced and inclusive growth."

The agenda ahead continues to be huge be it in trade reform, the Sustainable Development Goals, the Africa Partnership and Climate Change. The G20 has made a major contribution to setting the global governance agenda. To conclude it can be said that the G20 has made a serious contribution to making globalization fairer and more sustainable while transforming the processes of international negotiations.

References

1. Declaration – Summit on Financial Markets and the World Economy, 15 November 2008, Washington United States, www.g20.org

2. The Global Plan for Recovery and Reform, 2 April 2009, London, United Kingdom, www.g20.org

3. Declaration on Delivering Resources through the International Financial Institutions, 24 April 2009, London, United Kingdom, www.g20.org

4. Declaration on Strengthening the Financial System, 2 April 2009, London United Kingdom, www.g20.org

5. The Leaders' Statement – The Pittsburgh Summit, 24-25 September 2009, Pittsburgh, United States, www.g20.org

6. The G20 Toronto Summit Declaration, 26-27 June 2010, Toronto, Canada, www.g20.org

7. IMF Staff note to G20, 26-27 June 2010, Toronto Summit, Canada, www.imf.org

8. The G20 Seoul Summit Leaders' Declaration, 11-12 November, 2010, Seoul, Korea, www.g20.org

9. The Seoul Summit Document, 11-12 November, 2010, Seoul, Korea, www.g20.org

10. The Seoul Development Consensus for Shared Consensus for Shared Growth, 11-12 November, 2010, Seoul, Korea, www.g20.org

11. IMF Report on G20 Mutual Assessment Process (MAP), 11-12 November 2010, Seoul Summit, Korea, www.imf.org

12. Final Declaration, 2-4 November 2011, Cannes, France, www.g20.org

13. G20 Leaders' Communique, 2-4 November 2011, Cannes, France, www.g20.org

14. The Cannes Action Plan for Growth and Jobs, 2-4 November 2011, Cannes France, www.g20.org

15. IMF Staff Reports for the G-20 Mutual Assessment Process, November 3-4, 2011, Cannes Summit, France, www.imf.org

16. G20 Leaders' Communique, 18-19 June 2012, Los Cabos, Mexico, www.g20.org

17. G20 Leaders' Declaration, 18-19, 2012, Los Cabos, Mexico, www.g20.org

18. G20 Leaders' Declaration, 5-6 September 2013, Saint Petersburg, Russia, www.g20.org

19. G20 5th Anniversary Vision Statement, 5-6 September 2013, Saint Petersburg, Russia, www.g20.org

20. G20 Roadmap Towards Strengthened Oversight and Regulation of Shadow Banking, 5-6 September 2013, Saint Petersburg, Russia, www.g20.org

21. G20 Leaders' Communique, 15-16 November 2014, Brisbane, Australia, www.g20.org

22. G20 Leaders' Communique, 15-16 November 2015, Anatalya, Turkey, www.g20.org

23. G20 Leaders' Communique, 4-5 September 2016, Hangzhou, China. www.g20.org

24. Hangzhou Action Plan, 4-5 September 2016, Hangzhou, China, www.g20.org

25. G20 Leaders' Declaration, 7-8 July 2017, Hamburg, Germany, www.g20.org

26. G20 Hamburg Action Plan, 7-8 July 2017, Hamburg, Germany, www.g20.org

CHAPTER - XII

THE RISE OF CHINA IN THE INTERNATIONAL MONETARY SYSTEM

Today China wields unprecedented influence on the International Monetary Fund, and this chapter presents the Rise of China as an economic superpower.

The rise of China as an economic super power, the second largest economy in the world, the largest in purchasing power parity, contributing to 1/3rd of global growth and 15 percent of global exports represents the greatest economic transformation the world has seen in the last 30 years. Successive waves of reform have reduced poverty and catapulted China to middle income country status, accompanied by an infrastructure boom with an array of roads, airports, high-speed rail systems, high-rise buildings and other infrastructure. Over 600 million people were lifted out of poverty, life expectancy and literacy have increased significantly. The growth model was based on high investment, relatively inexpensive labor, productivity enhancing foreign direct investment and strong global demand.

Since the initiation of economic reforms, China's economic growth has been marked by periods of cyclical surges in economic activity and inflation followed by periods of retrenchment, with 2 cycles in 1980s ending in hard landings. Particularly notable is the 1986-90 cycle which began with the relaxation of monetary and fiscal policies. Inflation rose to 19 percent in 1988, and efforts to curb inflation meant growth slowed sharply. The 1991-97 cycle was initiated by a rise in central and local government spending and easing of bank credit. By 1992, an investment boom was witnessed with GDP growth exceeding 14 percent. Liberalization of food prices and public sector wages led to massive inflation. Inflation peaked at 24 percent in 1994. China adopted policy measures to cool the economy. These steps included an increase in interest rates, tightening central bank credit to banks and limiting investment approvals. China eventually achieved a soft landing of the economy with inflation in single digits by 1996 and reduced food prices. The credit boom of 1991-97 cycle led to weaknesses in financial sector, rise in non-performing loans in the banking system as banks funded State Owned Enterprises with little regard for credit risk.

China – The 1991-97 Economic Cycle (in percent change)

	1991	1992	1993	1994	1995	1996	1997
GDP	9.2	14.2	13.5	12.6	10.5	9.6	8.8
Fixed Investment	13.2	26.2	36.7	14.4	11.5	11.8	9.3
Fiscal Balance	-2.2	-2.3	-2.0	-2.7	-2.1	-1.6	-1.8
Consumer Prices	3.4	6.4	14.7	24.1	17.1	8.3	2.8
Domestic Credit	20.2	22.8	38.9	26.1	22.5	21.5	16.3

Source: People's Republic of China: 2004 Article IV Consultation – staff report; staff statements and Public Information Notice on Executive Board Discussions (www.imf.org)

The Asian Financial Crisis

The East Asian financial crisis left China largely unaffected. The Chinese economy fared well. GDP growth was marginally lower than the previous years of 9 percent, inflation was at a 5-year low, exports grew at 20 percent contributing to a US $ 40 billion trade surplus, foreign direct investment was US $ 45 billion and foreign exchange reserves reached US $ 139 billion by the end of the year.

Yet in the region there was gloom. Severe economic recession was witnessed in the crisis hit countries of East Asia further aggravated by the

Russian crisis and the financial strain in Latin America. As global recession threatened, China called for concerted global action in strengthening the architecture of the international financial system. Dai Xianglong said that the speed of liberalization in the crisis hit countries exceeded the pace of enhancing economic management abilities. There was no consensus on effective management of capital flows, and the impact of liberalization was felt on economic security and social stability in East Asian countries. China recommended that the IMF should establish a mechanism for monitoring short-term capital flows and movements of speculative capital. They also supported strengthening of the Fund's early warning system based on enhanced information disclosure and transparency.

Dai Xianglong said that the Chinese Government had taken a highly responsible stance during the Asian Crisis and turbulence in the international financial markets. Further he said that great efforts were made to preserve the financial stability in the Hong Kong SAR. He said:

> "First China sustained its rapid economic growth. Against the backdrop of a substantial slowdown in exports of Asian Countries, we have adopted a vigorous fiscal policy and increased money supply appropriately to expand infrastructure investment. Secondly, China has maintained the stability of the RMB exchange rate. Since the foreign exchange system reform in 1994, China adopted a managed floating exchange rate regime. In the interests of regional stability and growth, we have maintained the stability of the RMB and pursued a non-devaluation policy. Thirdly China has taken measures to expedite structural reforms and to prevent and reduce financial risks. The Chinese Government successfully achieved the target of retrenching 50 percent of employees in the ministries of the State Council. State owned enterprise reform is progressing and breakthroughs have been achieved in provincial reform, with the objective of increasing the Central Bank's independence. The Ministry of Finance has issued state bonds of RMB 270 billion to recapitalize the state owned commercial banks."

Despite the optimism of Dai Xianglong, there were several critiques. Nicolas R. Lardy said that China's financial and banking system suffers from inadequate central bank independence and lax regulation of commercial banks. Three of the four largest banks do not event report their consolidated balance sheets. Non-performing loans are classified by lenient standards than international norms and there exist losses due to fraud, corruption and other lending irregularities, with serious financial crimes on the rise. Despite these vulnerabilities it was felt that China was not affected by the Asian financial crisis as the currency was not convertible for capital account transactions. China's capital flows were largely for direct investment with a long term horizon. There was hardly any exposure of foreign capital flows to bank deposits, bonds, stocks or any other financial assets which could be sold in the market instantly.

The 1998 Asian crisis focused on the need for fundamental structural reform in China – money losing State owned enterprises and weak banks. Efforts in this direction included reorganization of regional branches of the People's Bank to reduce political interference and injection of 270 billion RMB into the four largest state owned banks. The classification of non-performing loans was aligned more closely with international standards, and the central bank tightened supervision and regulation of banks and financial institutions.

The Dai Xianglong Years

Dai Xianglong served as the 10th Governor of the People's Bank of China from 1995 to 2002. It was in his tenure that the reorganization of the People's Bank of China (PBC) was undertaken. The PBC removed all its provincial and municipal branches which were headed by local politicians and established regional branches to strengthen independence of the Central Bank. Reform of Commercial Banks was pursued with the establishment of 4 asset management companies to purchase the non-performing assets of wholly state-owned commercial banks thereby reducing the commercial banks' non-performing loans. The PBC established a supervisory council in each commercial bank, adopted international loan classification and accounting standards and recapitalized the banks. Dai Xianglong focused on stabilizing the balance of payments and the RMB exchange rate. To boost domestic demand, the PBC undertook 9 interest rate cuts in Dai's tenure earning him the moniker "the Governor who cuts interest rates." Strong growth and strong export performance were witnessed all through his tenure – above 7 percent growth and 20 percent growth in export performance.

Dai Xianglong's views on the role of the international reserve currency, fund surveillance and capital account liberalization represented a roadmap for future Chinese policy makers. He said that

> "The role of international reserve currency played by a few countries' national currency has been a major source of instability in the international monetary system. The fluctuation in interest rates increases uncertainty in trade and huge risks about in the international financial market. The current financial system cannot solve the balance of payments imbalance, which has repeatedly been the cause of the international financial crises. To solve the problem of an international reserve currency, the international community should consider the additional allocation of SDR's and create conditions to increase their use, and strengthen the Fund's function of providing liquidity to its members."

China also considered that regional financial cooperation to be a helpful complement to the existing international financial system. Economic integration in the Asian region was represented by the Chiang Mai initiative. China became an active participant in financial cooperation based on currency swap arrangements introduced among ASEAN countries and China, Japan and Korea. In 2002, as a net debtor and low income country China made contributions to reducing debt burdens of HIPCs and the poorest Nations.

The Zhou Xiaochuan Years

Zhou Xiaochuan served as the 11th Governor of the People's Bank of China from 2003 to 2018. He was consistently ranked as the most influential policy makers of his generation and oversaw China's transition as the second largest economy in the world. A man praised for his intellect and diplomacy, Governor Zhou is called "China's most able technocrat."

China: Selected Economic Indicators 2000-2015

INDICATORS	2000-2007	2008-2010	2011-2014	2015-2017
Real GDP	10.5	9.8	8.1	6.8
Consumer Prices	1.7	2.8	3.2	1.8
Unemployment Rate	3.9	4.2	4.1	4.1
Current Account Balance	4.4	5.9	2.1	1.9
Gross Official Reserves (billions US $)	1018	2445	3606	3146
Nominal GDP (billions RMB)	16466	36018	56812	81344

Sources: 2017 Article IV Consultation for the People's Republic of China (page 43) and Modernizing China: Investing in Soft Infrastructure edited by Lam and Schipke, 2017 (page 27)

Zhao Xiaochuan's long tenure can be divided into 3 distinct phases

(a) The 2002-2007 period wherein he strove for exchange rate flexibility, capital account liberalization and reform of the banking system at a time when China had favorable medium term prospects for maintaining strong growth and continuing its integration into the global economy. In this period China played the role of modest, debtor country to the Bretton Woods institutions adopting a cooperative approach.

(b) The 2008-2010 period, in which period China had to formulate a response to the global financial crisis, handle near term domestic risks particularly to the property sector, local government finances, credit quality and put in place sustained rebalancing policies for rebalancing of growth towards private consumption. It was a period when China urged the IMF to consider the inclusion of the RMB in the SDR basket to improve the attractiveness and liquidity of the SDR as a reserve asset.

(c) The 2010-2017 period, in which period China pursued policies of Renminbi Internationalization, Financial Sector Reform and underwent the transition to a sustainable growth path and reforms. In 2010, the IMF rejected the RMB's attempt to enter the SDR basket. But China did not give up and intensified its push. Finally in November 2015, the IMF accepted the RMB into the SDR basket, assigning it 10.92 percent of the total weight, below the US Dollar, the Euro, but above the Yen and the Pound Sterling.

Exchange Rate Flexibility and Capital Account Liberalization

On January 1, 1994 China introduced a market based, unified and managed floating exchange rate system. Under the new system, certain banks were authorized to sell and purchase foreign exchange. On December 1, 1996 the renminbi became convertible for current account transactions. In the inter-bank market the PBC limited the daily movement against major currencies, +/- 0.3 percent around a daily announced reference rate. For capital transactions, exchange controls were applicable. China imposed restrictions on domestic investments by qualified foreign institutional investors, approval of the National Council of Social Security Fund for investments abroad, restrictions on foreign borrowing plans of government departments, controls on FDI and investments on derivative transactions for purposes of speculation.

Post the Asian Financial Crisis, China adopted an exchange rate policy that fostered economic and financial stability while maintaining healthy, rapid economic growth. It was felt that exchange rate reforms and institutional reforms were integral parts of the overall reform endeavor and it was important to identify proper sequencing to carry out both these reforms. Full renminbi convertibility was a stated goal, and it was to be achieved through a gradual and deliberate approach. The reform of the exchange rate was to be carried out in tandem with reform of state owned enterprises, clearance of non-performing assets and conversion of state owned commercial bank operational mechanisms. China also pursued a gradual approach to capital account liberalization given the weaknesses in the financial system.

On June 21, 2005 China instituted a reform of the renminbi exchange-rate regime by moving to a managed floating exchange rate regime based on market supply and demand and with reference to a basket of currencies. This reform step had profound significance for maintaining macroeconomic and financial market stability. The Chinese government took measures to cultivate and develop foreign exchange markets. Hedging instruments like forward, swap were developed. A market making system and OTC in the inter-bank foreign exchange market was introduced. Enterprises were given incentives to retain more foreign exchange and some relaxations in capital account restrictions were given. The RMB exchange rate moved in both directions against the US dollar, and by March 31, 2006 the RMB had appreciated 3.2 percent against the dollar. The real effective exchange rate of the renminbi rose by 8.1 percent in 2005.

Banking Sector Reforms

The Chinese authorities placed banking sector reform at the center of their overall policy agenda. The Banking Sector reforms necessitated were recapitalization and restructuring of the Bank of China, the China Construction Bank and the Industrial and Commercial Bank of China. China injected US $ 45 billion into recapitalization of Bank of China and China Construction Bank. Moneys were transferred from international reserves to Central Huijin Investment Company which financed the recapitalization. A Central Banking Regulatory Commission (CBRC) was established with a number of performance assessment indicators, enhanced external oversight and strengthening corporate governance of banks. The other steps in the Banking Reform included development and monitoring of time-bound restructuring plans, adoption of a commercial focus and enhancements to the market infrastructure.

The period 2003-10, China strengthened bank's balance sheets, internal control systems, governance and credit risk management in state banks. As Chinese government provided financial support to restore capital adequacy, full provisioning for NPLs, the operating profits of Bank of China and China Construction Bank improved significantly. China allowed foreign ownership of Banks with Bank of America and HSBC procuring stakes in Industrial and Commercial Bank of China and the Bank of Communications respectively. The CBRC took steps to monitor large exposures, undertake on-site examinations and introduced a deposit insurance scheme.

China also focused on the activities of the Agricultural Bank of China (ABC) and the Regional Credit Cooperatives (RCC). Given the huge scale of operations and exposure to the agricultural sector, restructuring of the ABC and the RCCs was pursued.

By 2006, China was witnessing strong GDP growth of 10 ¼ percent, fixed investment was nearly 30 percent, trade surplus had surged to US $ 135 billion, foreign exchange reserves reached US $ 895 billion. It was expected that GDP growth would easily exceed 10 percent, rural incomes would continue to rise and consumer credit facilities expand. Inflation was below 2 percent. China was undertaking a range of reforms in the banking sector, fiscal sector reforms like adoption of VAT, higher social sector allocations for health, education and pensions while accelerating the development of capital markets.

Financial Sector Reforms

The Financial Systems Stability Assessment (FSAP) of China's Financial sector was undertaken as part of the Article IV consultations by the IMF in 2011. The FSAP underscored the importance of careful sequencing of Financial Sector Reforms given the interconnections between the reform processes. The five major areas covered by the FSAP included exchange rate flexibility, monetary policy framework, improvements in regulation and supervision, financial market development, interest rate liberalization and capital account liberalization. There are serious concerns of a growing mountain of debt, shadow banking practices and massive stock market swings.

Then came the Global Financial Crisis of 2008-10 which changed the world's perception of China's economic miracle.

China's response to The Global Financial Crisis 2008-2010

The Global Financial Crisis of 2008-2010 confronted China with the question of an international currency that will secure global financial stability and facilitate world economic growth. China felt that issuing countries of reserve currencies were constantly confronted with the dilemma between achieving their domestic monetary policy goals without carrying their international responsibilities. The crisis called for creative reform of the international monetary system towards an international reserve currency with stable value, rule based issuance and manageable supply to achieve the objective of safeguarding global economic and financial stability. Zhao Xiaochuan pleaded for reform of the international monetary system that yielded win-win results for all stakeholders.

"Special consideration should be given to giving the SDR a greater role. The SDR has features and potential to act as super-sovereign reserve currency. More over an increase in SDR allocation would help the Fund address its resources problem and the difficulties in the voice and representation reform. Therefore, efforts should be made to push forward a SDR allocation. This will require political cooperation among member countries. Specifically, the Fourth Amendment of the Articles of Agreement and relevant resolution on SDR allocation proposed in 1997 should be approved as soon as possible so that members joined the Fund after 1981 could also share the benefits of the SDR. The scope of using the SDR should be broadened, so as to enable it to fully satisfy the member countries demand for a reserve currency."

Persisting with its call for reform and future mandate of the IMF, China pressed ahead for immediate quota and voice reform. At the 12th Meeting of the IMFC at Istanbul, Dr. Yi Gang said that

"The current financial crisis, which originated in developed countries, has resulted in substantial losses for countries of the world. The failure of major international financial institutions to issue timely early warnings highlights the consequences of its misfocused surveillance. Only through the acceleration of fundamental reforms will the major financial institutions be able to discharge the mandate assigned to it by member countries. The persistently misaligned quota shares and under representation of emerging market and developing countries hamper Fund governance and even-handed surveillance. It undermines Fund legitimacy and effectiveness. It is critical that the Fund complete in a timely manner the reform objective announced by the G-20 leaders, namely a shift of atleast 5 percentage points of the quota shares in favor of emerging market and developing member countries. Building on quota reform, we support the broader reform of Fund governance. Emerging Market and Developing Countries should also have greater participation in management and staff."

Clearly China was pressing the demand it had made in 1999 in 2009, but the world was hearing its voice in a period of crisis as it represented the only country with a significant current account surplus and trade surplus and a double digit growth.

China's response to the Global Financial Crisis 2008-2010 was quick, determined and effective. It comprised of 3 broad strands – a major fiscal stimulus, an extraordinary credit expansion and re-pegging the renminbi to the US dollar. There was an increase in spending on capital projects and a 31 percent increase in credit. Growth picked up in 2nd quarter of 2009 and reached 9.1 percent, inflation remained modest, and reserve accumulation was rapid, reaching over US $ 40 billion/ month. The balance of payments saw dramatic changes with a fall in export volumes and foreign direct investment. There was an export rebound and by July 2009 exports were above their pre-crisis level with particular strength in electronics and light manufacturing. China's fast paced recovery had significant positive trade spill-overs to the global economy. The economic recovery enabled further reform of the renminbi exchange rate regime. On July 19, 2010, the People's Bank of China announced a return to the managed float exchange rate regime allowing for +/- 0.5 percent intraday movement from a central parity of the US dollar-renminbi spot exchange rate. Between July 2005 and July 2008 the Renminbi had appreciated by 1 percent per month. Once again in July 2010, a similar trend was witnessed.

2011 Spillover Report

In 2011, the IMF formulated a spillover report to examine the external effects of domestic policies in 5 systemic economies – the S5 economies comprising of China, Euro Area, Japan, United Kingdom and the United States. The spillover report highlighted the significance of China's influence on the world economy. The report said that as the world's most central trader, China's capacity to both transmit and originate real shocks was rising, clearly China had an important stake for the world in its stability. Its export oriented growth model was seen as a source of stresses and economic rebalancing was felt essential. Currency appreciation was important to the process of rebalancing. A failure to rebalance the growth model would imply unprecedented increases in export market share. China's policies could affect global capital flows and the large purchases of reserve currency assets reduces their yields and it is unclear what the net effect of closed capital account is and what opening up would do.

In response to large capital outflows in 2015/16 the Chinese authorities allowed some currency depreciation, used foreign exchange intervention and applied a wide range of measures to stem capital outflows. China launched a number of policies like "Going Global", "One Belt One Road", "RMB Internationalization" and "Made in China 2025" to provide impetus to capital flows. The high domestic savings searching for yield and diversification drove capital outflows. China liberalized capital inflows before outflows and FDI flows.

The IMF recommended that China's transition to a sustainable consumption-based growth is desirable benefitting the global economy and reducing longer term risks, even if it entails a medium term slowdown. However, the IMF said that given its size, openness, high investment rate, high import content of its investment and exports, a slowdown in China is likely to have strong global spillovers. The negative spillovers will weigh on global growth but the effects will vary with the country's level and type of exposure to China. China's rebalancing away from investment has contributed to a slowing demand for and prices of commodities. Financial spillovers from China are on the rise through strong trade linkages and rapidly rising financial linkages.

Renminbi Internationalization

From 2011, China facilitated a gradual increase in the international use of the renminbi. This was done by deepening bilateral monetary cooperation with 28 bilateral currency swap agreements signed, steadily developing offshore RMB markets and RMB clearing banks in 14 countries and regions. There has been a buildup in renminbi deposits in Hong Kong SAR and an increase in issuance of renminbi denominated "dim-sum bonds". There was also a relaxation of capital controls to allow the return of offshore renminbi to mainland China. The expansion of the international use of the RMB has occurred largely in the Hong Kong SAR which has an open capital account, highly regarded legal system and strong regulatory oversight provided by the Hong Kong Monetary Authority. The Bank of China acts as the clearing bank and a payment infrastructure has been created. Sales of renminbi financial products were also conducted in London as part of the plans to expand the offshore renminbi business to other financial centers.

At the 3rd Plenum of the 18th CPC Central Committee in 2013, it was announced that China would seek to "speed up the process toward capital account convertibility." China introduced partial or full convertibility on 35 out of 40 items on the IMF's classification of capital accounts. Zhao Xiaochuan says that China has adopted the concept of managed convertibility, while retaining capital account management in four items, which are widely adopted by most countries.

The RMB was officially included in the SDR currency basket on October 1, 2016. The Chinese authorities felt that it is a significant milestone in the process of RMB internationalization and an acknowledgment of the progress in China's economic development, reform and opening up. They also felt that it's was step that would help increase the representativeness, stability and attractiveness of the SDR and improve the international monetary system. China published its foreign reserves, balance of international payments and international investment positions in US Dollar and SDR terms and has issued SDR denominated bonds in China.

On December 22, 2017 the monetary authorities of Japan and China approved allowing Japanese Corporations to issue RMB based bonds – the Panda bonds in China. That said, Japan is yet to sign any of the 4 initiatives to advance RMB internationalization. These four initiatives being bilateral currency swap arrangements, RMB Qualified Foreign Institutional Investor Status, RMB payment settlement system and the Asian Infrastructure Investment Bank.

Despite China's efforts for RMB internationalization, the dollar is likely to remain the preeminent global reserve currency. The structure of political and legal institutions and the limited financial market development make it difficult for the RMB to become a major reserve asset. Despite China's efforts, the RMB's use in international transactions fell by about 30 percent between 2015 and 2016.

Quota and Governance Reforms at the IMF

On December 18, 2015, the United States Congress approved the 2010 Quota and Governance Reforms of the IMF. The Managing Director of IMF said:

> "The United States Congress approval of these reforms is a welcome and crucial step forward that will strengthen the IMF in its role of supporting global financial stability. The reforms significantly increase the IMF's core resources, enabling us to respond to crisis more effectively and also improve IMF governance by better reflecting the increasing role of dynamic emerging and developing countries in the global economy."

Following the Quota and Governance Reforms, the Fund's quota resources increased to about SDR 477 billion from SDR 238.5 billion.

More than 6 percent of quota shares shifted to dynamic emerging market and developing countries from over-represented member countries. China became the 3rd largest Member after United States and Japan. However, the Chinese authorities continue to feel that the 2010 Quota and Governance reform has not significantly closed the gaps between calculated quota shares and their actual weight in the global economy. Hence China has called for continued reform momentum in completing the 15th general review of quotas within the agreed time.

China's Influence in the IMF

China wields considerable policy influence in the IMF post the IMF quota and governance reforms implemented in 2015. China's influence on the IMF Executive Board has grown significantly and no important decision on the Executive Board can be taken without an indication of China's consent. China issues gray statements on almost all topics coming before the Executive Board. It has a presence in the IMF management. Zhu Min was appointed as Special Advisor to the Managing Director from May 3 2010 to July 25, 2011 and then was appointed as the 4th Deputy Managing Director.

Tao Zhang was appointed as the 4th Deputy Managing Director of the International Monetary Fund on August 22, 2016 having served as Executive Director on the IMF from 2011 to 2015. Tao Zhang represents the elite Chinese bureaucracy well versed with the Fund's program design, review and execution. As Deputy Managing Director Tao Zhang has the institutional support, the stature and credibility to influence IMF decisions.

Tao Zhang's positions as Acting Chair and Deputy Managing Director have been highly supportive of Low Income Countries. In a Conference in Port of Spain, he assured the Caribbean Prime Ministers of the IMF's deep commitment to helping Caribbean countries in navigating the challenges of low oil prices. Further, he has supported the international community and the IMF to provide assistance and encouraged IMF staff to refine their recommendations to make policy more effective in addressing LIC's development needs.

Tao Zhang identified several African countries namely Chad, Mozambique, Republic of Congo, Ghana and Mauritania as countries with elevated debt distress and advised them to undertake fiscal adjustment programs to deliver stronger economic performance. He has assured IMF support for advising low income countries on how best to balance borrowing to finance development and manage debt related risks, roll out the revised low income debt sustainability framework and strengthen technical assistance in critical areas such as public debt reporting and management. As Acting Chair and Deputy Managing Director Tao Zhang has pressed for timely completion of reviews and disbursements.

China's Presence in International Institutions

China's influence in international institutions is at an all-time high. It has strategically positioned itself to set-up new international institutions where it wields considerable influence. China has a voting share of 6.09 percent in the International Monetary Fund and 5.5 percent in the Asian Development Bank. It is the 3rd largest member in both institutions. Further, China is a member of the African Development Bank, the Caribbean Development Bank, the Inter-American Development Bank and the European Bank for Reconstruction and Development. China has also tried to create alternate international institutions – the Asian Infrastructure Investment Bank (AIIB) was established in Beijing in 2014 with 21 member countries of Asia under the Presidency of Jin Liquin. By 2018, the membership of AIIB has increased to 84 member countries. China also established the BRICS New Development Bank in July 2015 and established a contingent reserve arrangement to address short-term balance of payments crisis. China successfully hosted the 2016 Hangzhou Summit of the G20 leaders. The Hangzhou consensus of the Leaders of G20 was based on a vision to strengthen the G20's growth agenda forging synergy in fiscal, monetary and structural policies; promoting global trade through greater openness and inclusive growth.

Conclusion

China's unprecedented financial clout is visible in the International Monetary System. The journey traversed is remarkable and the RMB's inclusion in the SDR basket of currencies is representative of China's rise in the international monetary system. From merely supporting the IMF's various policy measures, China's positions have become far more strident following the IMF's Quota and Governance Reform. In 2017, it has called on the IMF to continue its quota and governance reforms to ensure that the IMF is strong, quota based and well resourced. It has further said that the IMF should continue improving its surveillance capacity. China has said that the IMF should enhance its research and put forward suggestions on key and common challenges faced by member countries and provide early warning signals. Further China has said that the IMF should press ahead with international monetary system reforms to address the deficiencies in the international monetary system. There remains a huge domestic economic policy agenda which China needs to address, and the implications of its policy decisions will have a lot of impact on the global economy.

References

1. Eswar S. Prasad., "Gaining Currency: The Rise of the Renminbi" Oxford University Press, 2017

2. Blyth Mark and Maxfield Sylvia., "A New Financial Geopolitics? The US – Led Monetary Order in a Time of Turbulence, Foreign Affairs, January 2018

3. Lam Raphael, Rodlauer Markus, Schipke Alfred., "Modernizing China" International Monetary Fund 2017

4. Miller Ken., "Coping with China's Financial Power: Beijing's Financial Foreign Policy"., Foreign Affairs, Volume 89 Number 4 July/ August 2010 pp 96-109

5. Posen Adam S., "The Post American World Economy: Globalization in he Trump Era" Foreign Affairs, Volume 97 Number 2 March/ April 2018 pp 28-38

6. Conable, Barber B. Jr, Lampton David M., "China: The Coming Power" Foreign Affairs Volume 71 Number 5 Winter 1992/93 pp 133-149

7. Lardy Nicholas R., "China and the Asian Contagion" Foreign Affairs Volume 77 Number 4 July/ August 1998 pp 78-88

8. Eichengreen Barry., "The Dollar Dilemma: The World's Top Currency Faces Competition" Foreign Affairs Volume 88 Number 5 September/ October 2009 pp 53-68

9. Economy Elizabeth C.., "The Game Changer: Coping with China's Foreign Policy Revolution" Foreign Affairs Volume 89 Number 6 November/ December 2010 pp 142-150

10. Zhou Xiaochuan., Governor People's Bank of China, Statement at the International Monetary and Financial Committee Dubai September 21, 2003 www.imf.org

11. Zhou Xiaochuan., Governor People's Bank of China, Statement at the Ninth Meeting of International Monetary and Financial Committee Washington DC April 24, 2004 www.imf.org

12. Zhou Xiaochuan., Governor People's Bank of China, Statement at the 2004 Annual Meetings of IMF and World Bank, October 3, 2004 www.imf.org

13. Zhou Xiaochuan., Governor People's Bank of China, Statement at the 12th Meeting of International Monetary and Financial Committee Washington DC September 24, 2005 www.imf.org

14. Zhou Xiaochuan., Governor People's Bank of China, Statement at the 13th Meeting of International Monetary and Financial Committee Washington DC April 22, 2006 www.imf.org

15. Zhou Xiaochuan., Governor People's Bank of China, Statement at the 14th Meeting of International Monetary and Financial Committee Singapore September 17, 2006 www.imf.org

16. Zhou Xiaochuan., Governor People's Bank of China, Statement at the 17th Meeting of International Monetary and Financial Committee Washington DC April 12, 2008 www.imf.org

17. Zhou Xiaochuan., Governor People's Bank of China, Statement at the 21st Meeting of International Monetary and Financial Committee Washington DC April 24, 2010 www.imf.org

18. Zhou Xiaochuan., Governor People's Bank of China, Statement at the 22sr Meeting of International Monetary and Financial Committee Washington DC October 9, 2010 www.imf.org

19. Zhou Xiaochuan., Governor People's Bank of China, Statement at the 27th Meeting of International Monetary and Financial Committee Washington DC April 20, 2013 www.imf.org

20. Zhou Xiaochuan., Governor People's Bank of China, Statement at the 30th Meeting of International Monetary and Financial Committee Washington DC October 11, 2014 www.imf.org

21. Zhou Xiaochuan., Governor People's Bank of China, Statement at the 31st Meeting of International Monetary and Financial Committee Washington DC April 18, 2015 www.imf.org

22. Zhou Xiaochuan., Governor People's Bank of China, Statement at the 33rd Meeting of International Monetary and Financial Committee Washington DC April 16, 2016 www.imf.org

23. Zhou Xiaochuan., Governor People's Bank of China, Statement at the 34th Meeting of International Monetary and Financial Committee Washington DC October 8, 2016 www.imf.org

24. Zhou Xiaochuan., Governor People's Bank of China, Statement at the 34th Meeting of International Monetary and Financial Committee Washington DC April 22, 2017 www.imf.org

25. Zhou Xiaochuan., Governor People's Bank of China, Statement at the 35th Meeting of International Monetary and Financial Committee Washington DC April 22, 2017 www.imf.org

26. Zhou Xiaochuan., Governor People's Bank of China, Statement at the 36th Meeting of International Monetary and Financial Committee Washington DC October 14, 2017 www.imf.org

27. Wei Liang., "China: Globalization and the Emergence of a New Status Quo Power?" Asian Perspective Vol 31 No 4 Special Issue on "The BRICSs Countries in the Global System" (2007) pp 125-149 www.jstor.org

28. Ciorciari John D., "China's Structural Power Deficit and Influence Gap in the Monetary Policy Arena", Asian Survey Vol 54, No 5 (September/ October 2014) pp 869-893 www.jstor.org

29. People's Republic of China: 2004 Article IV Consultation – Staff Report; Staff Statement; and Public Information Notice on Executive Board Discussion November 2004 IMF Country Report 04/351 www.imf.org

30. People's Republic of China: 2005 Article IV Consultation – Staff Report; Staff Statement; and Public Information Notice on Executive Board Discussion November 2005 IMF Country Report 05/411 www.imf.org

31. People's Republic of China: 2006 Article IV Consultation – Staff Report; Staff Statement; and Public Information Notice on Executive

Board Discussion October 2006 IMF Country Report 06/394 www. imf.org

32. People's Republic of China: 2006 Article IV Consultation – Staff Report; Staff Statement; and Public Information Notice on Executive Board Discussion October 2006 IMF Country Report 06/394 www. imf.org

33. People's Republic of China: 2010 Article IV Consultation – Staff Report; Staff Statement; and Public Information Notice on Executive Board Discussion July 2010 IMF Country Report 10/238 www.imf.org

34. People's Republic of China: 2012 Article IV Consultation – Staff Report; Staff Statement; and Public Information Notice on Executive Board Discussion July 2012 IMF Country Report 12/195 www.imf.org

35. People's Republic of China: 2014 Article IV Consultation – Staff Report; Staff Statement; and Public Information Notice on Executive Board Discussion July 2014 IMF Country Report 14/235 www.imf.org

36. People's Republic of China: 2015 Article IV Consultation – Staff Report; Staff Statement; and Public Information Notice on Executive Board Discussion August 2015 IMF Country Report 15/234 www.imf.org

37. People's Republic of China: 2016 Article IV Consultation – Staff Report; Staff Statement; and Public Information Notice on Executive Board Discussion August 2016 IMF Country Report 16/270 www.imf.org

38. People's Republic of China: 2017 Article IV Consultation – Staff Report; Staff Statement; and Public Information Notice on Executive Board Discussion August 2017 IMF Country Report 17/247 www.imf.org

39. Hangzhou Action Plan, 4-5 September 2016, Hangzhou China www.g20.org

40. Zhao Xiaochuan: Reform of the International Monetary System dated 23/3/2009 www.pbc.gov.cn

41. Statement of Dr. Yi Gang, Deputy Governor of the People's Bank of China at the 12th Meeting of the IMFC Istanbul dated 6/10/2009 www.pbc.gov.cn

42. Statement by Mr. Dai Xianglong Governor of the People's Bank of China at the 1998 Annual Meeting of the International Monetary Fund and World Bank, Washington DC, October 6, 1998 www.imf.org

43. Dai Xianglong., Statement at the Fifty-Third Meeting of the Interim Committee of the Board of Governors of the International Monetary System, September 26, 1999 Washington DC www.imf.org

44. The People's Republic of China Selected Issues IMF Country Report No 17/248 August 2017 www.imf.org

45. The People's Republic of China Selected Issues IMF Country Report No 16/271 August 2016 www.imf.org

46. The People's Republic of China Spillover Report – 2011 Article IV Consultation June 27, 2011 www.imf.org

....

CHAPTER - XIII

CONCLUSION

It's time to look back on the various research questions pursued in the book and present concluding findings some of the key issues of Fund policy namely even-handedness of Fund surveillance and Spillover Reports of systemically important economies, Asymmetry in IMF's handling of crisis in Europe and Asia, Fund's developing positions on capital account convertibility, Fund's engagement with civil society and the IMF positions vis a vis India.

Even-Handedness of Fund Surveillance

The 2008 Global Financial Crisis necessitated significant changes in improving the even-handedness of Fund Surveillance. The Fund responded by adopting the 2012 Integrated Surveillance Decision for Modernizing the Legal Framework for Surveillance and the 2014 Triennial Surveillance Review. The significant changes made included integration of bilateral and multilateral surveillance, a systemic analysis of risks and spillovers, micro-financial surveillance examining the structural policies and lastly cohesive expert policy advise which focused on fiscal policy, growth and sustainability implications. The Fund also adopted the 2012 Institutional view on Trade Liberalization and Management of Capital Flows. Today, there is optically greater even-handedness in Fund Surveillance. Yet there exist serious concerns on the nature of Fund engagement with advanced economies and the extent of Fund influence through policy advise.

Traditionally, Member Countries attach significant importance to Fund Surveillance of their economic policies. The IMF recommendations in Article IV consultation reports represent important policy inputs. Fund

Surveillance covered the core areas of exchange rate policy and directly associated macroeconomic policies. There were times when the Article IV reports have also dealt with structural and social policies in addition to economic policies. Statements on economic policy of member countries from the IMF can have tremendous impact on market performance in most economies. The IMFC has held that "effective and even-handed IMF surveillance across the whole membership is central to promoting high and sustainable growth in member countries and to crisis prevention." Even-handedness and uniformity in treatment of member countries is essential for IMF's credibility and legitimacy.

The 2014 Triennial Surveillance Review contained a Review of Even-handedness of Fund Surveillance. The guidelines say that "Fund Surveillance must be even handed, whether large or small, advanced or developing and should pay due regard to countries' specific circumstances." There has been a long standing perception that Fund Surveillance is biased in favor of large advanced economies. In the advanced economies, the Fund was seen accepting the policies of the authorities. It was often felt that the Fund did not sufficiently press for fiscal consolidation in advanced economies, and FSAPs were not uniformly critical across the advanced economies. It is important that 60 percent of the Mission Chiefs to advanced economies felt that they were under pressure to dilute the candor of staff reports to avoid upsetting the country authorities. The issues of consistency in Fund advise were raised in handling fiscal policy, monetary policy, financial sector issues, external sector issues and even in structural issues.

But the limits of even-handedness of Fund Surveillance in advanced economies is a lacuna that is not entirely of the Fund's doing. The Fund simply does not have the same presence in advanced economies that it has in emerging market economies. The Fund may say the right words, but has few listeners.

In the Fund's 2018 Article IV consultation with the United States, the Fund raised significant concerns over the recent trade policy proposals that could have damaging effects beyond the US economy, trigger retaliatory responses, and undermine the open, fair and rules-based multilateral trading system. The Fund urged the US authorities to work constructively together with their trading partners to reduce trade barriers and resolve trade and investment disagreements without resorting to harmful unilateral actions. The United States chose to ignore the Fund advise.

In the 2018 Article IV consultation with China, the Fund underscored that trade tensions should be resolved in ways that support and strengthen the international trading system and the global economy. The Fund also recommended that progress in rebalancing the current account should be accelerated by more decisive structural reforms to support consumption, reduce inequality and pollution. The Fund recommended China formulate a holistic policy framework for reducing tensions across rebalancing dimensions. China chose to ignore Fund advise.

The United States published a list of US $ 50 billion worth products from China that would be hit with 25 percent tariffs. China retaliated with US $ 50 billion list of US goods for tariff hikes spiraling a trade dispute with the United States. The United States responded with tariffs of 10 percent on US $ 200 billion of Chinese goods following the retaliatory action by China. Trade hostilities continue to escalate as the United States seeks to address its trade imbalance with China which currently stands at US $ 372.5 billion. The Fund has remained a bystander in the trade dispute which threatens to undermine the international trading system developed after decades of consensus building.

An examination of the Article IV consultations of Japan and Euro Area member countries indicate the Fund's limited oversight of the international monetary systems and the difficulties in ensuring even-handedness of surveillance.

In the 2018 Article IV consultations with Japan, the Fund encouraged the Japanese authorities to adopt enhanced financial sector policies to contain financial stability risks and strengthen financial sector oversight along the lines of the Financial Sector Assessment Program recommendations. The Fund encouraged the Japanese authorities to move towards full risk based prudential supervision and strengthen the corporate governance across banking and insurance sectors. The Japanese Authorities response was that they did not see the need to sharpen the Council for Cooperation on Financial Stability framework at this stage as the framework was built on Japan's past experience and key attributes.

In the 2018 Article IV consultations on Euro Area Policies, the Fund has held the view that there will be no winners from Brexit, as integration between the European Union and the United Kingdom has strengthened significantly over time reflecting the shared gains from the EU single market. The Fund held that the departure of the United Kingdom from the European Union will represent a loss not only to the United Kingdom but also to EU-27, as it will result in higher barriers to trade, capital and labor mobility and will have a long term effect on output and jobs throughout the region. To say the least, economic realities are far from political realities. The Fund has also advised the EU member countries for better compliance and enforcement of fiscal rules to focus on a single fiscal anchor. The EU monetary union removes the exchange rate as a shock absorber and national fiscal policies alone can provide buffers against risks. That said, the national fiscal policies have been drifting and there has been little or no fiscal adjustment in a number of EU member countries.

In comparison, Fund advise in India has received a lot of media attention. The August 2018, Executive Board assessment of India's article IV consultations has featured on the front pages of the Times of India and most other Indian dailies have prominently cited that "India's economy is an elephant that's starting to run". The IMF endorsement of India's macroeconomic performance continues to be capture both media and government attention.

Despite the Fund's explicit commitment to even handedness of Fund Surveillance it is difficult to overcome the deep rooted perception that the Fund is not even handed. It is almost impossible for Fund staff to take more strident positions in advanced economies and even more unlikely that the advanced economies will give the same level of attention to Fund advise. Perhaps a realignment of quota and increased voice for emerging markets in coming years will help overcome this perception. In the interregnum, the Fund has created a mechanism for addressing issues of even handedness in a transparent and well-substantiated manner.

The Fund's work in Financial Sector Regulation

The 2008 Global Financial Crisis witnessed 24 countries experiencing banking crisis. In 2009, the G20 adopted a regulatory reform agenda to be implemented by Financial Stability Board (FSB) and the Basil Committee on Banking Supervision (BCBS). The G20 has resolved that all financial markets, products and participants shall be subjected to regulatory oversight. The IMF's work on macro-financial surveillance was to be integrated with the work of the Financial Stability Board and the Financial Stability Forum. The Financial Stability Board has started publishing the list of Global Systemically Important Financial Institutions (G-SIFIs) since 2011 coordinating and regulating the G20's financial regulation agenda.

The Fund had commenced the Financial Sector Assessment Program (FSAP) in the aftermath of the financial crisis of the 1990s as an important tool for assessment of financial stability and development needs. The FSAP participation is voluntary, the focus of the assessment is broad and comprehensive and country requests are prioritized on the basis of systemic importance of the country. In 2009, consistent with the regulatory reform agenda, the G20 decided to participate in the FSAP which was hitherto voluntary. The FSAP assessment was expanded to systemically important countries on a 5-year cycle. The IMF has coordinated with the Financial Stability Board in examining the impact of the regulatory reform on emerging market economies. The IMF has also been publishing the multilateral policy issues report and the consolidated spillover report.

What are the salient features of the regulatory reform agenda? The steps are creation of a global framework for creation of resilient banks and banking systems, enhanced regulation of large interconnected institutions, and better supervision of a complex financial system. There remain aspects of the regulatory reform agenda that need to be completed. These include solvency framework for insurers, intensifying supervision of systemic institutions, cross-border cooperation in data sharing and reigning-in excessive risk taking by corporates.

The Fund has achieved significant progress in the global regulatory reform agenda by establishing a new set of international standards, guidance and best practices. Systemic oversight has enhanced and the coverage of the entire financial sector in the FSAP provides timely evaluation on status of implementation of reforms in both FSB and non-FSB countries. The downside risks in the coming years are waning multilateralism, regulatory fatigue and increased cyber-security risks for financial inclusion. Can we say the probability of crisis has reduced to zero? While several weaknesses have been compensated, the Fund itself acknowledges that no regulatory framework can reduce the probability of a crisis to zero.

India's 2017 FSSA

In November 2017, the IMF approved India's 2017 Financial System Stability Assessment (FSSA). The 2017 FSAP indicated that India had undertaken major reforms in financial sector from the 2011 FSAP. The major reforms included strengthening financial sector oversight, deepening markets and fostering financial inclusion. A Financial Stability and Development Council was notified for improving the intra-agency cooperation. The FSSA said that unifying the oversight of all commodities markets would promote efficient market functioning and modernize the sector. The Fund said that the Indian financial sector is facing considerable challenges of high non-performing assets. India's key banks appeared resilient but the stress tests showed a group of public sector banks highly vulnerable to further declines in asset quality and higher provisioning needs. The 2016 Insolvency and Bankruptcy code introduced a modern framework to deliver progress in NPA resolution. Government has announced a recapitalization plan for PSBs and has sought consolidation across several PSBs. The Fund has supported the Indian policy initiatives of bank recapitalization and the Bankruptcy code as also greater policy coordination between the financial sector regulatory agencies, it did push for greater regulatory autonomy to the Reserve Bank of India in banking supervision.

Spillover Reports

As part of the G20 mutual assessment process and the strengthening multilateral surveillance in the World Economic Outlook (WEO), the Global Financial Stability Report (GFSR) and the new Consolidated Multilateral Surveillance Report, the Fund formulated Spillover Reports from 2011. The Spillover reports explore the external effects of policies in five systemic economies: China, Euro Area, Japan, United Kingdom and United States. Spillover reports fill a gap between the domestic focus of a country reflected in Article IV consultations and the multilateral surveillance in the WEO-GFSR. The Fund has clarified that the Spillover Reports are not multilateral consultations of the nature that the Fund had convened in 2006 to reach policy consensus to resolve global imbalances.

The Fund has said that changes in government expenditure has large and more persistent spillovers than tax revenue measures, particularly over a longer horizon. Further fiscal policy shocks emanating from the

United States can have a global impact with large effect on Canada and Latin America as compared to modest impact of shocks from France and Germany which are particularly relevant for Europe. The Spillovers are amplified for recipient countries whose currencies are pegged to the source of the country's currency. Accommodative monetary policy actions in advanced economies created positive spillovers for many emerging market economies. This coupled with a decline in oil prices from 2014 till 2018 had created a spillover-rich environment boosting exports from emerging markets.

Spillovers from US Dollar appreciation has been an area of concern. Sustained US Dollar appreciation since 1980s was usually associated with crisis in emerging market economies, as also tighter US monetary policies vis a vis Europe and Japan. A country's vulnerability to US Dollar appreciation depends on the currency composition of foreign currency debt. The corporate debt stock in emerging markets has risen significantly and several corporates have foreign currency exposure. The Spillover Report suggests that the corporate sector risks remain moderate and no major vulnerabilities have emerged as a result of US Dollar appreciation in the Country's balance sheets as yet.

Capital Account Management and Exchange Rate Management

The IMF had long held the orthodox view that free flow of capital across the globe can have important benefits for countries and for the global economy. Capital flows can help a country's financial sector become more competitive and sophisticated. The 2008 Global Economic Crisis brought forth the significant risks posed by capital flows and the need for greater vigilance. The IMF came up with a more nuanced institutional view representing a remarkable shift in the area of capital account management.

The key feature of the IMF's new institutional view says that capital flow liberalization needs to be well planned, timed and sequenced in order to ensure that the benefits outweigh the costs. The countries with extensive and long-standing measures to limit capital flows are likely to benefit from further liberalization in an orderly manner. The Fund has reiterated that capital flows can have substantial benefits for countries but at the same time they also carry risks. Capital flow liberalization is generally more beneficial and less risky if countries have reached a certain threshold of financial and institutional development.

The stated policy goal of India and China and several Emerging Market Economies is that a fully open capital account should be the eventual goal. The forward path in both India and China has been calibrated on a cautious basis with evolving domestic policy consensus. China has pursued RMB internationalization as a major policy intervention and accorded higher priority to this initiative ahead of exchange rate liberalization. The Fund's institutional view is consistent with the national policies being pursued by the major Asian economies.

It is important to understand the IMF's work on capital inflows, exchange rate management and capital controls post the 2008 global economic crisis. In the aftermath of the 2008 global economic crisis, Central Banks in advanced economies pursued unprecedented expansionary unconventional monetary policies with Federal Reserve leading the way, followed by the Bank of England, the Bank of Japan and the European Central Bank to stimulate growth and employment. Unwinding the quantitative easing policies meant that the Central Banks in the Emerging Market Economies had to increase their policy rates. The monetary policy decisions of advanced economies had large spillover effects for emerging market economies.

The IMF has taken incremental steps to enhance policy collaboration, monitor and manage capital flows, and broaden the financial safety net. That said, Reserve accumulation has been the preferred form of global financial safety net for emerging market economies for defending exchange rates against potential volatility. The IMF has tried to strengthen the global financial safety net by introducing new instruments like the precautionary lines of credit where purchases can be made when necessary. The Fund has been recommending well sequenced financial deepening and opening of key Emerging Market Economies. Deeper domestic markets and asset diversification are expected to enable EMEs to better cope with the capital flow volatility.

The International Monetary System needs to provide in the coming years, greater role for emerging market economies in the global governance structures, to promote a sustained policy dialogue and build cooperation on improved capital account management.

The IMF's position vis a vis India

My 16 months of research work indicates the cordiality and respect with which India is held by the IMF's management. In recent years, Fund management has been supportive of India's strong policy actions including fiscal consolidation and anti-inflationary monetary policy. The synergy in views between India's top policy makers and IMF's senior management ensured that each of India's 3 Standby Arrangements was successfully concluded and repayments were always made on schedule. The close relationship between Dr. M.Narasimham and Jacques de Larsiere is perhaps the most striking of the IMF management supporting India's program request with its entire might. High levels of support were witnessed in the tenures of subsequent Managing Directors Michel Camdessus, Dominique Strauss-Kahn and Christine Lagarde.

India's macroeconomic performance stands out over the past 25 years. After the 1991 crisis and stand-by arrangement program with the IMF, wherein significant structural reforms were witnessed, India experienced high growth surpassed only by China and East Asian countries. India's growth rate reached 6 percent of GDP by 2000 and 9 percent by 2007. Business confidence was high, current account deficit remained manageable and the fiscal consolidation path was in accordance with the Fiscal Responsibility Legislation. Inflationary pressures were contained by appropriate monetary policy action and supply side measures. India's external reserves mounted to its highest ever levels, short term debt reduced sharply and constituted a very small amount of the country's external liabilities. Capital flows were buoyant and financial markets were stable. By 2016, India became the world's fastest growing major economy. India's rise from a debtor country to a creditor country at the IMF with significant increases in its voting rights reflected in higher quotas, represents a remarkable success story. The Article IV consultations of the IMF on an annual cycle have reflected the resilience and growth of the Indian economy over the past 25 years.

Has India influenced IMF approach

India has supported the IMF's strictly limited gold sales in 2009-10. In the first phase of the IMF's exclusively off-market transactions to interested central banks and other official holders, at market prices, the Fund sold 200 metric tons of gold to Reserve Bank of India. India's influence is also seen in the Fund's flexible view in the liberalization and management of capital flows taking into account the specific country circumstances. Post East Asian Crisis, the India called for well-planned and sequenced capital flow liberalization to minimize adverse domestic consequences. Post 2008 crisis, India's strong presence on the G20 has enabled it to push strongly for the quota reform in the IMF. India's constant support of PRGF programs in African countries has been well documented. India has supported the IMF's engagement with member countries through enhanced technical assistance. The MOU between India and IMF for establishing the South Asia Regional Training Centre is a significant forward step in the collaboration.

New Priorities and Policies for the Fund

The key policy priorities of the International Monetary Fund for 2018 are to enhance resilience, rebuild policy space and implement reforms to sustain growth upswing, to collaborate within a multilateral system and address shared challenges, upgrade tools to develop tailored policy solutions and improve governance of the Fund. As part of the multilateral surveillance, the IMF would be publishing Flagship Reports presenting the analysis of the lessons learnt 10 years after the Global Economic Crisis in addition to the regular publications. Analytical work is being undertaken on the resilience of emerging market economies to tighter financial conditions in the backdrop of gradual withdrawal of monetary policy stimulus in advanced economies. On structural issues the IMF seeks to develop a comprehensive work program on digitalization and formulate a strategic framework on social spending. The Fund's work on Digitalization would cover policy advise and capacity development in digital areas including Fintech, Big Data, Cyber Risks and GDP measurement as also seek to improve its internal practices on economic data management.

In the areas of international financial architecture, the IMF would collaborate with the G20 in presenting the IMF Institutional View on Capital Flows in Practice and the IMF Taxonomy of Capital Flow Management Measures. The IMF has said that it would present the Latest Developments on Financial Regulatory Reforms and the AML/ CFT Strategy to the G20.

Further the Fund and the World Bank will jointly formulate the Debt Sustainability Framework for Market Access Countries. The IMF in collaboration with the G20, would work on the issues of buildup of debt in public and private sectors following a long period of easy financial conditions.

The IMF has stated that it would continue efforts to completing the 15th General Quota Reform to maintain a strong, quota based and adequately resourced Fund at the center of global activity by 2019. The Fund management has said that further dialogue is necessary on the Independent Evaluation Office's recommendations for a stronger, more representative, more accountable, effective and efficient Fund.

To conclude it is important to note that there is strong momentum behind the global expansion despite the trade risks and financial markets volatility presenting the downside risks. To sustain the upswing countries have to adopt open and rules-based multilateral trade systems that work for all and to durably reduce the global imbalances. India would play a key role in the IMF further improving its policy tools to evolve with changes in the economic environment to support its global mandate and the member country's needs.

References

1. 2014-Triennial Surveillance Review– External Study – Evenhandedness of Fund Surveillance., www.imf.org

2. Selected Decisions and Selected Documents of the IMF., 39th issue – The Acting Chair's Summing Up – Evenhandedness of Fund Surveillance – Principles and Mechanisms for Addressing concerns, Executive Board Decision 16/16, February 22, 2016., www.imf.org

3. United States: 2018 Article IV Consultation – Press Release; Staff Report and Statement by Executive Director for United States dated July 3, 2018., www.imf.org

4. People's Republic of China: 2018 Article IV Consultation – Press Release; Staff Statement and Statement by the Executive Director for the People's Republic of China dated July 26, 2018., www.imf.org

5. Japan: 2017 Article IV Consultation – Press Release: Staff Report and Statement by Executive Director for Japan dated July 31, 2017., www.imf.org

6. 2018 Article IV Consultation on Euro Area Policies, dated July 18, 2018., www.imf.org

7. Global Financial Stability Report – A Decade After the Global Financial Crisis: Are We Safer?., International Monetary Fund, October 2018., www.imf.org

8. Review of the Financial Sector Assessment Program: Further Adaptation to the Post Crisis Era., International Monetary Fund, September 2014., www.imf.org

9. India: Financial System Stability Assessment – Press Release and Statement by the Executive Director for India., International Monetary Fund, December 2017., www.imf.org

10. Spillover Notes – Fiscal Spillovers: The Importance of Macroeconomic and Policy Conditions in Transmission, Special Taskforce, International Monetary Fund., October 2017., www.imf.org

11. 2015 Spillover Report., International Monetary Fund, July 23, 2015., www.imf.org

12. 2015 Spillover Report, International Monetary Fund, dated July 23, 2018., www.imf.org

13. IMF Multilateral Policy Issues Report, 2014 Spillover Report, dated July 29, 2014., www.imf.org

14. 2014 Spillover Report, International Monetary Fund, dated June 25, 2014., www.imf.org

15. 2013 Spillover Report – Analytical Underpinnings and Other Background, dated July 3, 2013., www.imf.org

16. Euro Tragedy: A Drama in Nine Acts, by Asoka Mody., www.ft.com

17. The Acting Chair's Summing Up – The Liberalization and Management of Capital Flows – An Institutional View, Executive Board Meeting 12/105 dated November 16, 2012 EBM/12/105., www.imf.org

18. IMF Survey: IMF Adopts Institutional View on Capital Flows, December 3, 2012., www.imf.org

19. The IMF and Recent Capital Account Crises: Indonesia, Korea, Brazil., IEO Publications, International Monetary Fund, September 12, 2003., www.imf.org

20. Macroeconomic Issues Facing ASEAN Countries., "Exchange Rate Policy and Macroeconomic Management in ASEAN Countries"., The International Monetary Fund., July 18, 1997., www.elibrary.imf.org

21. Problems of International Money 1972-85., "Exchange Rate Management and Surveillance since 1972"., The International Monetary Fund., August 9, 1996., www.elibrary.imf.org

22. Blanchard Olivier, Rogoff Kenneth and RajanRaghuram., "Progress and Confusion: The State of Macroeconomic Policy" The MIT Press., April 2016., www.elibrary.imf.org

23. Communique of the Thirty Seventh Meeting of the International Monetary and Financial Committee dated April 21, 2018 www.imf.org

24. Communique of the Thirty Sixth Meeting of the International Monetary and Financial Committee dated October 14, 2017 www.imf.org

25. Communique of the Thirty Fifth Meeting of the International Monetary and Financial Committee dated April 22, 2017 www.imf.org

26. Chirstine Lagarde, Managing Director., "Boosting Growth and Adjusting to Change" Remarks at Northwestern University September 28, 2016 www.imf.org

27. Christine Lagarde, Managing Director., "Statement by the Managing Director on the Work Program of the Executive Board" Executive Board Meeting, June 18, 2018., www.imf.org

28. Christine Lagarde, Managing Director., "Statement by the Managing Director on Argentina", August 29, 2018., www.imf.org

29. Christine Lagarde, Managing Director., "The Window of Opportunity Remains Open: The Managing Director's Global Policy Agenda Update", August 19, 2018., www.imf.org

30. Christine Lagarde, Managing Director., "Statement of the Managing Director on the Independent Evaluation Office Report on Governance of the IMF: Evaluation Update", September 27, 2018., www.imf.org

31. Press Release no: 18/96., "IMF Managing Director Christine Lagarde calls for G20 Policies to Make Growth More Resilient and More Widely Shared", March 20, 2018., www.imf.org

32. Group of 20., "The IMF's Institutional View on Capital Flows in Practice", July 30, 2018., www.imf.org

33. International Monetary Fund., "Information Note on Modifications to the Fund's Debt Sustainability Assessment Framework for Market Access Countries", Prepared by Policy Development and Review Department, July 1, 2005., www.imf.org

INDEX

A

Ahluwalia, Montek Singh xvi, xviii, 68, 94, 114, 151, 154, 180, 184, 198

Anatalya Summit November 2015 215

Anti-Globalization Protestors xiii

Articles of Agreement xv, 9, 11, 16, 28, 43, 110, 230

B

Bank for International Settlements (BIS) 73

Board for Industrial and Financial Reconstruction (BIFR) 83

Bretton Woods Conference 3, 8, 21, 43, 158

Bretton Woods Institutions 158, 206

Brisbane Summit November 2014 214

C

Cannes Summit 2011 211

Central African Economic and Monetary Union Policies 13

Chancellor of Exchequer xiv

Chavan, Y. B. 54

Compensatory and contingency financing facility (CCFF) 66, 98

Contingency Financing Facility 75, 76, 107, 178

Contingent Reserve Arrangement (CRA) 44

Country Ownership of Fund Programs 15

Currency Meltdown 33

D

Das, Shaktikanta 155

Debt Crisis 5

Debt Sustainability Framework (DSF) 18

Deshmukh, Sir C.D. 8

E

East Asian Crisis 17, 25, 155, 252

Eastern Caribbean Currency Union Policies 13

Emerging Market Economies (EMEs) 25

Enhanced Heavily Indebted Poor Countries (HIPC) 17

European Crisis 25, 41, 43, 44, 213

Eurozone crisis 167

Extended Fund Facility (EFF) 16, 50

External Investments & Operations (DEIO) 73

F

Federal Open Market Committee's (FOMC) 126

Financial Sector Assessment Program (FSAP) 7, 247

First credit tranche arrangement (FCT) 66

Fiscal Responsibility and Budget Management Act (FRBM) 140

Flexible Credit Line (FCL) 16, 128, 208

Fund-Bank Annual Meeting xiii

Fund Surveillance 13, 21, 128, 166, 187, 243, 244, 246, 254

G

Global Financial Crisis 36, 138, 140, 148, 153, 161, 203, 206, 229, 230, 243, 246, 254

Global Systemically Important Financial Institutions (G-SIFIs) 247

Great Depression vii, 4, 25, 26, 27, 28, 43, 45, 46, 168, 210, 218

Great Recession vii, 4, 12, 25, 38, 43, 44, 46, 168

H

Hamburg Summit July 2017 217

Hangzhou Summit September 2016 216

I

IMF Executive Board xiv, 1, 6, 11, 21, 22, 56, 149, 168, 169, 183, 188, 190, 191, 198, 234

Independent Evaluation Office (IEO) 19, 45, 198

International Debt Crisis 25, 31, 32, 43

International Financial Institutions 35, 206, 207, 208, 219

International Monetary and Finance Committee xiii, 133

International Monetary Fund (IMF) i, iii, ix, 9, 49, 158

  Articles of Agreement 9

  Creation of IMF 8

  Criticism of 18

  Evolution of 3

  Quota Reform 10

J

Jalan, Bimal xviii

K

Korean economic crisis 33

L

Lahiri, Ashok xv, xviii, 177

Latin American Debt Crisis 25

London Good Delivery (LGD) 73

London Summit April 2009 207

Long Term Fiscal Policy (LTFP) 61

Los Cabos Summit 2012 212

M

Micro-Financial Surveillance 13

MRTP Act 50, 58

N

Narasimham Committee on financial sector reforms 90

Narasimham, Dr. M. xvii, xviii

P

Paris peace conference 4

Pennsylvania Avenue xiii

Peoples Republic of China ix

Pittsburgh Summit: September 2009 208

Policy Support Instrument (PSI) 18

Poverty Reduction and Growth Facility (PRGF) 17

Poverty Reduction Strategy Paper (PRSP) 17

Precautionary and Liquidity Line (PLL) 16

Q

Quota Reform 10, 169, 178, 253

R

Rajan, Raghuram xv, 130

Rangarajan, Dr. C. xviii, 71, 120, 161

Rao, Narasimha 74, 184

Rapid Financing Instrument (RFI) 16

Reddy, Y.V. xi, xvii, 121, 126, 158

Reserve Bank of India (RBI) 49, 52, 142

S

Saint Petersburg Summit 2013 213

Seoul Summit 2010 210

Shroff, A.D. 8

Singh, Manmohan 74, 77, 78, 81, 87, 89, 90, 93, 95, 97, 141, 155, 184

Subbarao, Dr. Duvvuri xviii, 128, 129, 163

Subramanyam, Arvind xv

Suez Crisis 25, 28, 30

T

Technical and Financial Services 14

The Evolution of IMF 3

Toronto Summit - June 2010 209

Triennial Surveillance Review 12, 23, 243, 244, 254

W

Washington DC Summit: November 2008 205

West African Economic and Monetary Union Policies 13

World Bank xiii, 4, 8, 9, 23, 25, 52, 53, 55, 84, 85, 88, 89, 101, 111, 133, 158, 163, 175, 177, 181, 182, 198, 206, 210, 238, 241, 252

World Economic Outlook (WEO) 31, 46, 248

World War II 4, 158

CPSIA information can be obtained
at www.ICGtesting.com
Printed in the USA
BVHW072303240719
554279BV00004B/16/P